Down and Out
In South East Asia

By Alex Watts

By the same author

Down And Out In Padstow And London

* * * ~ ~ ~ * * *

Down and Out In South East Asia

By Alex Watts

Copyright 2013 Alex Watts

Published by CreateSpace

* * * ~ ~ ~ * * *

Cover design: Harjit Kaura

ISBN-13: 978-1490500355
ISBN-10: 1490500359

To my grandmother Jane (1915 - 2013),
who passed away while I was in Cambodia.

To my mother and father,

and to Erica, Dan, Denise, and Eloise.

Sitting quietly,

Doing nothing,

Spring comes,

And the grass grows by itself.

- Zen proverb

* * * ~ ~ ~ * * *

CHAPTER ONE

THEY SAY location is everything in the restaurant business, but for me it wasn't about finding the perfect spot - just something cheap enough to buy. Yet there was hardly a cheaper place to buy a restaurant than SE Asia - and if I couldn't do it here, I wouldn't do it anywhere.

I'd tried everything from slaving in cramped furnaces in low-end kitchens, to toiling 17-plus-hour days in Michelin-starred restaurants, to my last job, working outside doing film location catering on Thailand's beaches, with my top off - the breeze blowing away the sulphurous stench of the onions. And none of them had worked out.

The only thing I hadn't done was run my own place. I'd been drifting too long, like some sozzled flaneur. Like some hammock-weary fool. It was time for action. Time for self-actualisation, as the shrinks call it. Time to realise my potential and find meaning in life, however more ambitious than talented I proved, and however more talented than prudent.

I figured I had just about enough savings to eat my way through the north of Thailand, and then Cambodia and Vietnam, researching the local street food, and collecting recipes for the restaurant, until I found the right place. Whatever I had left, I'd use to buy the business and the pots and pans I'd need.

I dreamed of a beach shack on a white-sand island, boiling crabs straight from the boats, and washing off the sweat of the kitchen with regular dips in the sea. Or perhaps a river barge on the Mekong Delta, with tables on deck, sparkling with glass and silverware?

Or maybe a small noodle shop tucked away in a steamy side-street in Saigon, with a few Western dishes thrown in for misty-eyed expats yearning for a taste from home? Or, if it was as cheap as I'd been told, a guesthouse with its own plot of land, overlooking the Sea Forest in remote north-east Cambodia, picking vegetables grown in the Martian-red soil?

The only thing I knew for certain was it wouldn't be the hideous, overbuilt megalopolis where my gastronomic road trip started in February 2011. They say you either love or hate Bangkok, and it had taken me all of five minutes to realise it was the latter.

The place was filled with huge, air conditioned shopping malls selling expensive designer clothes and watches. There was even a shop on the eighth floor of one selling Lamborghinis. All I could see was mile after mile of mall after mall.

Outside, deformed beggars and other hapless victims of Thailand's unbridled capitalism held out cups. Some had babies in shoals draped across their shoulders. Buddha Shmuddha, I thought. The contrast in wealth was obscene. I'd never seen such unabashed materialism - not even in Beijing.

I sat in a ringed-off area and watched a live band, then headed back in the general direction of my hotel. The traffic was so bad, it took 15 minutes just to cross the street. I couldn't see why anyone bothered with taxis. It was far quicker to walk, even in the suffocating heat and smog, and soon I was sweating like a Geordie in a maths test.

THE STREETS were full of conmen and hustlers. I'd seen some pretty good ones in my time, but the ones in the Thai capital were so confident, they laughed at you all the way through it. One tuk tuk driver offered to show me round the city for an hour for 40 baht (just less than £1). No-one does anything in Bangkok for 40 baht. Even the beggars turn their noses up if you give them less than that. But I was bored and went along for the ride - just to see the game being played.

The driver grinned at me through his rear view mirror, asking what hotel I was staying at and therefore how much money I had, and quickly deviated off the route. First stop was an Indian tailors. If he turned up with a farang, they paid for his gasoline, he claimed.

Then it was a pit stop at the "Lucky Buddha temple". A smartly-dressed man with impeccable English was peering through a window at the monks praying inside. He told me he'd been a monk there, and was paying the place a quick visit while his girlfriend went shopping. Then, seamlessly, he was on to the engagement ring he'd just bought her for 30,000 baht (about £700).

He said it was fashioned like the one Prince William had inherited from his mother Diana's £21m estate and given to Kate Middleton, with an oval blue sapphire in the middle, surrounded by a cluster of 14 diamonds, and would be worth double when the Royal wedding took place two months later. Then he wrote down the name of the wholesaler, and said they had "sole copyright" for the ring in Thailand. Copyright! Everything was copied in Thailand. I'd even seen a T-shirt with "Tuna" above a Puma logo.

"You have girlfriend?" he asked. "You should buy one for her. She will be very happy..."

I headed back to the tuk tuk and the game continued, this time to his "other shop", which by incredible coincidence turned out to be the wholesaler the snake oil-peddling monk had just mentioned. I said no, but he got angry and said I only had to pop in for a minute so he could get his precious juice. Staff pounced on me, offering me iced tea, and giving me the hard sell. I decided to cut to the chase.

"Have you got a Lady Di ring? You know the one the Queen of Hearts wore - England's rose?"

There were conspiratorial whispers and glances. How did the farang know? And such a chubby one, still smelling of milk? Then the owner - a moon-faced Chinese woman with gold teeth - was called over. She only had one left. If I'd arrived a few minutes later, I'd have been completely out of luck. She was soon punching numbers into a calculator, telling me I could have it for £3,800 - and £2,500 would definitely be her last price.

"Me only wholesaler in Asia with copyright!" she said, her teeth and half-moon spectacles gleaming over the jewel cabinets.

She carefully opened the box holding the priceless ring and let the light catch its large, central stone of 12-carat blue glass. It was so impressive, I half expected it to say Garrard of Mayfair on the box, or at least Gerrard of Mayfart. I took her card, told her I'd think about it, and got back in the tuk tuk.

"You buy?" the driver jerked, his head wagging away like a Chihuahua pounding a chair leg. Then he was badgering me about massage parlours.

"Only 3,000 baht!" he continued. "You not like lady? You ladyboy?"

"Look, no more selling!" I shouted.

He sulked for a few seconds and was soon back to "boom boom bars", saying he knew a good place just round the corner in Soi Cowboy. I jumped out at the next set of lights, threw 100 baht at him, and stuck to water taxis after that.

I SHOWERED for the third time that day, and walked the streets around Nana Plaza red-light district, taking in the Bangkok noir. The place was as seedy as it was depressing.

Ugly, pock-marked, tattooed sex tourists in Harley-Davidson wife-beaters were clenching beer bottles menacingly and leering at the street, ready for the night. Many had beetroot faces, farmer's tans, and hacking coughs from 60-a-day habits. Some were sickly thin and walked with sticks, and looked like they had weeks to live.

It was appalling to see the desperate, young Thai women fawning over them. In day light, it looked far worse. You could see just how old and repulsive the men were, and the dead fish look in the girls' eyes. Take away the pretty women, Thai-style techno, and constant screams of "welcooome" and "massarrr", and it looked like Blackpool on an extremely bad trip.

I sat in a hotel bar and read the local news on the internet. There was a story about a German expat who'd been killed by his pet cobra. He lived alone and they'd only discovered his body when a maid noticed the smell. Apparently he'd run out of money, and therefore grown lonely. He bought a 3ft-long cobra from a man in Pattaya, and it had bitten him as he slept. Or he'd just dangled his hand over it and waited for the bite.

The Thai police had invited the local press along, as they always do when a farang is involved. The website had posted a video showing the man's green, decomposed body slumped on a bed, and another of officers catching the snake.

The clip finished with the camera panning into a picture of the man on the mantelpiece. Next to him was a young Asian woman. It was an undignified end, and I wondered what Thai men really thought about the hordes of Chinese, Korean, Malaysian, Japanese, Iranian, Russian, European, and American tourists and businessmen coming over to have sex with their women. What was really going on behind those smiles?

The only hint I'd seen was when I'd been sitting at a food stall surrounded by Thais slurping noodles. A drunk Scouser had suddenly shouted out: "I fucking LOVE Thailand, mate!"

"No, you love Thai women," said a pony-tailed Asian man on a nearby table.

"I love Thai men AND women," the Scouser replied, but you could tell he was lying.

I sipped away at my ice-cold beer as the last of the light faded, the car lights came on, and Bangkok put on its neon clothes and waited for the hustle and shrieks of night. Groups of young girls and ladyboys were lining up in the car park outside Nana Hotel, waiting for customers.

A skeleton in a dress stopped at my table and asked if I'd finish my beer can. She told me she'd been forced to walk the streets when her mother got stomach cancer. She said the only way to get morphine was from the army, and it was expensive. But she couldn't see her mother suffer, so she slept with men and bought the morphine, and then she buried her mother and was left with no family. And there she was, toothless, her looks ravaged by ice, collecting empty cans for a few baht coins. She was 25.

I went back to my hotel room and lay on the bed thinking about what a miserable place Bangkok was. The land of smiles, the land of cheek-clenching piles more like. I hadn't seen a genuine grin since I'd got there. But then that was no surprise. A smile in Thailand means absolutely nothing - it's just a way to hide thoughts and feelings. And if they hated those sex tourists as much as I did, I knew exactly what they were thinking behind those dizzying pearls.

THE NEXT morning, I packed my backpack, crammed my books into my lap-top bag, and caught a bus from Bangkok to the relative tranquillity of Kanchanaburi, a small town surrounded by temple caves hewn into the limestone hills, and home to the famous River Kwai Bridge.

I'd read a lot on Twitter about the street food at the night market (Th Saeng-hchuto), and after a tour of the vendors – flogging everything from catfish to chickens' feet – I sat down at a stall specialising in pink eggs. And as the elderly stallholder, like everyone else at the market, spoke English as good as my Thai, I still have no idea what the dish was other than some sort of slant on the Chinese delicacy one-thousand-year-old eggs.

I watched as the old man made the salad, and ate it with the sort of relish you only get with other people's cooking. I'll never forget that meal. It wasn't just his kindness and patience seeing some bleary-eyed foreigner towering over him, watching every knife stroke (and any cook will tell you how irritating that is), but its simplicity and fiery magic.

First, he cracked open two pink eggs, exposing translucent, dark-amber whites. Then he stretched an elastic band that was tied by one end to a rusty nail on his stall and sliced the eggs into quarters with it. He arranged them on a plate – their yolks oozing out like rotten aubergine – and proudly held them up for me to smell. Was that a faint whiff of ammonia? Sulphur? Mustard gas? Or some other chemical weapon left behind by the Japanese?

He grabbed a mixing bowl and threw in a handful of ginger cut into julienne strips. They were as skilfully sliced as anything I'd seen in any Michelin-starred kitchen, and there wasn't a mandoline in sight. He asked how many red chillies I wanted, and I held up five fingers.

He then pounded them in a wooden pestle and mortar, and added them to the ginger before seasoning with a little sugar, salt, fish sauce, and lime juice. Then he chopped up a sprig of coriander and finely

6

sliced a quarter of an onion and mixed the whole lot together and arranged it over the eggs.

What a blast of primary colours! There was only one drink worthy of such a salad and that was a massive bottle of ice cold beer. I sat down and tucked in as the Thais giggled away, pretending not to watch me. I admit the egg looked far from appetising, but I began wondering when I'd last had such a fabulous meal. The white had a gelatinous quality, and the yolk was rich, creamy, and soothingly salty. If this wasn't umami, then I was in the wrong game. It was definitely one for my restaurant.

I got back to my guesthouse and spoke to a chef called Apple, who ran a Thai cooking course for backpacking foodies. She explained that the eggs were preserved in a mixture of lime, clay, salt, and rice hulls for a few weeks – a method of curing eggs dating back hundreds of years. I'd seen them before in China, but the shells had always been white from what I vaguely remember. I asked whether the Thais put beetroot in to colour them, but she laughed.

"They're laid like that. They come from special chickens in the south of Thailand," she said.

I still don't know if she was winding me up, or whether the farmers fed them prawns or something. And when I did a bit of research on the web, I was no clearer. I found mention of a special breed of chickens in South America that apparently lay pink eggs. But they weren't really pink when you looked at the photos. All I knew was the only pink eggs I'd seen had been at Easter.

I SPENT the day searching for restaurants for sale on the internet. It didn't look too promising - most were well over my budget. Then I went to the market and wandered round the food stalls again. I thought about the painfully-trendy street food revolution in the US and London. Blah! Nonsense! Go to Thailand, I thought. They were doing food vans and motorbikes decades before they were so achingly 'a la mode'.

But then these weren't bored corporate pirates indulging their foodie passion by running a street stall selling heritage meats, hand-squelched juices, and banana and mustard exotic cheddar on a

Saturday, these people did it for a living. If they didn't get it right, their families went hungry. There was no monthly pay check to fall back on. No pension pots and healthcare packages like the Putney chutney makers.

My pirate copy of Lonely Planet claimed the market was home to the best fried mussels in batter (hoi tod) in the whole of Thailand. Even though the guide has a fairly comprehensive food section, I'd always been highly sceptical of such claims, and usually took them with a few buckets of salt. I mean, had the authors really tried every street food vendor in the country?

The stall was perched half-way into the market, and if customers were anything to go by, it certainly looked liked it had a great reputation. There was a large queue waiting for fish supper-style wrappers of hoi tod, and after ten minutes with nothing for company but a bottle of Tiger, I got to try them. But I was pleased for the wait - it gave me the chance to see every part of the operation, without standing there watching and taking pictures and making them feel uncomfortable like I normally do.

The cook had a flat wok in front of her, about the size of Pluto, heated by a Calor gas burner. She poured vegetable oil on to the wok and within seconds it was hissing and spitting like a cat being wrestled into a cardboard box. Next she added a few gallons of batter. I don't know what was in it, but Apple told me most hoi tod batters contain tapioca flour, seasoning, and soda water and eggs are cracked in later.

But she definitely didn't add eggs, not even pink ones, so they must have already been in the batter, which was about the thickness of single cream, and quickly formed a massive pancake. After a minute, she scattered in some chopped spring onions and coriander stalks, and a few tonnes of shelled raw mussels that were lined up on ice next to her stall.

Using two enormous spatula-type weapons, she kept pushing the mussels around until they were covered in crispy batter. After more circling action, she threw in half a minibus load of bean sprouts and let them wilt in the mixture. She then scattered portions of hoi tod, garnished with coriander, on to sheets of paper, folded them up with

8

a small pot of chilli sauce inside, and handed them out to the waiting crowd.

I grabbed mine and headed for a table. The dish was fairly tasty but under-seasoned, and needed the sweet chilli sauce. When I got back to Bangkok I tried them again, and they weren't as good. I'd have to take Lonely Planet's word that they were the best in Thailand.

AFTER ANOTHER miserably-hot, sticky day in Bangkok, I met up with an old school friend who had been living in Thailand for 12 years, and had just married his heavily-pregnant wife Pla. John picked me up in his four-wheel drive, and we headed south to the beautifully picturesque Rayong Province - an area where tourists are thankfully as rare as nine baht notes.

On the way we stopped at Khao Chee Chan, which also goes by the name Buddha Mountain. Standing at nearly 400ft tall, it is said to be the biggest Buddha image in the world, and was carved into the cliff using lasers and then filled with gold leaf.

Later, we visited a couple they knew, who'd built a beautiful house on a piece of land overlooking lily fields near Rayong. When they bought the land, it was completely overgrown and home to a pond that the neighbours had stocked with fish. They cleared the jungle and left the tallest trees, and built a prefab house in the middle of the plot.

I was very jealous. Although they were cut off, Jim and his Thai girlfriend Fi were living the good life and had filled the garden with vegetables and fruit tree saplings. Two years later, they were living off the land, eating bamboo shoots, lemon grass, basil, galangal, tomatoes, aubergines, bananas, huge mushrooms grown in boxes, and eggs from their hens and ducks.

When they fancied a change, they caught a few fish from the pond and fried them in breadcrumbs or made Thai curries. They were living there happily with their three Huskies and two Cocker Spaniels, and no children.

I walked around the fruit trees, dreaming of leasing a similar piece of land, and building a small restaurant, cooking fresh produce from the garden. As I say, I was very jealous of the fabulous climate they lived in, and the mangoes they picked each morning. Until they told me about the snakes, that is. They were being plagued by deadly cobras from the lily fields at the bottom of the garden. They had put up fine mesh fencing, but still they came in.

Only the day before, Fi had screamed as they were letting the dogs out of the car, and Jim turned to see a 6ft-long black cobra a few feet from them. Jim had killed quite a few with his hoe, but this was much bigger. He threw a stick at the snake, but missed, and it rose up and made lunging motions at them. Fi kept screaming and eventually it slithered away into next door's garden.

The dogs had been less lucky at times. Despite their size, the Huskies gave snakes a wide berth, but the bravest Cocker Spaniel liked to grab them and shake her head violently, and batter them to death on the patio. A couple of months before, she had run into the house howling in pain and pawing at Jim's leg, her eyes swollen after an encounter with a spitting cobra. They had just got her to the vet in time, but she still lost an eye.

But it was the stories of the king cobra that most worried them – and whether it had any offspring. Years before they moved in, the neighbours said they had seen a 20ft-long monster near the pond. They were alerted by the sound of frogs being eaten – apparently frogs make a particular shriek when they're being swallowed by snakes. Knowing how deadly and fast the world's biggest venomous serpent is, and its enormous striking range, they took no chances and blasted the thing to death with a shotgun.

Poor Jim and Fi were clearly still shaken by the cobra encounter when they showed me round their land, but then I suppose it was one of the downsides of living in a beautiful country. We fed the fish and I promised to catch a few and barbecue them that evening.

Then we packed up the cars and headed out to Khao Chamao National Park to visit the waterfalls. We stopped off at a restaurant on the way to buy food for the trip - beautiful roast duck and rice that came with bags of satay sauce, and soy sauce with chillies. And then we bought dried, salted pork similar to biltong, and parcels of rice, minced pork, and lily seeds wrapped in leaves.

But when we got to the park, the guards on the gate spotted the food and confiscated it. They were flabby and greedy-looking and looked like they hadn't bought a meal for years. We handed over our delicious food, and my beloved ice box full of beers, and the guards went through the motions of writing down our number plates, saying they would return it all on the way out. They even said we weren't allowed to take water bottles in, which considering the heat was ridiculous.

We paid the entrance fee (which was seven times more for foreigners) and prepared for the steep ascent into the jungle. Thai families were openly carrying water bottles and huge picnic hampers up there. Some even had ice boxes, and I could hear the cheery rattle of beer bottles. I thought about those guards and my lovely ice cold beers. The buggers would probably be on their second one by now – can in hand, munching on a duck drumstick, waiting for the next farang to arrive.

I hadn't come prepared and had to walk through the jungle in flip-flops. After 20 minutes of climbing over rocks and vines, the sweat was pouring off me, and I thought about those lovely cold cans again. Thirty minutes later, I had a pounding headache from dehydration and began to lag behind after stubbing my toes numerous times.

I tried not to think about cobras. If they were that common in Jim's garden, how many would be out there in the jungle? They're not in the trees - they ARE the trees! Flip-flops would offer no protection. If I was bitten, I'd be dead by the time I got to the bottom.

Eventually, we got to the waterfall, stripped off our clothes and plunged into its deep ponds. The water was filled with black fish, which I found out later were a species of carp called tor soro. There were so many of them, you brushed against them as you swam, and if you sat on the rocks they came up and nibbled your feet, with the sandpapery rasp of a cat's tongue. Some must have weighed 6lbs and would easily have fed a family of eight.

But their numbers and size were down to the fact the Thais didn't touch them. The locals said if you eat the fish you become dizzy, which is how the waterfall got its name, Khao Chamao - meaning "to get drunk" in Thai. The fish apparently eat berries from overhanging trees, which don't affect the fish but cause humans to hallucinate.

Now, I've always considered myself an adventurous cook, and it would have been easy catching one of those fish. And I did think about getting some wood together and cooking one by the side of that waterfall just to see what would happen. But I just couldn't bring myself to do it.

Maybe someone a lot madder and braver than me, like Anthony Bourdain or Bruce Parry, would have done it. Or at least have got one of their film crew to try it first. But I was too worried about getting back in flip-flops as it was without running around being chased by imaginary cobras.

I CAUGHT a budget flight to the northern Thai city of Chiang Mai. It was the only flight I'd been on that had a chilli rating on the on-board menu. I found a cheap hotel, and then headed out to the night bazaar.

It wasn't the best timing - there was a major food poisoning investigation there following the death of a New Zealand backpacker. Two friends who had eaten the same seafood curry had survived, but were seriously ill in hospital.

But any health concerns were put firmly into context by the nerve-jangling journey to the market and back. I wanted to walk there, and was enjoying the relatively cool climate after the seething cesspit of Bangkok, but after the 58th tuk tuk driver slowed down and beeped his horn at me aggressively, I gave in.

I slid into the back and the driver sped off, cutting up two mopeds, narrowly missing a stray dog, and taking the first bend at such a speed that it made the back wheels wobble. The contraption's brakes were down to the metal and we hurtled over a canal bridge and almost into the back of a passing car.

When the driver did actually stop at a red light, he looked at me in his mirror, cranked up his radio, and said: "Why you go to night market? Many ladies, many bars here!" At another stop, he tried again: "You want lady massage? I take you there..."

12

Finally, after another test of wills and his shot brakes, he dropped me off at the night bazaar. The place was filled with tourists and I headed around looking at the stalls, and then stopped off at a restaurant called Seafood Mho-O-Cha, boasting "the best and fresh seafood in Chiang Mai", like all the other signs.

The fish were packed in ice and looked almost as fresh as anything you'd get on the quayside, even though Thailand's second city is hundreds of miles from the sea. There were the usual mud crabs, blue swimmer crabs, lobsters, prawns, and fish, and then I saw something I hadn't seen before - sea snails piled up like fat, brown conches.

I asked the manager how they cooked them, worried they might turn out dried to foul-tasting grit like the cremated clams I'd had in Bangkok. She said grilled, so I asked how she would have them, and she said something I didn't understand, so I went for that.

Trying to put Chiang Mai's seafood scare out of my mind, I bought a beer and a Sang Som rum, and a steaming pot quickly arrived at my table. The waiter removed the lid and I was hit by a delicious smell of kaffir lime leaves, chillies, and the sweet scent of fresh and best seafood. I hadn't eaten all day, apart from three mussels a barman had given me that were as small as a manicurist's thumbnail, and got stuck in.

The broth was splendid. It was hot and sour, and filled with whole pink shallots, Thai basil sprigs, lemon grass, thick coins of galangal, and slices of red chilli. The snails were beautifully cooked, and much firmer than whelks. There was no chewiness though, just like you get when you order fresh whelks at a decent seafood stall on some wind-swept pier in England.

I finished the meal and drank the soup and sat there wondering whether to have another pot. The manager returned and I thanked her for her recommendation and asked for the name of the dish again. She asked someone else and said it roughly translated to "Thai-style sea snails cooked in a traditional clay pot" and was a speciality of the restaurant, and the only place you could get them in Chiang Mai.

Full and content, I headed out through the market again, but my good mood was quickly destroyed by another tuk tuk driver. It was obvious he hadn't heard of my hotel, but kept pretending he had. After another Grand Theft Auto race through the streets, he headed the wrong way past the canals and kept ignoring me when I told him to turn round.

He took me up a couple more dark streets, and suddenly I was outside a neon-lit building in the middle of nowhere. It looked more like a boutique hotel than a go-go club, but it was obvious what it was from the scantily-clad women outside.

The driver turned off his engine and the girls descended. The trouble with chrome chariots, apart from the criminal bastards who drive them, is they offer no protection to pulling arms. There are just two poles at the back, meaning you can get attacked on three sides. But after a few minutes, I managed to get him to drive off again.

Then it was another chicane through the canal area, and more areas I didn't know, and this time he dropped me off in the centre of Chiang Mai's red light district.

"Bar here," he kept saying. "Many beautiful ladies for you!"

I'd had enough. I'm not a prude, but there was no way he was going to get his free gasoline kickback from me. I scowled at him, and told him I wasn't going to pay him and walked off down the road.

I went into a bar and ordered a drink, and the driver followed me in, trying to get commission from the owner, who pointed out that all I'd ordered was a beer, and there was no money in that. Eventually he left, and sat outside in his tuk tuk staring at me darkly.

When I left, he shouted at me again, and things looked like they were going to turn nasty, so I jumped in another tuk tuk and kept glancing round half expecting him to be following. The new driver quickly got lost and after a few minutes we were on the city ring road. I started getting panicky, thinking he was in cahoots with the first driver, and we were going to end up in some horrible Tarantino lock-up.

But there was no man in a mask, thank Buddha, and after another 20 minutes of dark alleys, he somehow found my hotel, which by then had closed. I eventually managed to find my way in, past the air conditioning units, rubbish bags, and rats at the rear of the guesthouse, and thankfully my room key fitted the back door.

I headed off to bed, trying to restore my mood by wishing excruciatingly painful deaths on all tuk tuk racketeers, and thinking about how I could never go to an amusement park again. "Wanna go on the scary ride?" they'd be saying. "I've BEEN on the scary ride!" There was only one thing for it – the next day I'd hire a mountain bike.

AFTER A couple of sizeable bar tabs, I got to know the guesthouse owner and convinced her to let me do a bit of work in the kitchen with my two new cheffing chums (let's call them Dave and Si because they deserve their own TV show - more than the two Hairy Bastards anyway).

Si wore a wolf hat for some reason. It was a novelty take on the traditional chef hat, and I didn't ask why he was wearing it. I can only guess it might have had something to do with the whisky we'd been drinking.

But as I was a guest in his kitchen, it was none of my business, and quite frankly would have been rude of me to ask. It was his kitchen, and if he'd decided to don a Pope mask, then it was absolutely his right to do so. One thing you learn in cooking is never to question a chef's judgement - or even his fashion sense - if you're on his turf. It's just not done.

Anyway, it was a simple exchange – I showed them how to cook some European dishes and they taught me two Thai meals in return. Like many restaurants in tourist areas in Asia, the place had a Western food section for people who like to eat sausage, egg, and chips wherever they are in the world.

Their restaurant, in the old walled city, already had steak and ale pie on the menu, so I showed them how to make steak and red onion pudding. When I taught them how to make pizza – and how ridiculously profitable it is – they were delighted. There are mugs in

Chiang Mai who happily shell out £6 for a distinctly average pizza, when they can get a bowl of wonderful massaman curry for less than £1.

They cooked two meals for me at the end of the evening – fried prawns and enoki mushrooms in oyster sauce, and the goddamned hottest tom yam soup I have ever tasted, or hope to ever taste, in my life.

They said it was how they ate it, but they were grinning away like alley cats in a sardine factory when I tucked in. Thais have a great sense of humour when it comes to chilli, and find it extremely amusing tricking farangs into eating ludicrously potent dishes. And as chefs very much share the same level of schadenfreude, Thai chefs should never be trusted.

It was interesting seeing how they cook in restaurants in Thailand - everything was prepped first and put in bowls, ready for each step of the recipe. I once did a short stint at the Dorchester Hotel in London, and used to watch the chefs in the Oriental Kitchen, and it reminded me of that – blindingly fast. Faster than any chefs I've ever seen.

If you wonder how your freshly-made tom yam soup arrives five minutes after you order it in Thailand, then this is how they do it. The beers didn't seem to slow them in the slightest, or the wolf hat. So two wonderful dishes in minutes. Eat your heart out Jammy Oliver – but then these were proper cooks, not overweight, healthy-eating gurus lecturing people about obesity and Turkey Twizzlers.

They lit up the stove and got a wok and a soup pan on the go. They put a tablespoon of vegetable oil in the wok and a pint of water in the pan. Soon the oil was smoking and the water bubbling. In the meantime, Si finely chopped a handful of red and green bird eye chillies.

Dave prepped the ingredients for the oyster sauce dish and put them in a bowl – chopped spring onions, sliced red chillies, enoki mushrooms, raw prawns, roughly-chopped shallots, and bottled oyster sauce. Si threw lime leaves, lemon grass, basil leaves, galangal, sliced button mushrooms, spring onions, and the chopped chillies into the soup and let it bubble away. He then chopped up chunks of a white fish, which had a very similar texture to haddock, and sliced a large red chilli.

While he did this, Dave put a generous spoonful of tom yam paste into the soup. There was no stirring; he just let the heat of the water do the mixing. He then poured in a tablespoon of condensed milk (some chefs add coconut cream, but it is far better without coconut, which to my mind turns it into a completely different soup). The condensed milk amalgamates the flavours, lends sweetness, and thickens the soup slightly. To balance it, he added a small ladle of freshly-squeezed lime juice.

Si, meanwhile, chopped a large tomato into eight pieces, and roughly chopped a couple of shallots and put them in yet another metal bowl (I felt sorry for the potwash). They went in the soup, and then he added the fish, which in that heat needed less than a minute to cook.

There was an explosion of flames as Dave threw the enoki bowl into the smoking oil, and tossed the wok a few times, before stirring it all round with a ladle. And that was it – the meal was pretty much done in the time it had taken us to gulp down a big bottle of beer each, which wasn't long. Si then chopped up some coriander and spring onion tops and chucked them in the soup and served it. I was glad I ate the enoki dish first – it really was wonderful and melted in my mouth, and I wouldn't have been able to taste it otherwise.

As I say, the tom yam was extremely hot, and reminded me of the time I'd been talked into eating a phall by a notorious curry-muncher, and soon I was weeping away like an Oscar winner as Dave and Si smirked.

Just breathing air into my mouth afterwards was painful, let alone smoke. But although I can't pretend I didn't suffer the consequences, it was a fantastic meal, and one that I'd definitely have on the menu should I ever be lucky enough to run my own place somewhere, anywhere, in SE Asia.

IN THE back streets of Chiang Mai, I came across a plant I'd never seen before. It resembled sprouting broccoli that had gone to seed, or perhaps unripe elderberries, and was bubbling away in a pork belly and pig's tail stew.

I turned to Twitter, and eventually found out it was called sadao - the fruit and leaves from the neem tree, whatever that is. Apparently, you can get it in jars in the UK, but I'd never seen it, and I was lucky enough to be in SE Asia when it was in season. I grabbed a plastic stool near the little Buddha shrine tucked away at the back of the street stall, and waited as the dish stewed away over charcoal.

The locals were queuing up for their evening meal. It reminded me how much of a takeaway nation Thailand is. Food at street stalls is so cheap, healthy, and delicious that many Thai households don't bother to cook themselves – it's cheaper to buy it.

They carry the dishes home in little plastic bags and then eat together. Walk past an open window at supper time, and you can often see a family crouched on the floor picking through bags of brightly-coloured food, all chomping away happily.

As the locals ordered their barbecued fish, minced pork, vegetable curries, and batter cakes made of tiny fish, I tucked into one of Chiang Mai's famous spicy sausages. It was like a fresh chorizo in texture, with little squares of moist fat. The heat hit me straight away and then the lime and coriander.

It was wonderful and had all the salty meatiness of a good banger. I've had some very poor sausages in Asia since – including one that was so sickly sweet I gave it to a flower-selling toddler, who wouldn't eat it either. But the sausages at that stall were the best of the lot.

Eventually, the stallholder came over and handed me a polystyrene tub full of pork sadao. It reminded me slightly of the soups they serve in greasy spoons in South America, designed, like all peasant dishes, so that a little bit of meat goes a long way. There were slices of green beans, onions, and tomatoes in there, as well as pig's tail and a fatty chunk of pork belly. But it was the sadao that was the star. It was slightly bitter and had a faint taste of celery – one of my favourite flavours.

The broth was thin and very subtle compared to most Thai dishes. It had been pepped up with garlic and Thai basil, but only a touch. The little heat there was came from white pepper - the seasoning Thai cooks used to spice dishes before the gold-seeking Portuguese arrived with their chilli plants.

I've often found it curious how the chilli pepper - something so endemic to modern Thai cooking - has only featured in its dishes for a few hundred years. But then I suppose you couldn't get fish and chips in England before Sir Walter Raleigh sailed home with the friendly potato. I sat there and sucked the bones and had another helping.

When I got back to the guesthouse, the owner told me how sadao grows near temples in the walled city and is revered for its medicinal qualities. I showed her the pictures I'd taken on my iPhone, and she gave me the basics on how to make it.

You start by frying pounded garlic, and then add slices of onion and pieces of pork. You add water and boil it rapidly for 20 minutes, and then add tomatoes and basil. You simmer it for an hour or so, and then throw in the sadao for the last five minutes. I've no idea what sadao tastes like in jars, but if you ever get a chance to try it fresh, jump at the chance.

I SPENT the next week chatting to monks, visiting temples, and narrowly avoiding becoming a Buddhist. I thought about heading north up to the sleepy Mekong River towns of Chiang Rai Province and the famed Sukhothai ruins. But I thought the food wouldn't change much, and would be disappointing compared to northern Thailand's gastronomic capital.

I wanted to leave its signature coconut milk-and-curry noodle soup dish, khao soi, to last. And I wanted to order it in what many locals say is the best restaurant to eat it in – the Thai Muslim-run Sophia restaurant tucked away in a back alley near the night bazaar.

But both times I cycled there, they had run out. Instead, I tried posh and peasant versions in and around the walled city, and I have to say the latter won hands down. There was something vital and hearty missing in the expensive restaurant offerings. They were too decorated and precise, as often happens when humble street food gets a gourmet makeover.

Mostly, the seasonings are already mixed into the broth – and that is the way it is served in the city's night bazaar. But look carefully if you go there, and you can get it the traditional way, where garnishes of pickled mustard greens, chopped shallots, fried chillies, lime quarters, and coriander are served separately in plastic containers and mixed in by the diner at the table.

You also get a range of types: the usual contenders of chicken, prawn, pork and fish, and sometimes beef, and in one restaurant I had frog khao soi, which was revolting. Yet however it comes, the basic components are the same: crispy fried egg noodles on top of boiled noodles in a spicy coconut gravy sparsely furnished with meat.

You notice how sweet the sauce is when you taste it without the pickled vegetables, which are deliciously hot and sour. Thais love fermented vegetables, the more pungent the better, and often order them as a side dish or bar snack - which helps explain why so many seem to have taken to roasted pork knuckle and sauerkraut served in German restaurants in Thailand.

Sadly, I never got to eat at Sophia's. But the steamed beef khao soi I had during the Sunday Walking Market, when roads are closed off and the town is filled with local hill tribes flogging art and crafts, was the best of the lot. The chopped nuggets of shin were succulent and full of flavour. And the sauce was blisteringly hot – or at least it was when I stirred in a second helping of soused greens.

My other regret was not trying hung lay, a northern-style pork curry made by frying and then simmering pieces of pork shoulder with garlic, ginger, turmeric, sugar, soy sauce, stock, and mild curry powder. I ate it in a restaurant when I got back to Bangkok and it was fantastic.

There is a similar recipe in Keith Floyd's guide to SE Asian food, Far Flung Floyd, which was one of six books I'd managed to cram into my laptop bag. Floyd had been told by the "culinary European gurus" he met in Bangkok that the dish, like the rest of the food in north-west Thailand, was strongly influenced by Burma, but "could find no evidence to support this theory".

He then ranted about how food book editors were obsessed with regional variations of cuisines, saying: "What they fail to realise...is because of things like aeroplanes, lorries, trains, refrigerators, regional cooking has gone out of the window. And you can just as easily eat duck Hanoi-style in Mandalay, Paris, Peking or London as you can in Saigon."

I wondered whether to take a similar approach as I continued my journey to the SE Asian culinary crossroads of Cambodia, a veritable truck-stop of migrant food from China, Thailand, Vietnam, and much further back India, and get less tangled up in tedious, pointy-headed details about regional influences and recipe origins, and just enjoy the food for what it is, and not care where it's from.

I mean how far back should you go? The first tribes that left Africa and headed east? Or aeons later, when Indian traders brought their pounding dried spices trick to the sub-continent? Or later still, to when the great Khmer Empire ruled much of present-day Thailand, Laos, and Vietnam?

There is no point banging on about whether tom yam soup was originally Thai, or in fact Khmer, as I would learn many Cambodian chefs claim. Or whether the tussled-over spicy meat salad called lab is in fact Laotian rather than Thai, or for that matter whether nasi lemak is truly Indonesian or Malaysian, or spag bol is English or Italian.

I mean, when a dish is cooked with different methods and ingredients in different places can one country still claim it as their own? Especially in Cambodia, a country which has seen centuries of invasions and mass migration. Life is far too short for that.

CHAPTER TWO

I HAD a few hours to kill before my flight to Cambodia's capital Phnom Penh, and was scribbling notes in a hotel foyer, listening to Johnny Cash's Pack Up Your Sorrows: "No use rambling, walking in the shadows, trailing a wandering star. No-one beside you, no-one to guide you, and nobody knows where you are."

There was something in his voice and lyrics that always helped chase away the black hound. But I was soon interrupted by an annoying student who'd spotted my white earphones and wanted to borrow my iPhone charger.

His name was Craig and he had graduated in some sort of trendy design course at London's Goldsmiths College, where he said "they make you think outside the box". He was irritating in the extreme. He had just spent two months on the horrendous shopping mall island of Hong Kong and was full of stories about a guy called Rob he'd met there.

Rob was 50 and from Ohio, and had got divorced from his wife and planned to travel the world having sex with as many women as he could. He was apparently an ecstasy dealer and hoped to fund himself by setting up a drugs lab in China, or being publicly executed. Before he left, he managed to persuade Craig to lend him $200 for his visa, claiming he was waiting for funds to clear.

I looked at the ginger 22-year-old lounging on a chair, sipping beers he'd brought into the hotel lobby. He reminded me of my early 20s, a time when I thought I knew everything, and was more than happy to share my incredible knowledge with anyone bored enough to listen. Somehow I couldn't shift him, and before I knew it had agreed to meet him for my last few hours in Bangkok.

I left my room early, hoping to disappear into the sticky, fish sauce streets, but he was already slouched across a sofa in the lobby. He moaned about every bar we went to - either they were too noisy or too quiet - and haggled over the price of every drink.

To maintain even the most rudimentary grip on sanity in Thailand, you have to accept you're going to get ripped off, and tips are expected everywhere. Your bar bill is often inflated - thanks to the way they get you to pay at the end of the night. Once your 'check bin' tub is stuffed full of bills, it's difficult to argue whether you've had 10 drinks or 12.

Of course, it works both ways. John had told me he'd spent his first seven years in Bangkok drinking in a huge beer garden every night. He was famous there for being the only man capable of drinking enough booze to win three Tiger Beer T-shirts in one sitting.

So legendary were his drinking skills, when he worked in a Japanese fishing port they used to parade him through the streets with his arm raised like a champion boxer. He must have spent thousands in that beer garden, but never once in all those years had the owner bought him a drink.

One night there was a power cut, and the generator broke down at the same time. Hundreds of people ran for the door. The security guards couldn't stop them. The lights came back on, and the bar was empty apart from dozens of unpaid bill tubs.

Craig started waffling about the prescription drugs they sold in pharmacies in Thailand. Rob had told him all about them. Before I could stop him, he was going through a feeble story about how his friend had left his prescription at home and needed some Xanax. The woman behind the counter quickly turned angry and he scuttled off.

We played some more pool, and this time Craig haggled over the price of the table as well as the drinks. The girl who served us had track marks up her arms. She was clearly out of her head on heroin, and had trouble racking up the balls.

A chain-smoking Brit with scaly skin asked for a game and kept licking his lips as he told us about the bar girls in Bangkok and Pattaya. He was a grotesque human being, and could not have looked more smug if doctors had suddenly announced smoking is good for you after all.

"Go on their tattoos," he said. "If they've got a flower, or a Buddhist sign or something, that's okay. But if it's a scorpion or snake..."

"Or dragon?" Craig said.

"Or dragon," he replied, "then go for someone else - there's plenty to choose from."

He licked his lips again, and wandered off.

As we played, small groups of Russian tourists bought tickets from a man in the street and then disappeared up a narrow stairway. We bought two tickets and followed them up. The dingy room had mirrors on the walls and ceiling, and in the centre was a stage with seven poles. Around it sat expressionless Russian couples.

Girls in bikinis came out and blew out candles, inserted ping pong balls, and then handed out balloons to the crowd. One of them handed Craig a balloon. Someone tapped him on the shoulder and told him the darts were sharp and not to stick the balloon near his face. They inserted blow pipes and darts and began bursting the balloons.

The first pop was met by a small round of clapping from the Russians - it was the sort of respectful, subdued clapping you might get in the early rounds of a croquet tournament. The finale was a musical duet to a background of Asian hip hop. The music would stop and one of the girls would fill in with a trumpet. The other played a whistle.

The Russian women looked on glumly. They were mostly middle-aged, with wide hips, bulging stomachs and large gold, hooped earrings. I wondered what was in it for them. Craig thought their husbands had taken them there to show how good their lives were in comparison. I wasn't so sure. The way some of those Russian women were looking with their blank, unimpressed expressions, they seemed to be thinking: "This is nothing. In Russia, we do this with Kalashnikov bullets - blindfold!"

I got out when a naked girl lay on stage and they brought out a massive python. Craig followed me down, and then he was off trying to persuade a drunk Norwegian man to sell him his T-shirt. It had

"The Less You Care, The Happier You'll Be" on the front. He asked Craig where he was from, and when he said England, refused to sell it to him. Craig followed him up a side street, and I seized my chance and gave him the slip. I'd been trying to find the right chance all night.

I'D NOT heard great things about Cambodia, and was wondering what to expect as we flew over the bright green, patchwork paddy fields into Phnom Penh - a city of heart-breaking poverty and extreme wealth fast rising from the ashes of one of the world's worst genocides.

John's wife Pla had warned me how dangerous the place is, and how Cambodians will steal the pennies from a dead man's eyes. But you can be unlucky in any city, and I'd met a lot of people in Thailand I wouldn't trust with a bag of chips.

In Bangkok, a drunk Canadian had told me how he'd recently crossed the Koh Kong border from Cambodia and was full of stories about how dodgy the country was, and how he was drugged and robbed one night. He talked about the armies of gold-toothed, Hawaiian shirt-wearing paedophiles swarming the streets, the acid attacks happening on every corner, and how you could pay a police officer $150 to get someone assassinated.

"Man, it was a pretty fucking lawless place, I can tell you" he added. "I stayed at one hotel man, and the security guard asked his eight-year-old son to pull up his T-shirt. He was covered in little tiny circles, man. They'd burned him with incense sticks to toughen him up. That fucking sucks!"

He told me the food was even worse. But for some reason, Cambodian cooking had always intrigued me. I can't say I'd ever picked up the Yellow Pages, and thought "I could murder a Cambodian..." But I'd always been interested in cuisines that hadn't been done to death.

For years, trend-spotting listicle scribblers had been saying Cambodian food would be the next big thing - and not just travel writers with room to fill. In its food trend predictions for 2008, three years before I got there, the Conde Nast-owned website Epicurious boldly predicted that "Cambodian is the new Thai" and described its noodle dishes, curries, and stir-fries as a triangulation between Vietnamese, Chinese, and Thai cooking.

I remembered when Rick Stein had filmed his Far Eastern Odyssey TV series, a French food expert had told him the country was a meeting point of all the culinary roads of Asia - a place where you could get the best of Indian and Chinese food with a piece of fresh bread on the table.

Gordon Ramsay had just made a similar programme called Gordon's Great Escape, but his trip through Cambodia was made up of shock-factor scenes of him spitting out duck foetuses and fried tarantulas, and harpooning frogs.

In nearly every emotional, hoarse-voiced clip, Ramsay had remarked how the country was recovering from the "crap" of a civil war that had killed nearly two million people, and rediscovering traditional dishes that "were nearly lost for good" under the Khmer Rouge - something he probably thought was a local wine until he read the cartoon script his producers had written for him.

But whatever lay in store in Cambodia, I'd been told it was probably the easiest place to open a restaurant in SE Asia. John had told me it was impossible for farangs to run a business in their own name in Thailand - a Thai national had to own at least 50%. And that required a "huge amount of trust and stupidity".

Many expats put the lease in their Thai wife or girlfriend's name, and end up with nothing when the relationship sours, or the family arrives and they're forced out of the business. Some end up flying off a balcony, dying from a heart attack 40 floors below. Apparently, two expats a week die flying off condo balconies in Thailand.

"The only way you get can round it," John said, "is to marry a Thai woman, put half the business in her name, then have a baby. Then you leave Thailand for a few years, and return when the child is five. You put the business in the child's name, but you have power of attorney until the child is 18, meaning they need your signature as joint business owner to flog the business. That way you've got a window of 13 years, and they can't do anything about it."

He'd told me some horrendous stories. There was the retired Japanese guy who'd fallen in love with a 20-year-old bar girl and opened a restaurant with her. He'd given her father and brother a moped each, and bought the family a farm in Isaan, in north-east Thailand.

They got married three months later. He spent thousands on the three-day wedding. The whole village was there, scoffing spit-roast pigs and chickens, and at the end a Thai man appeared and said: "You can go now."

"What?" said the pensioner.

"You can go now - I'm her husband..."

Then there was the Swedish businessman, who'd ended up with two broken legs and a broken back when he went to renew his lease on a bar in Pattaya he'd been running for two years. The landlady, from a rich family who owned several hotels in the city, had told him to bring $10,000 in cash, but then refused to sign the contract unless he handed over another $4,000.

He withdrew the cash from an ATM, and she took the money, counted it, and refused to sign. He began filming on his phone. One of her bodyguards threw him over a 10ft ledge and then jumped down on to his back. The police investigated, but no-one was arrested - even though he had video of the landlady ordering her bodyguards to beat him. She was far too well connected for that.

I'd read that as a foreigner without major contacts, you couldn't buy land in Cambodia, but at least the lease would be in your own name. All you needed was a business visa, which you could get on arrival. Then it was just a case of buying a restaurant, putting your thumbprints on a few documents, buying a business licence for $60 a year, and paying $10 a month in tax, and $5 for the police who came sniffing round every month. And as for all the health and safety red tape and work laws strangling restaurants in the UK - forget it.

I CAUGHT a taxi from the airport, dropped off my bags at a cheap guesthouse near Riverside, and headed out into the baking streets of Phnom Penh.

According to my guide book, the city had been described as the Paris of the East until it became a ghost town during Pol Pot's murderous regime in the 70s, when the capital's entire population of more than 2.5 million people had been marched out into the fields to grow rice. His black-clad minions banned money, blew up the central bank, and turned the clocks back to Year Zero.

Many of the old French mansions still remained though, dating back to colonial Cambodge's first boom period more than a century ago, and it had once again, aside from the horrendous rubbish everywhere, sprouted into a beautiful city.

My first stop was the Russian Market (Phsar Tuol Tom Pong – and pong it certainly did). It was a warren of chaos like any crowded bazaar in SE Asia, but instead of being housed in a single building, the stalls had spread outwards in a mass of corrugated iron and cement. The low ceiling and throbbing heat meant when I got to the food section I was hit in the face by a putrefying mix of durian fruit and fermented fish with the full thwack of a 7ft-long Mekong giant catfish's tail.

If you can imagine what rotten fish and pork smell like when they've been sitting in a sauna for six hours then you're half-way there. It really was a massive assault on the senses. All seven of them, because after an hour I was sure I'd developed three different senses of smell – death (durian and dying fish), fresh (fruit, flowers, herbs, and vegetables) and grease (an unpleasant haze of cooking oil and clammy sweat).

The market got its name because Soviets liked to shop there during the Cold War. And given the legacy of Russian people's inscrutable taste, it was filled with fake designer goods, trinkets, souvenirs, and bling.

Soon I was chatting to the owner of a stall, which only sold one dish - spring rolls with noodles. The woman made them by rolling up shrimps, minced pork, lettuce, spring onions, crushed soya beans, basil, grated carrot, and noodles in wafer-thin rice wrappers and deep-fried them for 20 minutes. This made them far crispier and chewier than the sort you usually get. They were absolutely delicious and almost sausage brown in colour.

They were cut up like bangers too, and put on top of a dish containing three types of rice noodles – spaghetti size, vermicelli size, and big, flat shoe laces that melted in your mouth. The dish was finished with a sprinkling of ground peanuts and came with a jar of chopped red chillies in lime juice and vinegar. And soon I was dripping not only from the oppressive 35C heat, but the delicious chilli paste.

I CARRIED on through the streets, the sweat stinging my eyes, and stopped at a bar for a few cold beers. An American lawyer in his late 50s was standing outside rolling a joint. He told me he'd been living in Cambodia for 20 years, and how Phnom Penh had changed so much in that time and was now a "dynamic city".

"People slag off Cambodia, but it's one of the freest places in SE Asia, probably the freest," he drawled. "You can say stuff here and not disappear - as long as you don't say too much..."

He said he was now running a business in Vientiane in Laos - a place he described as "the city that never wakes" - and said an NGO worker had vanished there last week: "There's even CCTV footage of the police arresting him, then no-one saw him again. The knuckleheads! They're still denying they arrested him, or know anything about where he is. It's all on film man, and they're still denying it!"

He finished off his joint, got on his dirt bike, and roared off to join his friends at a posh restaurant on Riverside. I walked back to my hotel and passed Phsar Kandal, a rough old market near the Tonle Sap river, where the locals were buying freshwater fish, prawns, cockles, pork, beef, and vegetables, grown in the fine silt river soil.

Everywhere stallholders were scraping away at fish scales with small machetes, and pulling out guts. I wandered around looking at the small flapping catfish that they barbecued whole in bamboo canes. I watched as a man crushed sugar cane in a hitlerite contraption that had a pipe leading off so his wife could fill bottles with the creamy liquid. He pushed the cane through several times, folding the lengths

29

each time, and then for the last pressing added a segment of green orange, which gave it a faint taste of bitter marmalade.

I didn't like the look of the slabs of pork and beef sweating in the late afternoon sun. But the preserved fish looked splendid - little brown, dried fish, smoked fish, and bowls of prahok - Cambodia's notoriously foul-smelling fermented fish paste that tastes of blue cheese and is the backbone of Khmer cuisine. It all looked very promising, a culinary Phnomenon if you will, and I'd only just scratched the surface.

I SPENT the next few days walking the streets and taking in the breeze by Riverside, and seeing all segments of Cambodian life from mad-for-it grandmothers in pyjamas doing aerobics, to monks with their alms pots, to old men in freshly-ironed shirts and trousers squatting by their mopeds looking for the next ride, to the tuk tuk driver with 'Lexus 570' scrawled on his backboard, to the moon-faced official barely peering over the wheel of his supercharged Range Rover with its carte blanche Khmer flag and VIP sticker in the window.

One of only two countries in the world with a building on its flag, or so I'd been told by the dope-smoking American lawyer. Afghanistan, if you're asking. And that must say something. A reminder of the great empire that built Angkor Wat, and a hope that the good times might come once again. Just like Greece.

It was this naive hope, the continued smiles, and bright outlook I grew to love most. I'd escaped from the cold and the dreary faces of those who have plenty, but grumble about everything. I'd fled from the obsession with weather stories, and erosion of common sense and fun, to a country where most people have nothing but look pleased to have it.

But it was heart-breaking seeing the malnourished children who lived rough in the capital, especially when you saw the hundreds of shiny Chelsea tractors driven by Phnom Penh's elite. Some of the street kids were barely more than toddlers, owning nothing more than a grubby T-shirt, shorts, and flip flops. They scratched riel from tourists by begging, shining shoes, and hawking travel guides, quail eggs, bags of prawn crackers, and fruit.

Some worked as prostitutes, and many were addicted to glue, heroin, or yaba - a highly addictive, strawberry-flavoured methamphetamine sold in pill form. Nearly all of them were boys. Girls don't last long on the street, I was told - they are usually found and sold to brothels.

But there was one place that helped them - Friends, a huge complex where hundreds of street kids ate and showered every day. The NGO was set up to train the youngsters in a trade like cooking, welding, or hairdressing so they could find a job and get off the streets. Part of the organisation was Friends The Restaurant, launched in 2000 by an Austrian chef called Gustav Auer, to train them to become cooks and waiters. Over the years, it had helped thousands of street kids get jobs in the capital's restaurants and hotels.

After graduating, they usually walked straight into a $100 a month job - not a bad wage in this third world country. Sewing in a dark factory ten hours a day making clothes for retail giants like Wal-Mart, for instance, pays just $60 or $70 a month. Some worked for a few years, gaining valuable experience in kitchens, and then returned to the centre as teachers.

They were taught about hygiene and safety procedures - the first of three levels in their "hospitality vocational training" - and were then sent to Friends' sister restaurant Romdeng, where they were taught to cook traditional Cambodian dishes like beef fried with tree ants, pork fillet stuffed with toasted coconut, and grilled seafood salad with banana flower and seaweed. They then moved to Friends, where they learned international cuisine.

They spent half their time in the kitchen, and the other half front of house, so they got to learn all aspects of the restaurant business. Serving Westerners also helped them brush up on their English, a highly sought-after skill in Cambodia. The NGO bosses said that with the shameless level of corruption in the country (the Government is said to lose $500m a year, or 4% of its entire GDP, to corruption) the only way ordinary Cambodians could benefit from the booming tourist industry was by working in it.

FRIENDS WAS filled with holidaymakers and flashpackers when I arrived. The menu certainly looked interesting. There was roasted pumpkin and goat's cheese salad, couscous-crusted pork, tropical cheese cake with coconut Breton, mushroom and leek spring rolls, and young watermelon soup with prawns and paddy field herbs.

I went for their most popular dish, Khmer chicken curry. It had a lovely rich taste of fall-apart chicken, with a backdrop of coconut, potato, green peppers, and mild curry spices. And it was real thigh and breast, rather than the processed strips of meat, chemicals, and water you often get in Asian restaurants and takeaways.

Indeed, the difference between the traditional Cambodian curry and far runnier and spicier Thai curries was interesting. The meat had been cooked for a long time, as it should be in a decent curry, and was more reminiscent of Indian food in its heavy use of onions and potato. And its mildness and rich chicken stock flavour reminded me of Mediterranean stews, with their simmered-to-a-squelch green peppers.

They made it by pounding lemon grass, galangal, fresh turmeric, lime zest, star anise powder, garlic, and a half a dozen shallots to make Cambodia's traditional curry paste kroeung. They boiled down coconut milk until it had almost reduced to nothing, and then added the kroeung paste and fried it until it was fragrant.

Then they added fish sauce, fried it again, and added the chicken, potato chunks, and more coconut milk. They topped it up with chicken stock as the sauce reduced, and then added palm sugar, green beans, green peppers, onion chunks, salt, and mild curry powder. People ordered it with baguettes, which they sell on every corner in Cambodia – a legacy from its years as a French colony.

It was wonderful talking to those chefs and seeing the joy in their faces rather than the haunted looks of the street kids that bed down in dark alleys. The organisation had clearly done an amazing job in transforming their lives. And there wasn't a celebrity chef, dream academy, or film camera in sight.

WALK DOWN any road in Phnom Penh, and you'll see street food – sometimes an ingenious bicycle-driven cart hooked up to a car battery, sometimes a stall with a few plastic chairs to perch on.

There are old women pushing barrows of freshwater clams from the nearby Tonle Sap river that are slowly 'cooked' on a metal tray in the morning sun for an hour or two, baguette stalls serving num pang pate, Cambodia's version of Vietnam's famous banh mi, with its pate, pork belly and pickles, BBQ stalls selling chicken wing tips coated in sweet red marinade, and sometimes hawkers flogging fried tarantulas, bugs, and tiny, coiled snakes, who charge squeamish tourists $1 for taking pictures.

But the one thing I began to miss was meat. It was not that they didn't do it well. It was just that you didn't get much of it, which is hardly surprising in a country where meat is a luxury and used more as a flavouring than a main ingredient.

Yet that was certainly not the case at the strip of BBQ beef joints opposite the city's massive Wat Ounalom temple complex, which were a veritable meat-eater's paradise. And there was only one name on the salivating lips of the locals who flocked there – ko dut, a whole calf spit-roasted over charcoal and served in slices with raw vegetables and a bowl of prahok.

For me, there are few finer smells than the waft of scorched beef and greasy smokiness of yellow fat as it drips into hot embers. And what a splendid way to spend an hour – drinking jugs of Anchor beer and chatting to a cook spit-roasting a 50kg fatted beast in the blazing sun.

They would start the day by butchering and washing the carcass, and then fill the belly with lemon grass, lime leaves, and rice paddy herbs before sewing up the cavity with wire. Then they'd baste it in soy sauce and lime juice for flavour and colour, and constantly feed the coals as the beast slowly grilled for hours, and occasionally you'd get the pleasing crackle of dried reeds sticking out of its behind.

The cook carved hunks of pink meat, and then finished it off over the coals until the skin was crispy. Then he'd chop it up on his greasy wooden board and nestle the slices on a bed of sliced raw onions before they were snatched away by waiters. Lesser known cuts of the

33

animal were grilling away too, including the neck, intestines, and a part affectionately described on the menu as "beef's dick". In fact, the whole place was a temple to meat: barbecued goat, frog, duck, chicken, pork, eel, and octopus, and it had specialities for all of them.

The ko dut came with a tray of raw green beans, shredded banana flowers, white cabbage, and slices of green banana, carrots, cucumber, and green tomatoes, dotted with ice cubes to keep them fresh. And each added something to the dish – the crunchiness of the green beans, the bitterness of the unripe bananas, and the earthiness of the carrots.

I was so impressed with the dish, I half toyed with the idea of setting up a ko dut stall if my half-baked plan to open a restaurant in SE Asia came to nothing, and I was forced to return to the UK with my tail between my legs. I'm not sure how it would have taken off, and I knew I'd have more chance of getting hold of a Dodo egg in Blighty than prahok. But I reckoned hunks of spit-roast calf would go down well on an English common with the sound of leather on willow and the chink of warm beer glasses.

Of course, I knew I'd be facing far more stringent street food regulations in the UK, and would have to fill out forms giving details of everything from my inside leg measurement to the name of the calf before the council offered me a pitch. But, as I would learn, there was one ludicrous law that I wouldn't have had to worry about.

Later, the Cambodian government, in its wisdom, banned restaurants and stalls from spit-roasting cows in public – over claims they incited violence and were bad for the image of Cambodia. It followed a meeting by the Supreme Council of the Mohanikaya Buddhist order, which decided the sight of roasting carcasses glorified the killing of animals.

"Grilling cows in front of the restaurants is a show of support for violence in a country that believes in the Buddhist religion. It can instil the ideas of a massacre to a child and push them to commit violence in society," one council member was quoted in the local paper as saying. He explained that rotisserie chickens and whole roast ducks were not offensive because they were "small size" animals.

It was initially reported as a ban in Phnom Penh. But when I phoned a spokesman for Cambodia's Ministry of Information, he confirmed it would be rolled out across the country. "We don't want to see this kind of thing," he told me. "You can still sell it, but we don't want it being cooked in public. Restaurants can put it in the kitchen, but not on display."

Had they been into a Khmer restaurant kitchen? The vast majority were so tiny that if you put a dead calf in there, there wouldn't be room for the cooks. Other officials cited hygiene concerns about cooking in the street, which was ridiculous when you saw the state of many indoor kitchens, and the dozens of busy food stalls perched on every corner.

In fact, I only got food poisoning once in all the times I ate at that strip of barbecue restaurants, and I was convinced it was nothing to do with the beef – roasting meat and then finishing it off directly over red-hot coals is a good way of killing bacteria, regardless of whether it's done in public or not. It was far more likely to have been the accompanying tray of raw vegetables that emerged from the grimy dungeon of a kitchen overlooking the toilets, where the calves were later cooked.

The ban was widely ignored to start with - many restaurants said they hadn't even heard the news, let alone received a directive from the Government. And the owner of one restaurant thought I was winding him up, and it took a good couple of minutes for him to believe me.

"It's crazy," he said. "People love seeing the cow being cooked!"

As he sweated in the mid-morning sun, filling the animal's belly with herbs, a group of orange-clad monks wandered past from the huge temple complex across the road. They didn't cross the road, or clench their nostrils, or drench us in water, or throw rose petals at us to remove evil spirits, they glanced at the cow and smiled.

Sadly, the Cambodian government got tough with restaurants flouting the ban, and threatened to close them down. And soon you couldn't see a spit-roast calf on display anywhere - they were being cooked in kitchens and yards at the back. The only ko dut advertising allowed was on beer signs outside the eateries. Mmmm beer. Now that never causes violence does it.

It was ridiculous. However much it was against Buddhist sensibilities, grilled calf was one of the best meals I'd had in Cambodia. The government should have been showcasing those dishes, and promoting the country's badly-marketed cuisine, rather than ordering them to be swept off the streets. And if they really were worried about the sight of spit-roasts inciting violence, and being a bad image for Cambodia, perhaps they should have taken a look at the blood-thirsty tourists shelling out $10 a time to throw live chickens into crowded crocodile pens.

Or better still, the country's many shooting ranges, where drunken Americans could relive moments from their favourite Arnie films. They had stopped allowing holidaymakers to fire rocket launchers at live cows at $500 a pop, but they were still quite happily supplying "small size" animals for cack-handed tourists to blast at – provided you paid of course.

MOST DAYS, I ate chicken porridge soup (borbor sach moan) at the Central Market - a giant yellow, art deco dome with four arms stretching out into vast hallways, selling everything from seafood to fake Rolex watches. On one side, near Noodle Alley in the Chinatown area, were rows of food stalls. It was a seething sauna, but I'd been told they sold the best soups in town.

I quickly grew to love the dish. Maybe it was the heavy use of nutty, browned, but not burnt garlic (a common garnish in Khmer soups), or the herby fragrance of the chopped culantro sprinkled on top? Or the occasional limp crunch of bean sprouts poached in the heat of the broth? Or the pleasing discovery of a little piece of chicken or bone to suck on?

Or was it the soothing lightness of the chicken stock, hinting of lime leaf and lemon grass? Or the julienne strips of fresh ginger that were, like the bean sprouts, stirred in at the end moments before service so they take on an increasingly cooked texture as you finish the soup?

Because this was not a soup to be rushed. It took time to finish. And as a breakfast, which is when it is traditionally eaten in Cambodia, it was deliciously filling - and there was no bacon and eggs in sight. The great "all day English breakfast" as every cafe and restaurant seemed to describe fry-ups out here may leave you feeling stuffed for an hour or two with all that lovely grease and ketchup. But in my experience, it often leaves you craving a second breakfast – especially if bacon sarnies are involved.

But chicken porridge soup keeps you going all day. And that was just as well for a grizzled expat I met who was living on $2 a day for food, which he managed to achieve by eating two bowls of borbor sach moan every day - after he'd persuaded them to charge him the Khmer price, that is.

But it wasn't just the flavours. It was the love with which it was made. I honestly thought I'd met the happiest two women in the world when I went to their tiny stall at the Central Market. The twins had two small tables that customers would cram round, and gazed on happily, constantly joking and smiling, as they watched customers queue for space, and then dive into the condiment trays of ground pepper, sugar, fish sauce, lime segments, fiery red chillies, and fermented bean paste.

There were no wounded egos or chef tantrums – Khmer food is always served with plenty of condiments to balance the desired sweet, sour, bitter, and salty tastes of each diner. There was little arrogance in the kitchens out here, as I would learn, and no "right" way to flavour a dish. And it came as a refreshing change if you've ever had the misfortune to work for the sort of brazen, dogma-driven robots Michelin-starred restaurants spew out.

But it was not just the love and the bean sprouts and the zip from the black pepper, and the hit of lemon grass and ginger, and the soothing crunch of gizzards (easily the best part of a hen for my money), and the soapy richness of the cubes of blood pudding, and the wilful perfume of dusky, browned garlic. It was the gloop - the way the jasmine rice splits and thickens the stock, creating a greyish, cloudy sheen.

As has been repeated widely by sandwich toaster-endorsing celebrity chef Heston Blumenthal and others, many dishes take you back to a memory of childhood. For me, it was the chicken and rice dish they served at school. I think they called it "chicken a la king" but it was so long ago it's hard to remember.

It was chicken cooked in a creamy, yellow sauce that probably came courtesy of condensed soup - the base of many a casserole in those days. It always came with boiled rice and one or two triangles of fried bread. Fried the same chestnut brown as the garlic at the twins' soup stall.

There was something splendid about the way you stirred the chicken and rice together, the softening fried bread dancing playfully on your tongue. And it was that sort of texture you got from Cambodia's famous soup, especially if you bought a baguette to dip into it as I always did.

I became such a regular, I asked if I could watch them make it one day, and was surprised when my alarm clock went off at 4.30am and I actually got up. They started by putting five or six whole chickens in a huge soup cauldron. They filled it with water, threw in some chopped shallots and garlic, lime leaves, and a few bruised lemon grass stalks, and then raked up the charcoal and brought the pot to the boil.

Then they added enough peeled turmeric to turn the liquid a golden yellow. The spice is heavily revered by Khmers for its medicinal properties – and pregnant women have it rubbed into their bodies to keep their skin tight after they give birth. They let the stock simmer away for a couple of hours, topping up with water when necessary, and then seasoned it with salt, fish sauce, sugar, and plenty of pepper. They fished out the chickens and put them in a bucket to cool, ready to be prepped.

Every part of the bird was laid out on a tray, including the yolks taken from the hens' ovaries, which glinted like amber pearls and were absolutely wonderful. Diners chose which parts of the chicken they wanted, and the breast was shredded and carefully rationed, and laid on top.

In a smaller pot, they cooked the rice until it began to break up, and then put a scoop in each bowl - with a handful of blanched bean sprouts and some shredded ginger - to a rough proportion of one third rice to two thirds chicken stock, so it didn't completely smother the broth. When cooking for smaller numbers, the rice is boiled in the chicken liquor, but when you are dealing with vats of the stuff, and keeping it hot all day, you have to keep them separate otherwise the rice dissolves and loses its porridge consistency.

Lastly, they made the garlic garnish by finely chopping dozens of cloves, and heating vegetable oil in a frying pan. When the oil began to spit, they tossed in the garlic and stirred for 30 seconds or so until it was brown, but not burnt. Then they drained off the oil, and sprinkled the garlic on top with chopped culantro and spring onion greens. You should really try it - it's a blinder. And if it's excellent out here in the stifling heat of Phnom Penh, it must be even better on a dark, chilly morning in wind-swept Britain.

ONE NIGHT, I went to eat at a tiny bistro that was for sale in the middle of one of Phnom Penh's red light areas. The owner wanted $10,000 keyhole money - a third of the price of most of the bars for sale in the area. There were three years left on the lease, and the rent was $550 a month, according to the details on the agent's website.

I'd been sitting at a table for a few minutes, when I thought things were going to turn quite ugly for a second, and had visions of my iPhone being thrown on the floor and crushed under a weighty boot. The owner, a stocky, heavily-tattooed Frenchman, stormed over and said: "No photo!" as I took snaps of the menu. He demanded to know what I was doing and I assured him I didn't own a restaurant, and wasn't there to nick his dishes.

He calmed down after that, and said he was worried three or four restaurants might appear near his tiny bistro with identical menus. I felt like holding up a copy of his sacred menu – boasting French classics like coq au vin – and asking him which of the dishes he'd invented himself. But wisely thought better of it.

The owner was soon back to his charming self, and poured me a shot of absinthe. I necked it as he returned with a spoon and sugar lump. "You do already!" he said. I didn't want to upset him again, so I bought another one and let him unleash the green fairy, and pay homage to the memory of Toulouse Le Plot.

39

He was soon telling me of the years he'd spent in the French army while flicking through his menu, pointing to the cheapness of the drinks - just $1 for a glass of house wine. I asked about the specials on the blackboard, and he went off to his kitchen at the back of the bistro, and proudly returned with a vac-pack pouch of confit duck he'd cooked in a sous vide water bath.

I sat there looking at the bawdy madness of the street, thinking about what a strange place it was to have a French restaurant selling tripe and tete de veau hidden on a row of lady bars, next to a shady gambling den, as if to say, oh, find me if you must. Would I take a date there, I pondered. Probably not. But I was clearly wrong, and the tables began to fill with Frenchmen in femme-batteurs and their escorts.

Raw and ready might be one way to describe the street-side ambience. It was a real diamond in the rough. But the place certainly had character - the informal, neighbourhood dive ambience of a true bistro. The kitchen was small, but well fitted out, and I imagined myself cooking there every night, and sleeping upstairs in the wooden shack perched on top of the restaurant.

I thought about a book I'd read called The Art Of Simple French Cookery by Alexander Watt, a notorious gourmet who spent much of his life lounging around in Gallic restaurants, which perfectly captures the essence of the Parisian bistro in the 1950s.

No doubt beginning his day with pastis, moving on to red wine, and then finishing the night on brandy, Watt would gorge himself on bistro classics such as poularde Marie-Louise, boeuf en gelee, rognons a la moutarde, gibelotte de lapin, and always a plate of seasonal cheeses.

The accounts of his "gastronomic peregrinations" are a joy to read, as is his book, Paris Bistro Cookery, which adjoins the back of The Art Of Simple French Cookery like an upside down Siamese twin. As you flick through the pages, you can picture Watt swaying in the doorway of tiny Parisian kitchens, disrupting service as he scrawls into a grease-spattered notebook.

And something told me he would have approved of that tiny bistro, 6,200 miles away in Phnom Penh, and the cooking of its chef-owner. I kicked off with a plate of foie gras, which was tasty enough and had the usual coma-slipping texture, and came with toasted slices of white sandwich loaf – thankfully not the repulsive, sweetened variety you always get in Cambodia. After my main course arrived, the owner returned from the kitchen and caught me taking pictures. This time there was no hostility. He simply walked up to his friend at the next table and joked in French that I was Japanese.

My tournedos was wonderfully succulent, and full of well-aged, beefy flavour. It was topped with a rich red wine sauce, thick with melted shallots, and with a deeply sensual taste. The potato gratin was studded with garlic slices and extremely good. I checked the price on the specials board behind me, and sneaked another photo. There was definitely no 1 in front of the 7. How you could sell such a generous portion of fantastic food for just $7? He could hardly be making $1 gross profit on the meal, if that. It must have been a front.

I was given a shot of orange rum, and finished with a very decent cheese plate – goat's cheese, Roquefort, Camembert, and a surprisingly good version of that dullest of all fromages, Port Salut.

The bistro wasn't pretty or elegant. Nor was it trying to be. It simply represented an instinct to feed on good quality French food at a very wallet-friendly price. I thought about making the owner an offer - $10,000 was about all I could scrape together, and I knew the landlord would want at least three months' rent as a deposit - but he didn't look the sort to negotiate.

Besides, I wanted to check out the rest of the country first, and I'd always dreamed of a restaurant with a sea view. Nothing fancy - just a glimpse of the harbour would do. Phnom Penh was far too hot and chaotic.

CHAPTER THREE

I WAS on a bus south to Sihanoukville - the country's most famous beach resort, which sadly had become better known for its seedy sex industry and sewage sludge waters than its amazing seafood.

Slowly we left the dusty sprawl of the capital and passed through villages filled with rubbish. Sugar palm trees were dotted across the pancake landscape like green lollipops. Occasionally, we'd pass the gates of a pagoda, winged by mythical beasts in peeling gold paint. Rice paddies gave way to ponds full of lotus flowers. A small girl was canoeing in one of them. Then the farms stopped and we passed another strip of sweat shops producing cheap garments for the US and Europe.

The brakes squealed again and we stopped at a grimy restaurant next to a series of Buddha shrines at the Pich Nil pass - the halfway point between Phnom Penh and Sihanoukville. People were stopping to light incense and leave offerings of bananas and other foods. At the foot of one statue sat a pig's head swarming with flies. Some sprinkled holy water over their cars to bless them, and presumably protect them from accidents.

I found out later the spirit houses were dedicated to Ya-Mao, a deity said to oversee Cambodia's 280 miles of developing coastline. She was apparently the wife of a fisherman who spent months away from her at sea in Koh Kong. One rainy season she grew lonely and travelled by boat to meet him, but was swept away in a storm and drowned.

But her spirit lived on, and the fishermen and villagers began leaving offerings of phallic objects to her. Some said it was what she was seeking when she set out on her doomed trip. Others said she hated men and blamed her husband for her death, and wanted symbols of severed penises to placate her.

It reminded me of a story I'd read about in Thailand where wives would get revenge on their cheating husbands. They'd wait for him to go to sleep and then cut off his penis with a kitchen knife before throwing it out of the window of their stilt house to be eaten by ducks.

The saying, "I better go home or the ducks will have something to eat" was said to be a common joke among men in the country.

We passed through more villages offering guesthouses for $3 a night. Everywhere were signs for Prime Minister Hun Sen's Cambodia People's Party. The rest just advertised beer. The whole industry seemed to be based on mobile phone shops, moped garages, and noodle joints. People were gathered around stalls munching baguettes, whole sweet corn, and barbecued chicken wingtips. No-one seemed to be in a hurry to do anything. Concrete tubes, 3ft-wide, were piled up everywhere, waiting for more sewers to be dug.

But it was the horrendous amount of rubbish everywhere I noticed most. There seemed to be no pride in the beauty of that emerald countryside, no thought of cleaning up the litter filling the muddy market squares and village ditches. There were plastic bag graveyards beside every road, streams choked full of bottles and cans, and witches' knickers in every tree.

I'd never been in a country where people loved the sight of discarded plastic so much. You could be strolling through an idyllic stretch of countryside and find a lotus flower-filled pond with cows supping from the water, the late afternoon sun glinting away on the ripples, and there'd be mounds of sun-bleached bags and other human waste blighting the scenery.

We passed one picnic area overlooking a beauty spot, and it was as if each family had filled the car with every bit of rubbish they or their neighbours could get their hands on, and then chucked it on the ground.

And it was not helped by the fact that Cambodians seemed to use plastic bags for everything. Take the coconut – the perfect drinking device. The day before, I'd seen a young boy hawking them in a park in Phnom Penh. Whenever anyone ordered one, he tipped the coconut upside down and poured the liquid into a plastic bag and handed it to the buyer with a straw. When they finished, people just chucked the bags on the grass and then continued their journey in search of more plastic.

Another time, a Land Cruiser sped past me. A KFC Variety Bucket landed at my feet. I gave a universally-recognised gesture, and there was a screech of brakes as he pulled up sharply at a set of traffic lights. I picked up the bucket and was about to throw it in a bin, when I saw the driver still waiting at the lights. I caught his eye and he opened the window.

"You've dropped something," I said.

He looked confused and then saw his empty fried chicken bucket. I held it out towards him and he shouted at me, and then sped off. He clearly saw it as his right as a consumer to throw his Variety Bucket wherever he pleased.

When I'd talked to the Cambodian staff at my guesthouse, they said it was simply a matter of education – and many Khmers also get frustrated at the sight of rubbish everywhere. Kids see their parents chucking litter about so they do the same, and so the cycle continues. There are messages on Cambodian TV telling people not to litter, and signs on walls telling people to respect the environment, but it makes no difference.

One of the staff told me: "When I see a person throwing rubbish in the street, I get so angry. I tell them they cannot do, and think they don't know it's wrong, but they just get angry and say 'up to me!' Many have no education and are ignorant, others just don't care..."

There should be fines for littering, I scribbled, my pencil jiggling away over the potholes as green-fronded mountains rose up from the fields, and I knew we were near the coast. Cambodian police are very good at skulking in corners and hiding up alleyways jumping out on anyone who's not wearing a motorbike helmet, so they'd be just as good at catching litter bugs red-handed – if there was a bit of cash in it for them.

And it doesn't matter how many green T-shirt-wearing workers they employ to clean up the mess, it's impossible to finish a job that can never be completed. It would be far worse without recycling, of course, when there's 100 riel or so for each beer can or plastic bottle collected. But there's no money to be had scavenging for plastic bags or takeaway containers. It's such a crying shame in a country filled with banana trees. Why no-one has made takeaway boxes out of banana leaves is beyond me.

THE TUK tuk mafia descended as I got off at the bus station, quoting ridiculous prices.

"How much you pay then?" one of them snapped.

"I'm not paying you anything," I said and walked off down the road.

They were soon following me and the price quickly halved. I got a ride through the down town area to Ochheuteal Beach, and waited at the reception desk of a huge, shabby-looking guesthouse. A South African backpacker, covered in tattoos, was trying to convince the chubby man behind the desk to rent him a moped for seven days.

"Are you smoking" asked the manager. "No smoking here..."

The backpacker got aggressive.

"Why do you think I'm smoking?"

"No smoking here!"

"Why do you think I'm smoking?"

It went on for a bit so I picked up my laptop and backpack and walked off to the next hotel. The monsoon was thundering down and a backpacker had stripped off his clothes and was standing in the road, his arms stretched out and his face peering up to the heavens as if crucified.

"Oh yeah, baby!" he kept shrieking.

I didn't like the look of the place at all, and decided to find a new guesthouse the next morning. I unlocked my room, switched on the wheezing fan, and unstitched the hem on the curtains. I put my passport and cash in there, sewed it back up again, and then headed out for a beer.

"Skunk, coke, lady?" came the chorus from the moto drivers as I walked down the broken road to the beach.

I sat in a bar on the pier and looked out at the dark waves and the distant lights from the fishing boats. The beach shacks stretched along the sand as far as I could see. I watched the fire jugglers for a while - from a distance they looked like burning wagon wheels - and then headed back to my guesthouse, checked the hem on the curtains, and tried to fall asleep. The power went off, and soon sweat was pouring from my brow. I went out and drank some more beer and eventually fell asleep.

I SPENT the next few days eating at the local restaurants. It looked far from promising. Costa del Cambodia was so geared towards tourists and expats, with nearly every menu offering cottage pie, burgers, fish and chips, spag bol, schnitzel, and of course, pizza (some were of the 'happy' kind, where they lace the top with a sprinkling of the local oregano) that the chefs had either forgotten how to cook Khmer food, or they'd just eaten too much of the pizza. Or quite possibly both.

In an apparent afterthought, tucked away in an almost ashamed manner in the tiny Khmer section at the back of most menus, you always got what for some reason have become known as Cambodia's two most famous dishes (blame Lonely Planet) – amok (a sort of steamed fish soufflé in a coconut curry sauce) and the utterly revolting beef lok lak (stir-fried beef with chips and rice).

Anything seemed to be chucked into lok lak - from tomato ketchup to oyster sauce to sweet chilli sauce to the juice from tinned mackerel, and the beef generally varied in tenderness from the thickness of boiled leather to the tenderness of biltong soaked in water for two-and-a-half seconds.

In one of the better restaurants, they made it by dicing a piece of steak into smallish cubes, and then chopping up two cloves of garlic. They heated a tiny amount of oil in a pan, and then fried the garlic until it began to colour, and then threw in the meat to singe it slightly. They added a sprinkling of sugar and salt, and then cooked the meat for another minute or so before pouring in a little water, and adding a few glugs of tomato ketchup and oyster sauce to produce a velvety red-brown sauce. They served it with chips, lettuce, slices of tomato, and onion, and topped it with a fried egg.

46

But what Snooky - as it was imaginatively called by its large expat community - lacked in food, it certainly made up for in its nightlife, white sand beaches, undeveloped tropical islands, and blisteringly hot weather. The locals were so friendly, I found myself loitering in kitchens chatting to Khmer cooks, and eating what they ate rather than the stuff they knocked out for the tourists.

One evening, I shared a splendid meal of tiny smoked fish (trey chha-ae) with pickled cabbage. The fish had been pierced through the head with bamboo skewers, wrapped in banana leaves, and smoked over smouldering coconut husks until they were brown and crispy. They were then left in the sun to dry for a couple of days. They reminded me of smoked anchovies they were so strong in flavour. But the cabbage was the star. It was wonderfully sour and the perfect accompaniment for the salty fish and ubiquitous bowl of sticky rice.

My new friends were worried about me eating too much cabbage, saying my stomach wasn't used to it. I didn't know what they were talking about at first. They kept pointing at my paunch and saying "bad". I was starting to get quite embarrassed, and even made a mental note to go back on Gary Oldman's vodka, fish, and melon diet.

Then they started pointing at the cabbage juice. They obviously thought the only time vinegar is used in British cooking is when a few drops of malt are sprinkled over chips, but then that was no surprise given the dishes on the menu.

There was also a pork noodle soup that was fabulous. It was filled with beautifully soft slices of belly, deep-fried tofu, and banana flowers. The pork stock had been boiling all day, with the addition of chicken feet for extra gloop. It was rich and meaty like a good Vietnamese pho. But it was the contrast of the condiments that really made it – ripe tamarind fruit soaked in water, sliced red chillies, sugar, and shrimp paste (kapi). The shrimps are cleaned and then salted overnight before being pounded into a paste, spread into a thin circle, and dried in the sun for a few days.

And then there was the amok - or at least their version of it, which was much more like a fish curry than the soufflés they teach

47

holidaymakers to make at Cambodian cookery schools. Forget all the nonsense about steaming and serving it in stapled banana leaf cups - that was for the tourists. When they were cooking for themselves, they just steamed it in a bowl half-submerged in a pot of simmering water over a charcoal burner.

It wasn't a brilliant dish, but was intriguingly chameleon-like in character. It initially had a whiff of stew about it, with its flavour-soaked carrots and potatoes, but then drifted towards a creamy korma, and then you got a hint of lime leaf, like a Thai curry, but far less spicy. And then it changed again, and you got the taste of the eggs and coconut cream that had been mixed in at the end. Its final notes were the warmth of cracked black pepper and the buttery taste of prawns and white fish, and it suddenly changed again – this time into a rich chowder.

For some reason, it made me think of Moby Dick when Ishmael and Queequeg feast at the Try Pots, a rough inn famed for its chowder "plentifully seasoned with pepper and salt". And leaning back a moment, it started bethinking me of the fishiest of all fishy places I'd found myself in. I don't know if it was the intensity and freshness of the fish, the sea air, or the decidedly colourful characters that lived in the hazy bars in Sihanoukville. But I'd never sat down at a table before and been the only person who hadn't been to prison.

A WEEK later, I moved up to Victory Hill on the other side of town. A few years before, it had been the backpacking hub of Sihanoukville with enough customers to fill the sea with gold. But since then gravity had definitely moved down the hill to Ochheuteal Beach and the now-thriving Otres Beach area.

It had become so forsaken and run-down that even the tuk tuk drivers at the bus station, not even a mile away, pretended not to have heard of the place - presumably because they got bigger kick-backs from businesses in Ochheuteal.

"Victory Hill," I'd heard one expat say after getting off the bus from Phnom Penh. The tuk tuk drivers shook their heads and looked at each other, repeating the words. "Look I KNOW it exists," he said. "I own a fucking restaurant there..."

Apart from the odd chrome chariot dropping off groups of sex tourists in money belts, Victory Hill's trade seemed to be mainly barflies stretching out their invalidity benefits and pensions in the cheapest bars selling $0.50 handles.

Even people in Ochheuteal grumbled that business was down from last year's high season - which they moaned was heavily down on previous years. And Victory Hill seemed to have shouldered most of that pain. Business was so bad, some bar and guesthouse owners said that on their worst days they'd taken just $2. And when $50 went through the till, they thought they'd won the lottery.

They were not helped, of course, by the clientele, and the seedy reputation that stretch of lady bars and drinking holes festered in. As one Irishman, who had recently moved out of the place, put it: "It seems to be a magnet for the biggest arseholes from the four corners of the Earth." It was hard to argue. I'd never seen so many alcoholics and junkies in one place, and wondered whether it was some warped nominative determinism that a place called Victory Hill should be so full of losers.

Slowly an exodus was beginning, with a number of bar owners seeing the light, and selling their businesses to some other mug, and opening a new venue in Ochheuteal or Otres. Those who remained either claimed to have money and were running their place as a "lifestyle business", or were presumably trying not to think too hard about how a business model based on customers with no money was ever going to work. Crunch down the gravel most nights, and you'll see the depressing sight of empty bar after empty bar, with groups of women sitting outside looking bored and discussing noodles.

There were one or two Western-owned venues still doing a trade, but only the street of Khmer restaurants, identical in price and menu typos, were ever more than half full. But with the ludicrously cheap prices they charged, they could hardly be making more than 2,000 riel ($0.50) per customer - enough to pay the rent and give free accommodation, and a bit of spending money if you know how to live on a Cambodian wage.

As for the hobby entrepreneurs all living the dream, when they did try something new, they nearly always failed, they grumbled. The simple truth was there were not enough customers to support the ludicrous number of restaurants and bars in that small, seamy white ghetto that easily boasted the highest proportion of expats in Cambodia.

One night, I saw the owner of one bar hire a decent American three-piece covers band from Phnom Penh to try to drum up business. He'd spent tens of thousands fitting out his bar, but it was empty every night. He paid the band $150 for a two-hour set, but there were barely six customers in there. I walked back sometime later. The music was pumping, and then I turned and saw the misers lined up at a joint across the road, watching the band, but only paying $0.50 a beer.

The local business owners said it spoke volumes about the Hill. There was no support from anyone. And the $0.50 beers were killing everyone, they grumbled. Some joked that the way things were going, the place would soon turn into the Chicken Farm, a line of huts near the port where dogs were said to fight over condoms dropped through cracks in the floorboards. Those misers watching the music for free while drinking their cheap beer had a lot in common with those dogs.

MY GUESTHOUSE was run by an Italian cook called Marco. One night he served me a splendid dish of tagliere misto. The Parma ham and mortadella, and cubes of, as I know now, fontina and provolone cheeses were fantastic, but the thick slices of fresh salami were incredible.

He'd brought the salami back in a box from his home in Bergamo, Lombardy, where it had been freshly made by his neighbour. I'd never had one that "green", as he called it. It tasted like a very ripe camembert and danced on the roof of my mouth, crackling with umami bubbles on my tongue and gums, and then left an incredibly deep flavour of moist tartare.

As I tucked in, Marco chatted away about Khmer food, and how it was impossible to get flavours like that in Cambodia - a country where, he said, they have no idea what to do with pork, and just eat it fresh, missing out on all those magical products you get with the simple addition of salt, spices, air, and time. He said it was down to Cambodia's poverty-induced "eat for today, forget tomorrow" mentality (that and decent cold-storage facilities anyway).

"That's why they eat mangoes when they're green! And pick the grapes before they're ready! They eat food when they see food," he said.

I thought it best not to mention how some Italian families had eaten cats during food shortages in the Second World War. After the meal, Marco showed me the pizza oven he'd finished building in his outside kitchen three months ago. It was still in the testing stage. He was having trouble maintaining a strong heat flow.

"Anyone can throw a pizza in an oven, but the oven has to be right. The pizza must be cooked in three minutes," he explained.

He said he gets the fire going with dried vines and bristles from an old brush, and then puts big logs on, and lets them burn down for two hours. Then he sweeps the embers to the far side of the oven and places the pizzas straight on to the fire bricks near the opening.

Marco said the dome was made of fire bricks that he had laid without cement. When the special mix of imported cement, sand, and lime – again an old, secret Italian recipe – is sculpted on the outside it holds the structure together. He showed me the sloping chimney mechanism and how it is designed so the wood smoke sits six inches above the pizza.

ONE DAY, he organised a boat trip for his guests. There were four others there – an old Italian man who looked like Picasso, a strange, little Italian hippy who kept giggling to himself all day, a Canadian who'd gone travelling after losing his job as a financial consultant, and a French woman backpacking her way around SE Asia.

The weather looked good for the boat ride, and the early sun shone on our faces as the skipper navigated the pristine mangrove swamps and unspoilt islands dotting the waters off Sihanoukville. And then the Canadian sat next to me. He wouldn't stop talking. I couldn't believe my beautiful view and the quiet lapping of the mill pond sea were being ruined by someone blabbing on about earnings per share and P/E ratios.

Luckily, I got a break from the fiscal tedium when we stopped to fish. The trouble was getting your hook down before the hordes of small fish near the surface stripped it clean. But when I did get the prawn bait to the bottom, I got a bite each time, and pulled in a blue-toothed grouper and some kind of parrot fish, and two smaller specimens that I threw back.

The grouper had enormous bite. It felt like the line was caught on the bottom. But when I finally snagged it from its hole, it was easy to pull in, even with a fishing line wound round a plastic water bottle. The skipper threw my fish into the bowels of his boat. That was obviously his supper sorted out, I thought.

We got to Koh Ta Kiev, a beautiful island with a blissfully empty beach. It looked deserted apart from four fishermen holding a net in the water at the other end of the bay. At one point, a soldier appeared from the jungle and stood a few feet from our camp.

Our skipper had disappeared to talk to the fishermen, and Marco said the soldier wanted his "parking fee" for the boat. Apparently we couldn't just hand him the dollar because there was some sort of paper work required. He stood there for 30 minutes, and then questioned Marco about what we had with us.

"Just some food, some drink to make barbecue," he said.

The soldier was back again an hour later. Marco lit the barbecue and a joint and made some bruschetta with diced tomato, olive oil, and balsamic vinegar. He cooked some mullet-like fish and served them with dressed salad and cold rice. And then the Canadian, who'd been going on about my fish in the hull for the past hour, saying he felt sorry for them, asked why I didn't barbecue them as well.

I had a bad feeling about it for some reason. I don't know what was wrong with me, but I just couldn't bring myself to kill them. They were too pretty. Alright, it was the sharp blue teeth and vicious spines that put me off as well. But mostly it was that although I hadn't let anyone else think otherwise, I couldn't really swear what types of fish they were. And with their bright yellow spots and aquamarine iridescence, they looked too exotic, and too potentially poisonous.

After ten minutes, the Canadian was still going on about the fish despite my protestations that I was going to give them to the skipper for his supper. Then Marco said we should at least see what they tasted like, so I found myself back on the boat, trying to recatch the fish with a plastic container that had been cut into a dustpan shape. It wasn't easy. The fish had landed in puddles in the hull and were very much still alive. I knew what getting pricked by a sea bass spine can do to you, so I was taking no chances.

Every time I put my hand near the grouper, if it was a grouper, he was at me with his vicious jaws. In the end I scooped them into a plastic bag and bashed them to death in the shadows of the hull. Or at least I thought I had. The grouper, and it probably was a grouper, just wouldn't die. Normally you only have to hit a pollack or cod once.

But this thing was like the Rasputin of the marine world. Every time I thought I had the measure of him, he was suddenly back lunging at me with his frightening blue teeth. I was about to gut him with a knife that was as blunt as a spoon, when he came alive again in a flurry of horrible-looking spikes.

I was getting quite embarrassed by my cack-handed killing skills and wasn't being helped by the Canadian leering over me giving me advice. I tell you if he was on Mastermind, his specialised subject would be everything. He continued to poke his nose in as I scaled them in the sea.

"You don't need to do that, you don't need to scale them," he kept saying.

What the hell did he know, even if he had picked me up on my lack of knowledge about, as I know now, fontina and provolone cheeses the night before? He was only saying it because Marco hadn't bothered to scale his fish, and although they were delicious, I like the taste of crunchy, charred skin, not a mouthful of fish armour. I sprinkled the two fish with salt, olive oil, and black pepper and grilled them over hot coals. They were soon crispy black around the gills and spines, and then the Canadian reappeared.

"That's definitely cooked," he said, prodding the grouper, and it definitely was a grouper.

I was really beginning to regret telling him how I'd just finished writing a book about my failure to make it as a professional chef. He was continually trying to pick me up on holes in my cooking knowledge. Then Picasso stood by the barbecue.

"Do you know fugu?" he asked.

There was a discussion about blowfish and the dangers of eating them, and the inference that only highly-trained chefs were trusted to serve them. He pointed at the exotic specimens I was turning.

"Are you sure not same?" he chuckled.

It wasn't just the sun that made me sore that day as I basted in the heat of that supposedly unspoilt island, it was the fact they hardly ate any of my fish. Was it the blue bones? I'd experienced the same in Cornwall when I made what I thought was a magnificent meal of garfish. The customers had been put off by the green bones. But I wasn't in Padstow, I was among Italians. Surely they bathed in carnality and gastronomic adventure?

It soon became a scene out of Lord of the Flies. Not, unfortunately, with me nicking the Canadian's bottle-end glasses to make fire and forming my own tribe on one half of the island, but in a feast of flies. We packed up, buried the charcoal embers in the sand and took the fish back for Marco's menagerie of cats and kittens at the guesthouse.

They soon got stuck in, and for five minutes there was no mewing as they chomped away, concentrating on their food. One of the kittens was trying to gulp down a huge tail end of grouper. It was like a human eating a 3ft-wide salami. I sat there listening to the crunch of bones and the licking of fur. I was glad someone liked my fish.

THE NEXT night, I met a retired bank manager from New Zealand, who part-owned a restaurant on the Hill, and he convinced me that the next big thing in Cambodia would be the pork pie. He said expats and tourists were crying out for them, but he couldn't get them anywhere, and he'd had no luck making them.

"It's the pastry! I can't do the pastry," said Josh, rocking from side to side with a cigarette in his mouth. "I can do everything else. I've got this delicious jelly I've made in the freezer. Wonderful!" He smacked his lips. "There's a mincer in the kitchen, but the pastry, no. I can't make the pastry. Can I make the pastry? The answer's no..."

We sat around for an hour discussing the merits of pork pies and I thought that was pretty much the end of the matter. Then I saw him in Rodney's bar again the next night and he started going on about pork pies again. I may have mentioned that I'd worked as a chef. I may even have drunkenly boasted a bit about my pie-making skills. But at some point, I must have agreed to help him. Josh introduced me to his business partner Tom, who claimed to be an English gent who'd retired to the tropics after getting tired of the antiques trade.

"So you're the pork pie expert?" he said, shaking my hand. I knew I was in trouble. "I have to tell you, I'm quite a lover of pork pies," he added.

There was only one thing for it. I'd go back to my windswept, Wild West-style guesthouse, and do some pork pie research on the internet and then practise the pastry in their kitchen until I perfected it. I told Josh we'd need some lard. Luckily, he said you couldn't get it anywhere in Cambodia.

"Butter no problem. But lard? No. No lard. Forget it."

I got some recipes and tips from food writers, bakers, and chefs on Twitter, and spent the next night making notes as I read everything I could on pork pies. Some hot water crust pastry recipes use butter and even eggs as well as lard, but they all use lard to some extent. The only one I could find that used butter and no lard was Rick Stein's pork pie recipe. But I was dubious about that. I knew what he'd done to the Cornish pasty, and how he'd upset the locals by using the 'wrong' pastry.

I was convinced Tom - who clearly was the senior partner in the business (and what's that? Was I beginning to detect a faint Leicestershire accent?) - would be a stickler for a traditional pie crust. Stein's version also used anchovy essence in the filling, like Jane

Grigson's recipe, and I had doubts about what Tom would think of that, even if it was said to be a traditional Melton Mowbray ingredient.

I told them it was impossible without the lard. Then Josh had an idea. He could scoop off the fat that collected when he boiled down "bags of beef" for his dogs. I wasn't keen. I didn't like the sound of bags of beef in Cambodia, especially meat set aside for dogs. There were far too many people disappearing in the town.

I pompously told him the pork pie was all about a celebration of the pig, and involved pork done three ways - baking the fat-laden pastry, boiling the pork stock, and steaming the peppery filling. I waffled on about how the filling – flavoured with salt, pepper, thyme, sage, nutmeg, and perhaps mace or allspice, but probably no anchovy - is a tribute to cured and uncured pork, and its fattiness and texture, from the knife-chopped pork shoulder, to the coarsely-minced pork belly, to the finely-minced back bacon.

The succulent jelly (or gravy, as it is called in some areas) – with carrot, onion, bay leaf, thyme, pepper, and sea salt – is a nod to the satisfying gloop that pork bones and trotters bring to a stock. And the pastry is a celebration of how pig fat can produce rich, crisp, and yet moist pie crusts. In essence, I politely told him that the fat he'd get from his dog food would be no good, and that we needed pig fat.

"Oh, pig fat! You didn't say it had to be from pigs! Pig fat, no problem. Lard, no. Pig fat yes! We can get shit loads of pig fat. Leave that to me..."

By now, he'd shown me round his kitchen and I'd quickly gone off the idea. It was tiny. It made the Fat Duck's kitchen look like a cricket pitch. And the heat! It was 37C in the shade, but with no extraction unit and both ovens on making pizzas, it was like an inferno in there.

There was a fan in the corner, but when you turned it on, it blew out the gas rings. But worst of all, there were two Cambodian cooks sharing a surface space (the most crucial dimension in any kitchen) scarcely more than 3ft wide. There was no room to roll out the pizzas they were making, let alone pastry as well. And the two battered old

Cambodian ovens! It definitely wasn't the sort of kitchen to launch a pork pie empire.

THERE WERE a few more colourful characters sitting around Rodney's bar the next night. They'd all heard about the pork pie business. I was surprised how fast gossip travels in expat circles - even faster than kitchens.

One of them, a retired boxer from Manchester, who used to carry a football hooligan book about with him, which mentioned him on one of the pages, said he was hooked on TV cookery programmes. Then the rest were at it. They were all experts, and started swapping recipe tips, and talking about what celebrity chefs they did and didn't like.

"I loved Keith Floyd!" mused Rodney, wrinkling his Keith Richards face.

"Yeah he's fucking ace," said the boxer. "He's one of the top, top chefs. Haven't seen much of him on telly like...what's he doing now?"

"He's dead," I said, holding up a Sang Som in Floyd's memory. "He passed away almost two years ago."

"No! Get on! Really?" said the boxer. "That's the thing - you miss out on all that, living out here..."

Then they were on to the food they missed from home.

"A pork fucking pie!" said Rodney. "A proper pork pie - when you go in England. Oh! Beans, a couple of pickled onions, and I tell you what, I might have two pork pies. I fucking love them! Fantastic! I tell you, when I used to go to work..."

"I tell you what I'd have - boiled bacon! Cabbage and boiled potatoes, and gravy on it and that..." said a lorry driver from London.

"Liver and bacon!" came a voice from the back of the bar as the power went out for the second time that day.

As we sat in darkness, with Rodney cursing as he yanked away at the generator cord, there were calls for Colman's Mustard, Bovril, Walkers crisps, Hula Hoops, "proper" Cornish pasties, pickled eggs,

Yorkshire tea, and black pudding - products that seem to have taken on an exotic allure by being unavailable in the Kingdom.

Josh turned up. He still hadn't been able to get his hands on pig fat, much to my relief. I joked about how we could buy a whole pig from the market and render it down, and I could see he was going off the idea. Then I asked if you could get mace here.

"Mace, no. Nutmeg, yes," said Josh. "We can get shit loads of nutmeg, as much nutmeg as you fucking want, but no mace. No way! Why, do we need it?"

I told him the best pork pies had mace in them, and that we might as well do it properly.

"Well, you'll have to get on with it! I'm going home in nine days," said an old Australian called Dirty Derek. "Why don't you make a curry tomorrow night instead?"

It was brilliant. Everyone was in agreement. Curry! What could be even more British than a good old pork pie than curry! The fear and nerves vanished. A curry! If there was one thing I could make it was curry. I'd eaten at the only Indian restaurant on the Hill, and it'd been awful. I could corner the curry market. Become Mr Curry of Sihanoukville (small acorns). I had no qualms about curry – even in Josh's tiny kitchen. Then it turned out the boxer was an expert on curries too.

"I haven't had a good curry for years," he said, leaning back and stretching his arms. "I lived on the Curry Mile in the Wilmslow Road, the best fucking curries in the world, man..."

Then they were all discussing curries they'd had, and the nerves started to test again.

"Hey chef, what meat makes the best curry?" the boxer shouted over at me. "That's it! Fucking lamb," he replied, smacking the back of his hand. "It's alright, he does know his stuff..."

Josh said lamb was hideously expensive in Cambodia. He'd bought a 4kg frozen leg for his Sunday roast for $54. I told him I could get a massaged leg from Fortnum & Mason for that, and he pointed out that Fortnum & Mason wasn't round the corner. He said the cheapest meats were pork and chicken, so I decided on my trusty old, tried and tested chicken madras-style recipe.

"Yeah, but what about spices? What about all your cardamoms and that?" said the boxer.

"There's an Indian restaurant round the corner!" I said slightly irritably.

"Yeah, but what about your fenugreeks and curry leaves...you'll want them...I don't know, you're not in the right country for it..."

I became more drunk as the night wore on, and at some point told them I was going to make "the best bloody curry they'd ever had". It was a bold statement. Very bold. They looked the sort that got Christmas cards from their local Indian take-away.

I WALKED back to my guesthouse in the small hours, hoping I'd remember to turn my alarm on and be round at the restaurant at 8.30am to be down the market for nine. The alarm went off and I pressed snooze, then I pressed it again, and eventually woke up with a blinding headache at noon. I was four hours late for the market. I grabbed my lucky hat and headed over the road to the restaurant.

"How's your head?" said Josh as I arrived.

Tom was in the background fiddling with his computer. Somehow he'd managed to turn the screen upside down and had his neck tilted at a painful-looking angle, trying to read as he typed. He was in a wretched mood, and was already on gin.

"Good morning Pork Pie," he said, looking at his watch. "Well, I suppose it's afternoon now..."

Josh began fretting about what ingredients we'd need for the curry. It was all in hand, I assured him. He grabbed a tuk tuk and we headed down to the central market in Sihanoukville. It was like a pizza oven. Luckily, Josh didn't want to buy the chicken from there. But not for hygiene reasons, he just said they were too scrawny. He said he always bought imported ones from the supermarket. They were much plumper, but the Cambodians wouldn't eat them because they said the Thais filled them with chemicals to make them grow quicker.

Josh's restaurant order was already bagged up at the stall. I bought a sack of onions, a huge lump of ginger, two heads of garlic, a handful of chilli peppers, but no coriander. I wandered round the stalls. None of them had coriander. They were selling celery leaves, but no coriander.

But far worse, there were no dried spices anywhere. It wasn't a good start. We loaded up the tuk tuk with bags of rice, flour, and potatoes, and headed to the supermarket for spices. The second one was worse than the first, so we went back to the first one. Josh showed me the enormous range of vodka bottles. There was a bottle of local spirit with a cobra curled up inside.

"I bet that's got a bite," I said.

"Jesus no, that's for the Cambodians. Never touch the stuff. No way. Not in a million fucking years. Forget it!" he replied.

It may have had every vodka brand under the sun, but there was a very poor spice selection. You can buy anything in Cambodia from a live Russell's viper to a hand grenade, but cumin seeds? The answer was no.

I could imagine what the boxer was going to say. The only relatively cheap spice was ground coriander. You could get a small bag of it for $1.50 - but everything else was expensive, even by UK standards. A small pot of cardamom would cost an average Cambodian more than two day's pay. We were going to struggle to make a profit on the meal. But then it was only a trial, I suppose. They just wanted to see whether I could cook.

I bought ground coriander, ground cumin, cayenne pepper, turmeric, cinnamon sticks, black onion seeds, fenugreek, and a bottle of the snake liquor. It was far from perfect, but it was enough to make a decent curry. I'd put in plenty of ginger and garlic and pep up the cayenne heat with some finely chopped red chillies.

I thought about what I'd said the night before, and how I'd boasted that I was going to make them "the best bloody curry they'd ever had". I stood in the aisle flinching at the words. Then I consoled myself that a cook can only work with the ingredients and kitchen he's got, and I'd just have to make do. It would add to the challenge. But I knew they wouldn't suffer excuses. Then I thought about the boxer stuffing himself with his favourite curries on the Wilmslow Road.

I knew there was nothing wrong with my recipe though. I'd made it as a staff meal for the chefs at the Fat Duck. And they'd liked it, or at least said it was okay, which is a glowing accolade in cheffing circles, and they were three-star Michelin chefs, not a tattooed bunch of renegade food experts who'd found themselves washed up with the other bums, predators, pathological liars, pimps, alcoholics, junkies, and other flotsam on Victory Beach.

Then we had a major problem.

"I hope you're not looking for tinned tomatoes," said a miserable old Brit as we walked up the aisle.

He was enraged about not having tomatoes to go with his bacon the following morning. I was worried about not having tomatoes for 20 customers that evening. You can say what you want about using fresh tomatoes, but tinned tomatoes make a better curry, especially if you compare them to the bland, white-centred offerings you get in Cambodia.

"It's okay, it's okay, there's a tin in the kitchen," said Josh. "Yep, yep, I'm pretty sure there's a big tin in the kitchen somewhere."

Then there was more to come. The supermarket had almost sold out of chicken. All they had were chicken wings and breast. I remembered the boxer harping on about how breast is "tasteless mush", and the wings were no good, and then I thought about that stupid drunken boast again. We bought four big bags of frozen breasts for $16 and loaded up the tuk tuk, and called into a computer repair shop to send someone round to fix Tom's screen. He'd phoned up slurring about going for a massage because he'd got a crick in his neck.

Luckily there was a 2kg tin of tomatoes being used as a doorstop back at the restaurant. Dee, one of the Cambodian cooks, was serving a few customers. Josh told me to come back at 4pm when the broom cupboard kitchen would be quieter. I had between 4pm and 6.30pm to get a killer curry made before another two cooks turned up. Dee was finishing her last order when I returned. Josh was fretting around behind me.

"So what do you need? What do you need?"

Thankfully, he soon left us to it and returned to his card game with a loud, impish-looking Australian man on red wine. His name was Wayne, and he was blessed with an extraordinarily huge nose with blue veins running across it like Stilton cheese. He suddenly darted up from his chair, clutching a page from the Phnom Penh Post.

"Look, now we know what they really call us!" he bellowed furiously. "Even the fucking police!"

He darted around the bar, showing expats the offending police quote. It was a story about Cambodian fishermen rescuing 87 tourists whose party boat had capsized off Sihanoukville. The provincial police chief had blamed drunken passengers for dancing and making the boat sink. "It was caused by our long nose, who were too happy," he said.

Wayne rolled up the newspaper and whacked the bar top several times in fury.

"Pol Pot should have killed the whole fucking lot of them!" he screamed.

I BORROWED a chopper, board, and a plastic bag for the off-cuts and got to work on the sack of onions. Dee was standing around, watching me anxiously. She still had no idea what the strange long nose was doing in her kitchen. All Josh had said was "we make curry." She obviously wanted to chop the onions, but I wasn't taking any chances. The onions had to be right. I'd had enough set-backs already without ballsing up the onions.

I got her to peel some garlic, and then I realised just how good a cook she was. She blitzed the garlic, then started on the meat. I showed her how I wanted the chicken cut up, with six cubes out of each breast, and two minutes later there was a mountain of glistening, perfect cubes. She told me she'd started in the kitchen as a potwash at 14, and had worked for the past six years under a series of long nose chefs. It was in her blood.

I threw chopped onions, ginger, garlic, red chillies, and two scoops of sea salt into a huge pot with plenty of vegetable oil, and started cooking the curry sauce down. I didn't want to rush the sauce, but the clock was ticking and another order had come in to mess things up. I let the onions simmer for 30 minutes until they had that sweet, melted confit texture you'd use for onion marmalade.

I started thinking about the customers again. They were no doubt already down at Rodney's, swigging draught Angkor and talking about their curry. They'd probably even written out score boards. I knew they were waiting for me to mess things up. One of them, a huge pit bull of a man, had already cracked jokes about if his curry wasn't good enough, he wasn't going to pay for it. But as he'd survived five years in a Thai jail I wasn't going to argue with him.

Dee was fascinated by the curry, and I could tell she was taking it all in. I said Tom and Josh were lucky to have such a good chef, and told her to ask for a pay rise. I got her to sniff each of the spices as I threw them into the onions and explained how it was important to cook the sauce for a long time. I fried the spices for a few minutes and then added two fat cinnamon sticks and three bay leaves, and more water to stop the paste catching on the bottom.

Dee finished chopping the tomatoes, and added them to the pan. We'd let them cook down for another 45 minutes. It gave us 30 minutes to finish the dish. Josh popped his head in, and showed me the blender he'd promised. It was about the size of a Coke can. I had about five litres of sauce to blitz. I didn't have another big vessel to pour the pureed sauce into, and there wasn't the time or surface space to fill up a load of plastic containers.

I was just glad I'd finely diced the onions, and got Dee to do the same with the tomatoes. With plenty of oil and cooking it should almost go down to a smooth sauce, but again it wouldn't be perfect. Then Josh came back and said he couldn't find the grinder for the fenugreek. I thought about the boxer again and his freshly-made curry pastes on the Curry Mile.

The onions had almost dissolved by the time I put the chicken in. I let the curry gently cook for another 30 minutes or so. I added more salt and some lime juice, sugar, and tomato ketchup (the secret ingredient in Indian restaurants). It was as good as any I'd made at home, I was sure of it, but then it was hard to remember.

I was in foreign climes, nursing myself with gin and tonics to quell the afternoon sun, my mouth salivating at the very thought of curry. I was in no position to judge. But there was still something missing. I tried more lime juice and vinegar, but it needed more bite. Then I reached for the bottle with the cobra curled up inside.

It was 6.15pm when I turned the curry off and tasted it for the last time. I was dripping with sweat. I was as wet as a police officer during Songkran. I realised how out of practice I was, but I'd never cooked in a kitchen that hot before. Tom was hovering near the door, holding his neck. I asked him how hot he wanted it, saying it was just under the radar of what I'd call a medium-hot curry.

"Well, it can't be too hot, or the Western customers won't eat it," he grimaced. "But the Khmers will – they'll eat anything."

He washed a spoon and dipped in.

"Oh yes, that's good. It's got a kick, you can feel it," he said, clutching his throat as he swallowed. "I don't think it needs to be any hotter than that."

I wasn't convinced. I was sure the panel of food experts were looking for a hot curry. Tom and Josh went off in a huddle in front of the now fixed computer to work out a price. It really looked like they knew what they were doing. They decided on $4 for a bowl of curry with rice or a baguette.

I reckoned there were at least 16 servings in the pot – even with the huge portions they served. The ingredients had cost a maximum of $30, even if you took the tuk tuk into account, and it looked like I was cooking for free – there hadn't been any mention of money - so they were left with a $34 gross profit if they sold it all, plus whatever they made on drinks.

Normally in the UK, you'd go for a 30% food cost, meaning if you bought £30 of food, you'd sell it for £100. We were working at around a 50% food cost, but the overheads and wages are much less in Cambodia – the monthly rent on the restaurant was just $300, plus $20 to the police, and the odd crate of beer to the real police force in town, the tuk tuk drivers.

And as for wages, cooks and waiters get a paltry $15 to $30 a week for 12-hour days and four days off a month – which is why Tom and Josh rarely did anything at the restaurant. A 50% gross profit margin was good money in Cambodia, especially compared to some of the Khmer restaurants in town.

One up the road served a delicious chicken cordon bleu I'd ordered a couple of times. I had no idea how they could make it for the money. It was just 11,000 riel (just less than $3) for two big chicken breasts stuffed with slices of ham and cheese, and coated in Japanese-style breadcrumbs, and it came with salad and a mound of mashed potato. It was impossible to compete with prices like that.

I went back to my room, had a cold shower, and lay on the bed, bathing in the tickling chill breeze of the air conditioning unit. It felt good to be back in the kitchen. Very good.

I met Dirty Derek on my way to Rodney's bar. He was standing in the street, with a young Khmer woman under his arm, looking at Josh's specials board. Most nights he had cottage pie in there.

"You can't sell it like that! Gorr, how long did it take him to come up with that one?" he said.

We both looked at the board. All it said was: "Chicken Curry $4".

We headed up to the bar. Josh turned up later with a bowl of curry for his supper. All the food experts were there. I ordered another drink, sat at the bar, and waited for the verdict. I couldn't bear to turn round. The suspense was awful.

"Oh, ten out of ten," said the boxer. And I knew I was saved.

There were five orders and another three from across the street, and I don't know how many they'd sold down at the restaurant.

"That's a proper, proper curry! Yep, that's a good curry, Pork Pie," Josh said, smacking his lips, but he still made me pay for my own.

We chatted away until the small hours. By the end, Josh and Rodney were trying to persuade me to open my own restaurant. Josh said there was one going on the Hill for $13,000.

"You're never going to make a billion, no you won't make a billion. Will you make a billion? The answer's no," said Josh. "But you can make a good living here, especially if you can cook like that."

I went to bed happy and exhausted, but like everything in catering, it wasn't to last.

THE NEXT day, Josh told me they'd sold out of curry. I walked past in the afternoon, and there was a new sign up. I was furious. They'd stolen my recipe! I stood in the street for a while, wondering what to do.

The food experts had mocked Josh about his sign, and when he'd asked me what it should be called I said it was a madras-style curry. And there it was, less than 24 hours later in his spidery handwriting: "Chicken Madris $4."

Dee must have remembered everything I told her. She was certainly writing it all down in her Hello Kitty notebook. They'd got the spices I'd bought, so they knew what was in it, and I'd shown her every part of the recipe. I stood there steaming in the heat, then I returned to the restaurant.

Tom was slouched in the lounge, drinking gin. He smiled as I walked in. Not even a thank you. Not even the slightest bit of shame at stealing my recipe. I ordered a sandwich and coffee. As soon as Tom rode off on his scooter, I went into the kitchen. Dee wasn't there.

"You have chicken curry?" I asked the cooks.

66

There was a bit of confusion for a while, and then they realised what I was talking about.

"Yes, yes, one you made," one of them said.

It was impossible. Josh had said they'd sold out. I looked in the fridge. None of the bowls were covered. It was a world away from food premises inspections in the UK, and all those relentless, tedious manuals to document recipe procedures, and fridge temperatures morning, noon, and night.

Then I spotted a portion of what looked like my curry sitting uncovered on the bottom shelf with raw mince above it. I was delighted. The rage evaporated. My bruised ego was restored. They hadn't nicked my curry recipe after all – not yet anyway.

I met Josh in the street later and he asked about the pork pies again. He said he'd bought some belly and was rendering down the fat in his kitchen at home.

"Got to be right, got to be right," he said. "Leave it to me."

I suggested we experimented with the pastry first, filling the pie cases with chopped onions rather than meat. I said they'd still give off moisture, like meat, and it would be cheaper to crack the pastry first before moving on to the filling and jelly. But Josh said pork was cheap enough in Cambodia. It was roughly the same price as chicken breast – about $4.50 a kilo.

I STILL wasn't looking forward to the pastry, especially in that cramped kitchen. I needed to find bigger premises. That way I could set up a pop-up restaurant for a few nights, and experiment with the pie pastry at the same time. It would probably be Cambodia's first pop-up restaurant – there was no sign of another one on the internet.

I asked Rodney if I could use his kitchen. It had been well-furnished when he bought the lease two years ago, but he'd ripped it all out and given the equipment to Josh and Tom. But it was big enough and had the basics – two hobs powered by Calor gas, a sink, fridge, shelf space, and a tiny plastic chopping board. It would be fine for pot-based dishes.

And then it came to me – kebabs! I could start the pop-up with a few kebab nights over the Khmer New Year to get used to the kitchen. It would give me time to check out food suppliers. Then I could start on more cheffy dishes. There was even an unused bar upstairs that would take 20 covers at a push. Rodney said he was happy for me to put tables up there and do a few suppers for the wealthier expats in town.

They say it takes people a long time in business to discover that you need to make what customers want rather than what you want to make, and I was aware of making that mistake. It would probably be fairly tedious churning out kebabs, but they were the ideal food to get the name out there. You couldn't get a decent kebab anywhere in Sihanoukville. The nearest one was a five-hour bus ride away. I knew lamb was hideously expensive, so I'd go for pan-fried chicken doner-style kebabs. I'd made them a number of times in Blighty and they'd always gone down well.

I headed down to the supermarket the next day and bought 2kg of chicken breast, paprika, salt, white pepper, ketchup, vegetable oil, a decent knife, foil, kitchen paper, a large plastic container for the chicken, a bowl for the salad, and three small pots with spoons for the sauces.

Then I came across a major problem. The tortilla wraps were $5.50 for ten. It was much more than I was expecting, and they were small round ones, meaning I'd have to sell the kebabs as more of a snack than a meal. I wouldn't be able to sell them for more than $2.50, meaning a fifth of the food costs would just go on bread. It was disastrous, there was no way I could make a profit. Not that I expected to make any money. I thought about making the flat breads myself, but the kitchen was far too hot for all that.

I bought two packs of wraps, and reckoned I had just about enough chicken to make 20 kebabs. On the way back, I stopped at the market and bought half a huge white cabbage, tomatoes, cucumber, onions, garlic, limes, and chillies. I'd spent $40 including the tuk tuk fare. If I sold all 20 kebabs, I'd make $10 profit. And then there was Rodney's share to take into account. We still hadn't really discussed that.

Rodney chatted away non-stop as I prepped the chicken, and kept sticking his thumbs up and saying "lovely jubbly". Imagine David Jason 20kg lighter, with dreadlocks and Keith Richards' wrinkles, and you're halfway there. The facial resemblance was so strong that for the first year, Cambodian kids would run past the bar and shout "lovely jubbly" at him, much to his annoyance. Then he slowly joined in, and the catchphrase stuck from there.

"Everyone's talking about the kebabs, you know!" he said. "Dirty Derek phoned up earlier asking about them. He's having one! And I've got another three orders from the Finnish boys." He rubbed his hands together again. "Lovely jubbly!"

I chopped the chicken into thin strips lengthways and marinated them in oil, garlic, paprika, salt, and pepper. Then I finely shredded the cabbage and sliced the tomatoes, onions, and cucumber. I mixed the salad together and stored it in a bowl in the fridge. Then I made the two sauces. For the hot chilli sauce, I finely minced red chillies and mixed in ketchup, lime juice, and spices. For the garlic and mint yoghurt sauce, I finely chopped fresh mint, garlic, and cucumber, and added two tubs of yoghurt and plenty of salt and pepper and lime juice.

Then I tried a prototype. I got the largest frying pan smoking over the hob, dripped in some oil, and threw in a handful of chicken. After three minutes I let the chicken rest as I heated the smaller pan and toasted the tortilla wraps until they were puffy and slightly scorched.

I lay the tortilla on a tray, put chicken in the middle, spooned over the yoghurt and chilli sauces, and topped it with salad. Then I made a half-moon shape with the bread and folded both sides inwards and folded up the kebab. I rolled it in a piece of foil like a Cornetto. A Babnetto if you will.

Rodney came back a few minutes later, saying he couldn't find his other sandwich board to advertise the kebabs. He said he'd write out a sign on a piece of paper and stick that over his existing board.

"How do you spell chicken?" he said.

I told him I'd write the sign.

THE INITIAL trial of the pop-up restaurant turned out to be an eventful evening. But then, I suppose, what did I expect living so close to Serendipity Beach? It was New Year's Eve, and the place was dead. Many of the bars and restaurants had shut for the four-day Khmer holiday so the Cambodian cooks, waitresses, and bar girls could go home to their families. Some of them were travelling hundreds of miles to ramshackle farms and slums in northern Cambodia.

Two days on bone-cracking roads, and two days with their loved ones. It was tragic to think that some of the young mothers only saw their children two or three times a year, and then only for a couple of days. The rest of the time the youngsters are brought up by the grandmother while the mother sends money home. I could only wonder at the strength they had to get back on the bus, back to their tiny, shared rooms, knowing they wouldn't see their children for another few months.

But it wasn't just the ones with children or parents to support. One bar girl from Battambang had a Cambodian father and Chinese mother who had died in a car crash when she was 11, leaving her to bring up her younger sister and brother.

She'd been employed as a maid in a rich Khmer family's house, cleaning, cooking, and doing laundry all day for $7 a month and a small room for her siblings to sleep in. Occasionally, "uncles" would wander in at midnight, reeking of rice wine. Tears welled up in her eyes when she told me her story, and she turned away and wiped them.

"I say to Buddha when I pray, next time let me live anywhere, but not this country. Everything is wrong about Cambodia," she said.

Not that extreme poverty, trafficking, human rights abuses, the global food crisis, and Cambodia's Great Land Grab were of much concern to Rodney. He kept pointing at all the closed bars and rubbing his hands. By 7pm, he'd snared most of the alcoholics on the Hill.

All the food experts were in there, muttering about kebabs, and the best ones they'd had. And whether it was best with naan bread or pita, and whether they liked pickled green chillies in theirs, and one place they'd been to that seared the chillies for a second over the charcoal grill.

Then there were the culinary merits of minced lamb compared with slices, and the divisive issue of whether the chilli sauce should contain grated carrot, and whether it was a gentleman's right, by God, to insist on "crisp, fresh slices" from the elephant's foot rather than "stewed slices from the pot".

"You've got the slices, you've got the pita, they rip it open, cut it, you've got your meat, you've got your sauces. Doner kebabs! I fucking love them," said Rodney.

The boxer was there with his new Cambodian girlfriend. He'd met her in the street two nights ago. He started boasting about how he once lived above a shop "that sold the best fucking lamb doners in the world". When I told them I only had chicken they shook their heads, and sucked through their teeth like mechanics peering up from a bonnet, and I had to keep explaining about the price of lamb.

WE HAD chipped in $20 each to buy Akara, Rodney's bar manager, a single mattress and a double one for her parents for the Khmer New Year. They all slept on the floor of their wooden shack down the road. It was heart-breaking to see. I walked past on my way to the beach each day. Her mother and father would always be sat outside playing cards. Akara once muttered: "If my father work, family have mattress."

We always tipped her well, and Rodney paid her $150 a month in the high season – double the normal wage in Cambodia – and $100 a month in the rainy season. But most of it went to pay off her father's gambling debts.

"Her father not take care," Rodney would often say.

With the midday sun burning down, and 35C temperatures in the shade, it was miserable to see a family of six living in that 20ft by 10ft wooden shack without a fan or air con, trying to get to sleep on nailed boards, bugs below them, mosquitoes above them. Akara showered using a bucket filled from a water butt, but came in every day looking immaculate. None of us knew how she did it.

Josh and Rodney crept upstairs to get the mattresses and we all gathered round. It was a touching moment. Akara's face broke into a huge smile and then tears. Her father arrived later on a moped to take the mattresses home. We found out later he drove straight round to the pawn shop with them. I told Rodney I'd give my share of the kebab money to Akara. After that, they all wanted kebabs, and I had eight orders all at once.

It was easy juggling the food, the biggest problem was competing with the beer glasses. There was only one sink, so we battled for space. And talk about an open kitchen. It's one thing being on show in a restaurant, but at least you're tucked away behind aquarium glass like a zoo exhibit, or separated by a counter too high to jump over - you don't have to put up with people walking through the kitchen to get to the toilets.

It was impossible. The food experts were all far too curious, and kept stopping for a chat. At one point, a battle-scarred expat called Gary walked through. He was barred from most of the bars on the Hill, and had been in the country for three years without a visa. There were dark rumours about why he couldn't go back to the UK.

"What bread are you using for the kebabs, kiddo?" he said, venturing into my side of the kitchen. He was definitely past the water cooler. He was definitely off the toilet right of way I'd marked on the floor with yellow tape. He was definitely on my side of the kitchen.

"Wraps," I said. I told him I was using wraps.

"Fucking wraps! Jesus! Why don't you use pita bread, that's a proper kebab that."

I politely pointed out that it was just a trial and we were checking out suppliers, and it was easier to get fire-breathing midgets in Sihanoukville than pita bread, and tried to get rid of him. He was still hanging round as I wrapped the kebabs. I was annoyed with Rodney for letting him in the bar in the first place, let alone allowing him to loiter in the kitchen. But then it was my kitchen now. Rodney had told me himself.

"That bit's mine, this bit's yours. Lovely jubbly," he'd said.

I hate people hanging around in the kitchen, but this was a frightening looking man with a teardrop tattoo under one eye, meaning he'd killed someone or been raped in prison, or both, and my usual hints were lost on him. In the end, I was forced to put my arms up and walk towards him in an uncertain shooing manoeuvre. Luckily it worked and he lurched off.

My T-shirt was soon stuck to my back. It was truly unpleasant. I thought about cooking bare-chested, but I didn't want to put the customers off. Rodney had mentioned putting a fan in the kitchen. He had one standing idle in the bar. He came through at one point and joked: "I've been thinking about it. But I thought, no, I want the customers to smell the food! Then they'll order more!"

I wanted to teach Akara how to make the kebabs, but she was far too busy. Every time I showed her how to cook the chicken there was a shout from the bar. I didn't know how long I'd be in Sihanoukville for. There were other places I wanted to see along the coast that might be a good spot for a restaurant, and I wanted to make sure she could take over when I left. Even if she sold four kebabs a night, it would double her daily wage, and she could move out of that shack, and away from her thieving parents.

We sold all the kebabs in three hours. An Aussie called Wozza had three in a row, and the Finnish boys had two each. I cleaned down and went to sit with the others. They kept talking about the food and the Finns raised their thumbs. And then a fight broke out between Gary and the boxer's girlfriend. It turned very ugly, and people began to leave. I tried to calm it at one point, but Gary immediately eyeballed me.

"Believe me Tiger, you don't want to get involved," he growled.

He was right. I didn't. I went off and sat at the bar.

"You don't need this when you're trying to sell food," Wozza whispered to me as he paid his bill.

In the end, Rodney closed the bar and kicked everyone out. He spent the rest of the night muttering to himself in the mirror about how they were all barred, and how his friends had let him down. He brightened up after a couple of hours.

"Do you know something?" he said. "I love it!"

I went back to my room and lay awake for hours. The night had been a disaster. Even the thought of Akara's joyful tears was soured by the ugly scenes at the end. There would be no mention of the food on the expat forums and rocket-fuelled parish news grapevine, just the trouble.

Then I tried to make light of it. If it wasn't Cambodia's first pop-up night, and it probably was, it was definitely the first one to bar all its customers on the opening night. What is it about kebabs?

CHAPTER FOUR

THE OLD hands say living in Victory Hill is like wading through treacle. The longer you stay, the harder it is to move on, until you find yourself unable to even change hotel. And when some grand plan comes along like getting a bus to Phnom Penh, you get all of 200 yards up the road to the next hotel and spend another seven days with a bin fill of ripped-up bus tickets, and pretty soon you're down there with the rest of the bums.

But I managed to get out, and it all started with a late night conversation in the bar, when Josh and Rodney asked if I wanted to spend 10 days with them on Vietnam's largest island Phu Quoc, a place famed for its world-beating fish sauce, black pepper, and pearls.

The fang-shaped island – which was briefly captured by the Khmer Rouge during the Vietnam-Cambodia war - is only a short boat ride from Sihanoukville, or at least it should be. But because it's owned by Vietnam (an issue still hotly contested by Cambodians, who call the island Koh Tral), you have to travel for hours overland to the casino-swamped border crossing at Ha Tien, and then get a ferry from there, meaning the journey takes about seven hours instead of two.

They were talking about opening up a ferry route direct from Sihanoukville, but anything involving the foot-dragging Cambodian government takes years to arrange. There was an international airport already built in Sihanoukville, but due to squabbling between foreign investors and Khmer officials, it had been standing there empty for years. It was incredible to think the only plane in the port sat under a hangar in the middle of a Russian-owned nightclub, called imaginatively enough Airport.

Josh said he was hoping to persuade his wife Loung to go with us. But he'd been warned that Khmers aren't good travellers. The vast majority of the population have never been abroad – and are deeply distrustful of foreign food. Tom told him when he took his Cambodian girlfriend to Vietnam, the only thing she'd eaten in eight days was boiled rice.

You wouldn't think Khmers would be so picky when you see them tucking into bags of steamed ants, water beetles, and that wedding banquet of rat and snake meat Josh and Loung had invited me to that almost coldly furnished forth my funeral the next day. But it's not that Vietnamese food is so different, it's just that Cambodians view their sworn enemy as a marauding demon race who eat pickled babies and other unspeakable meats, and find everything about them hard to stomach.

Josh said we'd be leaving on the Thursday, and over the next two nights I taught Akara how to make the kebabs, and the night before I left I made a new batch of chicken for her. Then we headed off on a white knuckle taxi ride to the border. I was the only one with a Vietnamese visa. The others said you didn't need one as long as you told the immigration officers you were only going to Ha Tien. They said no-one ever checked your visa on the boat to Phu Quoc.

On the way, we almost hit a cow and two cyclists as the driver overtook on blind bends and threw his battered Toyota Camry over the pot-holed, red dust roads with one thumb permanently fastened to the horn. We passed salt beds outside the sleepy river town of Kampot, and saw an old woman loading salt into two baskets, which she carried on a stick on her shoulder.

Salt making is older than recorded history and was once used as a currency, and they need tonnes of it in Cambodia for prahok and fish sauce. Coastal fields, divided into squares, flood at high tide and the wind and sun evaporates the water leaving behind salt crystals, which are then raked into mounds.

We then stopped in Kep, a former colonial retreat for the French elite later obliterated by the Khmer Rouge, and had breakfast at its famous crab market. Wooden, ramshackle restaurants were perched on the rocky coastline. They were so near, they almost flooded at high tide. Nothing had been built there for years - it was definitely the water getting closer.

Families were dragging crab pots like sledges to position them 100 yards out for the tide change. Boys were spear fishing near the rocks as long-tailed fishing boats, painted toothpaste blue, waited for dusk.

A woman knelt over a reed bucket as she picked through dozens of blue swimmer crabs, grabbing them at the back, and tying their claws up with elastic bands to stop them nipping each other.

It was only 10am but the restaurant barbecues were already lit, grilling squid and fish as fresh as your hat. A group of Cambodian fishermen were sharing a bottle of Johnnie Walker Red Label and singing in one corner. They'd obviously just got back from a successful night on the waves.

We ordered plates of freshly-boiled crabs, grilled prawns, and stir-fried crabs with young green Kampot peppercorns - an incredibly aromatic spice long prized by chefs in Europe. Two years before, it had become Cambodia's first product to be awarded Geographical Indicator (GI) status like champagne and Melton Mowbray pork pies. But just 35 years before that, the country's pepper farms were all but destroyed by Pol Pot, who ordered his black-clad automatons to turn the palm-shaded vineyards into rice fields.

I watched as the cook chopped up the crabs, and with their legs still clacking, stir-fried them with garlic and fish sauce, before covering the wok to let them steam for a few minutes. She then threw in handfuls of green peppercorns, which Cambodians use like a vegetable, some oyster sauce and soy sauce, and then stirred it all together and served it.

The dishes came with tuk meric - an incredibly simple dip made from salt, black pepper, and lime juice. But my God it works. You get it with everything from hunks of barbecued calf to beef lok lak in Cambodia. But it goes best with freshly-boiled seafood, particularly blue swimmer crabs, which although contain little brown head meat, and virtually no morsels in the claws, more than make up for it with the generously fleshy chine.

In restaurants, they usually serve a mix of two thirds freshly-ground black pepper to one third salt, then carefully squeeze in two or three lime quarters and mix it in front of you. It might seem a laughably simple procedure that would scarcely trouble even the most cack-handed cook. But they take it as seriously as a chef de rang would the preparation of crepe suzette, pressed duck, or table-carved rib of beef, squeezing in the 'correct' amount of lime juice until there is the right moistness to the sauce. And if they are generous enough to give you the far superior red pepper, as they did in that restaurant, then it is out of this world.

It really was an incredible meal, and I knew I'd have few better days than that morning sat at the crab market, looking out to sea, watching those old women in their brightly-coloured hats checking their pots near the restaurant steps, while supping cold beer and dipping freshly-boiled crab into that incredible dip.

The crack of claws and chine, and that sweet meat magnified a hundred times by the pepper grown in the plantations behind the national park, sea salt raked from the neighbouring beds, and limes plucked from the orchards. It brought the fruits of land and sea in delicious harmony and offered the very best the pair have in a tryst of gastronomic delight.

In Singapore, they would have smothered those beautiful soft-shelled crabs in chilli sauce, in Vietnam it would take on an overriding taste of caramel, and in China it would most likely be in an MSG-laden sauce, thickened with cornflour. But there is something delightfully and deceptively simple about Cambodian food - which is why it's a shame it's so overlooked. It's the understanding of balance, simplicity, and the knowledge that fresh, local ingredients have a natural symmetry when served together.

As I dunked another chunk of chine into that dip, I thought about how my love for salt and pepper began when I was a toddler. The dripping on toast my grandfather used to make with meat jelly and fat from the Sunday roast would have been nothing without the liberal amounts of salt and pepper he sprinkled on top.

And then there were the salt and pepper sandwiches my father got me into - thickly-buttered, white spongy slices from a sandwich loaf fresh from the bakers, filled with nothing more than a generous sprinkling of salt and freshly-ground black pepper, as we sat in front of a roaring fire and drank cups of strong, brown tea during cold, wintry evenings, the rain lashing against the windows.

Just as good were the boiled eggs and soldiers we'd have in the mornings, with a small mound of salt and pepper on the plate. We'd plunge the soldiers into the runny, golden goodness, and then into the two condiments - a simple, delightful dip that would leap me forward to eating Khmer food more than three decades later.

As we left Kep, we passed a huge white statue of a topless woman gazing forlornly out to sea, and then one of a large blue crab, and saw more bombed-out and pillaged villas. And I imagined what the place must have looked like before the war. It really drove home the impact of the Khmer Rouge and the stopping of time in Cambodia.

IT TOOK at least an hour going through customs. A sour-faced official kept grilling me about why I had a visa for Vietnam and my travelling companions didn't. He clearly knew they were heading to Phu Quoc. Eventually his tone changed and he pulled out a wad of Vietnamese dong from his pocket and asked if I wanted to change some money.

We descended from the ferry into chaos on a long narrow pier crammed with motorbike taxis. We rented three beachside bungalows, surrounded by cashew nut, water apple, and star fruit trees. It was incredible waking up and picking a mango for breakfast.

It soon turned out Josh had the whole trip planned out in irritating detail. He said that night we'd head down the coast to a pearl farm owned by a few antipodean friends of his.

"They're big drinkers" he kept saying. "They're definitely big drinkers."

He said expats often converged there on Friday nights and it was traditional for everyone to bring something to barbecue. I knew what was coming next...

THE MARKET was a seething, fishy circus, and mopeds battled with pedestrians and stall holders along the narrow street. I bought 2kg of pork shoulder, tomatoes, onions, garlic, chilli, coriander, and limes to make kebabs. Then Josh remembered something.

"We need a banana for the monkey," he said. "Can we turn up without a banana for the monkey? The answer's no..."

The pearl farm was a stunning place, overlooking a deserted beach. The New Zealand owner and his bodyguards were as tough as Josh had described. But then they had to be. They had hundreds of thousands of dollars worth of pearls growing in the sea, and had an armoury of shotguns and high-powered spear guns to ward off pirates.

The monkey devoured the banana in seconds, but I didn't get too close. It looked friendly enough, but they kept it on a leash because the last one had bitten a customer's ear off. It was best friends with a small ginger cat. One of the pearl boys picked up the cat and put it next to the monkey. It immediately began cuddling the cat, and they sat there quite happily for a few minutes. The monkey had brought it up as a kitten and would carry it up coconut trees until it got too big to lug around.

We all gathered near the oyster beds to watch the sunset, and then there was a power cut and I had to prep the pork kebabs under torch light. It was an almost impossible task, and it was only the bluntness of the machete that stopped me losing a finger.

They told me they had a different method for producing pearls. Normally farmers nucleate the oysters by cutting opening the hinge and inserting a piece of grit, but they inserted a small pearl to speed up the harvesting process, which can take up to five years. Some of the necklaces they had on display in their museum were priced at $15,000.

We dug into the kebabs, and shared a huge red snapper between us, but there were no oysters to be had. We drank from pint glasses as rum bottles were passed around the table, and soon I was sitting in a brain-fogged haze, looking out at the dark sea and wondering at the undiscovered, man-eating leviathans it contained, while being mauled to death by worryingly-large mosquitoes.

Scores of squid boats were anchored in a long line against the horizon. There were so many out there, their lights looked like a distant motorway at night – a memory far removed from the tranquillity of that bug-filled paradise.

EVERY NIGHT we sat outside our beach bungalows, playing cards, listening to the gentle hum of the cicadas, walking up to the off licence to buy more crates of beer, and getting slowly bitten to death by sand flies.

During the day, we either lounged on the beach eating freshly-grilled seafood, or hired mopeds and rode around the island, visiting fishing villages that sold a potent liquor made from dried seaweed twisted like charred limbs. On the last day, Rodney came off. He was lucky to be alive, he kept telling us.

"It was horrendous. No, it was horrendous," he said. "I went through sand and the wheel started going. I've put the accelerator on, thinking it was a brake and it went. No chance! It was like a fucking horse - I've come off the bike, and it landed on my foot, and I was laying on the floor, in agony, you know - and pain - and this fucking bloke just drove straight past me!"

As the evening wore on, the tale became more exaggerated and frantic in the telling.

"But I'm lucky to be here, I tell you. I went in the air! I went five foot in the fucking air! Oh, I was out of the bike, alright. If I was on the main road, no chance, I would have been fucking dead! Very lucky, very lucky mate! Now I'm limping around like fucking Chester..."

"Chester?" I said.

"My Dylan, Mr Dylan. Do you remember Gunsmoke?"

"Oh yep, I remember Gunsmoke," said Josh, lighting another cigarette.

After a few more hands, the conversation moved on to bank security deposit boxes after Rodney told us about a gang who'd dug a tunnel from a sewer into a London vault.

"That takes real bottle that!" he kept saying. "Drilling into a bank, with all the alarms and that - get out of it!"

It was interesting hearing both sides of the conversation - Rodney had spent a quarter of his life in prison, and Josh had spent most of his as

81

a bank manager. Josh told us about the Nazi daggers, priceless paintings of old tramps, and huge piles of cash he'd locked away for customers.

When he first joined the bank, he had to carry a handgun and go for firearm training every six months. One afternoon he stopped off at a bar in his old Mercedes that was 20 times the size of him, and handed in his gun at the hatch. He returned to the bank later that afternoon, and his boss asked where his gun was. He had to drive back 40km to collect it. In the 80s, Josh had worn ties decorated with cartoon characters until his new boss pulled him up about his dress code.

"But the customers love it..." Josh had pleaded.

The ties went, and the only cartoon characters that stayed were the tattoos of Tweetie Pie on his left leg, and Bugs Bunny on the other. They couldn't take those away.

"Fucking pommie cunt!" slurred Josh, still enraged about the memory. "Was he a pommie cunt? The answer's yes. Would I still go for a beer with him, the answer's maybe..."

As we sat there supping beer, listening to the croaking calls of the geckos, and looking at the huge black millipedes crawling across the dirt, Josh had become a bank manager again. He was back behind his oak desk, dealing with customers and safety deposit boxes. I was still amazed you could put anything in them, and people wouldn't check. As Peter Cook had said, there's one law for the rich, in fact there are several laws for the rich, and very few for the poor...

"What about murder weapons?" I asked him.

"It's nothing to do with us! It's nothing to do with us - just like Switzerland. It's totally up to you what you put in safety deposit boxes..."

Rodney butted in.

"You could have the crown jewels in there and no-one would know - it's up to you. That's your fucking box!"

Josh lit another cigarette, and sat there with it in his mouth, swaying from side to side and mumbling words.

"One dear old lady, well she wasn't - she was an old bag. I don't know if she's still alive, the old bitch. She inherited a pile of money, and the whole safety deposit box was all $100 notes, absolutely jam packed full of them. And she said: 'The tax department isn't getting any cent of this!'

"And then when New Zealand changed their currency from one $100 to another, you know what I mean, a different style, she used to come in and take them all out, and get all new ones, and put them back in again. She was a mean old bitch! I played bridge with her daughter, she was mean too..."

THE NEXT day they left, and headed back to Sihanoukville. It felt strange being on my own again after two weeks of company. I usually like my own space, but loneliness crept in like a wounded badger. I stayed at the bungalow for two more days, and then booked a cheap flight to Ho Chi Minh City (Saigon).

I wanted to find out more about Vietnamese food, and see how the price of restaurants compared with Cambodia. But I wasn't too hopeful. The pearl boys had told me all about the mind-boggling bureaucracy you had to deal with in Vietnam just to get a business licence. It sounded even worse than Thailand. Cambodia was far more straight forward. I decided I'd spend a month or two in Vietnam, collecting recipes and seeing the sights, and then return to Cambodia to look for a restaurant.

I walked around the souvenir shops at Phu Quoc's impressively-modern airport and bought a scallop shell on a leather strap and fastened it round my neck. I told myself I'd hang it from the bar when I finally found my restaurant, and wouldn't take it off until I had.

On the flight, I scribbled a few notes about Vietnamese food. I'd heard mixed reports. Some people I'd met in Thailand and Cambodia complained that the Vietnamese didn't add enough salt to dishes, and the food was bland. But most cooks and food writers described it as deliciously fresh and healthy, with an abundance of vegetable and fish dishes.

Indeed, I remembered a story from Rick Stein's Far Eastern Odyssey about how the Vietnamese were supposed to have been born from a dragon and a fairy. One hundred eggs were hatched, and 50 rolled down into the sea and became fish, and 50 rolled up a mountain and became the Vietnamese.

"We're all descended from fish," mused Stein, sitting on a barge travelling through the Mekong Delta.

The boat's chef had cooked him stir-fried freshwater prawns with mango - a good example of the freshness and lightness of Vietnamese cuisine compared with the Chinese dishes it so closely resembles. He fried chopped onions and garlic in a wok, and then threw in fresh Mekong prawns, added a little water, salt, pepper, lime juice, and a spoon of cornflour mixed with water to thicken it. Then he added cubes of ripe mango, and tossed it together. It looked wonderful.

Floyd also had a great deal of praise for Vietnamese food. In Far Flung Floyd, he wrote about how it had been influenced for 2,000 years by the Chinese, and then Mongolian invasions in the 13th century brought hotpot dishes and charcoal-fired steamboats, before the French brought their baking skills in the 19th century.

But he said that Vietnam had "remained fiercely independent, taking the best of them, but maintaining its own distinctive style" with its generous use of fresh herbs, and preference for steaming food rather than frying.

He also wrote about Ho Chi Minh (he who enlightens), the great revolutionary leader, who trained as a spy in Moscow before forming the Vietnamese communist party and ousting the French and then the Americans from his homeland to finally achieve independence and unity for his country.

"He was apparently a well-liked and charismatic man. But much more important to us and not known by many, he worked as a pastry chef under the legendary Escoffier at the Carlton Hotel in London..." Floyd added.

And even less well-known, he also worked as a potwash at the far less salubrious Drayton Court Hotel in West Ealing during his time in

London, according to the BBC's Vietnam mavens. Humble beginnings indeed, I thought, as the plane touched down at Tan Son Nhat International Airport in the bustling city named after that former plongeur and Communist leader.

I CAUGHT a taxi to the backpackers' area in District One, and an old woman asked if I wanted a cheap room. She led me down an alley to a shabby hotel off Pham Ngu Lao, and then I hit the streets, sweltering in the tropical heat.

My mood wasn't helped by the appalling congestion. Ho Chi Minh City was an idiotic maelstrom of chaos just like every other Asian city I'd been to that views pedestrians as bottom of the food chain. Traffic priority was based solely on the size of your vehicle, and you needed 360-degree vision just to cross the road.

There were no enforced street laws - the road signs were purely for decoration. Mopeds rode on the pavement, the wrong way down one-way streets, in fact the wrong way down every street. The Vietnamese clearly hated walking just as much as the Cambodians and Thais, and mopeds were seen as a status symbol.

Everyone who walked wanted a moped, and everyone who had a moped wanted a car, and everyone who had a car wanted an SUV, and I was left with the sad realisation that the world would never be free of its addiction to gasoline – not when it was only a dollar a litre anyway.

It made me appreciate capitals like London and Amsterdam, which have embraced pedestrians and cyclists. In Ho Chi Minh City, all I could see was row after row of moped drivers, their faces covered in masks. It was like a million bank robbers had taken over the city.

Sometimes it took me ten minutes to cross a road. And even when the pedestrian lights were green, it meant absolutely nothing – moped drivers sailed through red lights as gamely as street walkers, so the only way forward was to take your life in your hands and dodge your way across packed roads as though you were in some weird Frogger game.

And to make matters worse, you couldn't judge the width of each moped because they could be carrying anything from 50 durian fruit to a family of six, some in the side-saddle position. Suddenly, a moped smashed into a taxi and shed its crates of beer. The road was covered in foam and brown glass. I'd been standing there waiting to cross just a few moments earlier, until I got bored and decided to carry on walking up my side of the street.

But I'm glad to say the traffic, as appalling as it was, was made up for by the food. The way they did seafood, for instance, was fantastic. You picked crabs, scallops, snails, winkles, mussels, clams, and other assorted molluscs, and then the stallholder weighed them on fixed scales and quoted you a price, scalping you accordingly, if you were a wide-eyed tourist.

Thankfully, they didn't cover the seafood in peanuts, which I absolutely detest, like they seemed to at every BBQ fish restaurant on Phu Quoc. Instead, they cooked it in sugar, which was sublime. You make the caramel sauce by simmering half a cup of sugar with a little water until the liquid is brown, then add some fish sauce and ground pepper to taste, and cool completely before using.

Some cooks recommend making it by caramelising the sugar in oil so that it turns toffee-coloured before you add the meat. This seals the meat, keeps in the marinade flavours it already has, and colours the resulting sauce, they say.

But I never saw any of the stallholders make it like that. They had their caramel sauce prepped in plastic beakers, ready for use, and there was no greasiness to the sauce. They fried finely-diced garlic and a smattering of red chilli in vegetable oil until the garlic was lightly browned, then added cracked, cooked crab claws, and raw shellfish and tossed them over a medium heat.

Then they added a ladle of caramel sauce, and continued to toss the seafood around in the wok. They covered it for a minute for the molluscs to steam open, and then added some herbs and spring onions, and served it on a metal tray with a saucer of tuk meric sprinkled with chopped chilli.

The taste was incredible. The lime cut the sweetness, and the sticky caramel coated the shells and gave them a lip-smacking, shell-sucking unctuousness that went brilliantly with my new favourite brew of green label Saigon beer poured over chunks of ice.

I soon learned to eat crabs like the Vietnamese, and crunch up the claws, shell and all. It was always a messy business, but a brilliant way to pass an hour watching the prostitutes, gangsters, hitmen, traffickers, perverts, dealers, and drunken English teachers who made up Saigon's many shades of noir.

THE NEXT day I escaped the traffic by strolling through a park near my hotel, and in typical communist style, there was a list of rules and regulations. Rule three stipulated visitors should not "be drunk, play gamble, participate in fortune telling and other evils". Oh, and "not tease animals". It was quite a list.

I sat down on a bench in the baking heat. An old woman was asleep in the shade. A police officer on a moped drove up and beeped his horn until she got up. Even sleeping wasn't allowed. But there was nothing about motorbikes. Not even the inadequately palm-shaded sanctuary of the park was free from mopeds.

Then a couple of Filipino girls sat on a bench next to me. One of them had seen the scallop shell round my neck and wanted to know all about it. We went to a street bar and bought some beers, and I told them about my love of cooking and how I was planning to open a restaurant in Cambodia, and they invited me round to their home for lunch the next day, saying they would cook me a Filipino meal.

I'd heard about the Filipino Blackjack gangs operating in the city, but I still went anyway. More out of curiosity than anything. But then there was a reasonable chance I could flog the story for a few quid - and I'd need every penny I could scrape together for the restaurant.

The scam generally works as follows: the fraudster will make up a story about how his (insert relative) is heading to your country and could you give some advice/assurance to (insert relative) while enjoying a lovely meal at their home. Then you'll be hoodwinked into a game of cards upstairs, frogmarched to a bank to pay off your losses, and end up walking home without your shirt - if you're lucky.

So I was prepared for the worst, when I met them at a noodle shop the next day and we caught a taxi to their "uncle's" house. On the way they asked me the usual questions about how long I'd been in the city and whether I knew anyone there. They might just as well have asked whether I had my bank card with me, what my pin number was, and whether I had a strong tolerance to Rohypnol. Eventually, after many unnecessary twists and turns, the taxi arrived at the house.

"Oh we didn't know our uncle would be here," they said innocently as we walked in.

JR, as he called himself, was a large, confident man, draped in gold, and his sole conversation was money. I was to drink an (unopened) can of Coke with him in front of the telly, while the women did the work in the kitchen. It was a two-storey house with a huge lounge and a spiral staircase leading up to the room where no doubt the card table would be.

He wanted to know how expensive it was in the UK, and nodded enthusiastically when I told him how much a coffee costs, or how much hotels are. Then he started asking whether I had a house, how much it was worth, whether I was married, had friends in Saigon – you know, the sort of questions that wouldn't raise suspicion in anyone. On and on he went, as I sat there like a gullible fool.

The interrogation continued as we sat down to eat mongo, fried fish, and prawns that you dipped in chopped garlic and vinegar. They said it was traditional for Filipino families to eat mongo on Fridays, and it really was a tasty dish – stewed mung beans, onion, tomato, prawns, and chunks of bitter gourd. It had been cooked by their aunt, who ran a restaurant in the Philippines. She told me how Filipino food is heavily influenced by Spanish food from its colonial past, and it reminded me of some of the rustic lentil stews you get in Spanish villages.

We shared the same food, but I watched every hand manoeuvre as they served. Then I felt a tingle. A mild rush. It was probably my imagination. My host was already on about how he worked as a croupier at a big casino. The next stage would no doubt involve being shown a fool-proof way of beating a casino, a couple of dummy hands of poker 21 (a venomously evil game that's like blackjack but involves bluffing).

Then there would be the dealer nose scratches he'd teach me to show I had a good hand, and then the sudden appearance of a rich businessman we'd supposedly set out to fleece. I'd win the first few hands, then the businessman would suddenly raise the stakes.

The pulse in my head got worse. Surely it was just paranoia? I'd watched every scrap of food and movement. Maybe it was that fish they'd left to one side? I still had a hangover, but it had suddenly got worse. Or at least I thought it had.

"What do you do for a living?" JR asked.

So I told him. It was the only card I had to play, so to speak, given the increasing fog. I told him I was a journalist and would be working in the city for a month or two, and had a couple of stringers there helping me. His expression didn't change, but something inside him did. He began lecturing the others about how difficult a job journalism is. He was clearly an expert on everything. Then he began a bizarre conversation.

"Because you're a reporter, nothing will happen to you in my house. Otherwise my name will be on the telly," he laughed, gesturing at the huge, flat-screen TV behind him.

It was a strange joke. I thanked him for his hospitality, stood up slightly unsteadily, but not nearly as badly as I'd feared, and headed straight to the front door. He was right beside me in a flash with another lecture.

"You know, you should never go to a stranger's house in Asia," he said. "You shouldn't just trust people like that. You don't know who they are..."

He kept on and on. He almost seemed concerned. I was being lectured on naivety and the dangers of fraudsters by the head of a Filipino blackjack scam gang. He was right though. And who would know better? I shouldn't have been there at all.

The blackjack is just a side show, it's not an essential part of the plan. It's just a way to break you down and put you in a powerless situation. A gun can do the same thing far quicker if necessary. It's just down to the witnesses who saw or didn't see you go in there. And I imagine no-one sees anything in some parts of Saigon. Not after a few bottles of Scotch anyway.

VIETNAM'S UNOFFICIAL national dish is the legendary fast food known as 'pho' - a steaming bowl of noodle soup, nearly always made from beef or chicken, and served with more fresh herbs than Antony Worrall Thompson can stuff into his pockets at Tesco. And what better place to try it than the country's most famous noodle shop, Pho 2000? It was where Bill Clinton slurped noodles in 2000, when he became the first American President to visit the country since the end of the Vietnam War, or American War if you live in Vietnam.

I'd heard a lot about the place on Twitter, and wanted to see how its food compared with the other pho joints I'd eaten in - from the elderly entrepreneurs with their portable kitchens carried on yokes on their backs, who you often see squatting and gossiping in rows on the pavement, doing more eating than selling. To the street stalls in steamy, drain-scourged alleyways - where you eat standing up. To the tiny, family restaurants with the kitchen out front, a pot of beef stock simmering on a charcoal burner, and sparrows pecking at the bean sprouts, to the characterless, air-conditioned outlets with their brightly-coloured branding, laminate menus, catchphrases, and slogans.

The restaurant - which bizarrely Lonely Planet website readers had ranked as the top visitor attraction in Saigon, and the 27th in the whole of Asia - overlooks Ben Thanh Market, a sweaty cavern of fake good stalls not far from where North Vietnamese tanks arrived 40 years before to spell a humiliating defeat of US forces.

Its refreshingly short menu (I've never liked the Asian custom of offering huge tomes with pages of dishes - it's an almost apologetic attitude that seems to say: "Hopefully you'll like one of our meals...") was pretty much just beef stew noodles (pho bo sot vang), shrimp spring rolls (cha gio tom), chicken curry with bread (ca ry ga), and beef ragout with rice (com ragu bo), but I was there for the beef noodle soup (pho bo).

The meal came with breath-taking speed, and that was another part of the canteen feel. The kitchen had been ripped out and replaced with US security money for Clinton's visit, and the owners had obviously decided to keep up the hygiene standards, because even though the Soviet-style white and beige decor needed a good revamp, the place sparkled. Even the spoons were wrapped in plastic.

It was a favourite with visiting dignitaries and Vietnamese leaders, and had long cashed in on its Clinton credentials. "Pho For The President" the restaurant frontage boasted. It was a strange advert given the devastation caused by America's offensive in Indochina.

But what was far stranger was why a restaurant that regularly found itself in such high company, and was presumably picked out for Clinton to showcase Vietnam's gastronomic excellence and noodle-fused national identity, was so spectacularly average. I mean the US President wouldn't just take visiting foreign leaders down to his local burger joint would he - even if he wanted to spin an all-American, man-of-the-people image?

The beef stock was so bland, it reminded me of the tins of cheap consommé my granddad used to buy when I was a kid. Traditionally, it should be boiled down marrow bones with scorched onions and ginger, star anise, cinnamon, cloves, fish sauce, and sugar. But clearly no-one had bothered. It tasted like water from the hot tap that had had a Tesco extra value horse stock cube dunked in it for a few seconds.

The paper-thin slices of onion, spring onion greens, and slices of slow-cooked brisket, cut against the grain and feathered to the point of falling apart, were tasty enough. But sadly there was no option to have the raw beef version (pho bo tai) or indeed the oxtail, tendon, tripe, and meatballs you find in a good pho.

It was perfectly alright, but bland, and I can see why Clinton ordered the chicken noodle soup (pho ga). I mean what do you do when you've picked out all the meat, and you're left with a mountain of rice noodles, without a decent broth to help them down? The word samey doesn't cover it.

But it must have been a difficult choice for the Vietnamese government to make, back in 2000. Choosing the closest thing Vietnam has to a national dish is fraught enough, but what about the garnishes? Small potatoes you might think, but people get very worked up about the thorny issue of leafy accompaniments.

Purists in the north – from where the dish is said to have originated – like it unadulterated, with just meat, noodles and a well-made broth. But by the time it had moved south with the Vietnamese who fled Communism, when the country was split into north and south rival states, the dish took on a more flamboyant identity.

There were rumours from the south, then disquiet and head shaking. There were tales that chefs had started to serve it with side plates of sliced fresh chillies, bean sprouts, thorny coriander, Thai basil, and lime segments. Others said it came with other foul abominations, like bowls of hoisin sauce and chilli ketchup – and that was how it was served at Pho 2000, and every other noodle shop I'd tried in Saigon and Phu Quoc. But this herby frivolity doesn't go down well in the north, where they are still true to the original.

So what a potentially explosive photograph it might be to see Clinton sipping papaya juice while scattering basil leaves and other horrors over what is after all a northern dish. The gaudy baubles of capitalism, or the no-nonsense, no leafy extras of communism?

And what about upsetting the Americans by choosing a dish so heavily influenced by cheese-eating surrender monkeys? Food historians generally accept pho came from the Hanoi area in the early 1900s, but in usual pointy-headed style, that's where agreement ends.

There is some debate about whether pho (pronounced 'fir') was a corruption of the French word for fire (feu) when colonialists introduced the classic French stew, pot-au-feu, to Vietnam. Others say the dish was around hundreds of years before the French arrived and is of Mongolian origin. But there is no denying that Gallic cooking shaped the dish – or that the French got the Vietnamese to start eating cows.

Traditionally with pot-au-feu, the cooking liquor is drunk separately as a soup, and the meat is heavily padded out with vegetables (substitute noodles), so you can see the hallmarks. But it is the tradition of making the broth with charred onions that truly separates it from many other Asian cooking styles – a nod to the French method of adding blackened onions to stock.

THE OTHER noodle shop I wanted to try was Pho Binh, which means, ironically enough, "peace soup". It was hard to imagine a restaurant that size was used to house 160 people, let alone launch an attack on American-led forces only 100 yards from the US military police barracks in Saigon. But that was the pivotal role played by the bustling eatery during the Tet Offensive in 1968, a turning point in the decade-long conflict.

The fact that the non-descript cafe was not easy to find only added to its character. I must have asked ten people for directions, only to discover I had passed the place several times. All that differentiated it from the hundreds of other noodle joints in the former heart of the city was a couple of plaques that had seen better days.

It was still a fairly popular spot for tourists, and the story was kept alive by the cleaner, who was only too delighted to tell tales of his comrades' bravery during the Vietnam War, especially that of its owner, Ngo Van Toai.

Ngo Van Toai had bought the three-storey house – 7 Yen Do Street – in 1966, and with money from Viet Cong coffers turned it into an undercover command post to co-ordinate attacks deep within American-controlled territory. He lived a double life, smiling at the diplomats and US soldiers he cooked for every day, while City Rangers from the communist north planned deadly assaults against them in a room upstairs.

A month before the 1968 spring offensive, he was told to start secretly bulk buying rice, wheat, and other foods – enough to feed 200 people a month. On the first day of the Lunar New Year, commanders gathered and encouraged the guerrillas on their suicide mission.

The co-ordinated strikes, including one on the US Embassy in Saigon, failed tactically, but proved a great political coup for the north. Pictures of the Tet Offensive were beamed into sitting rooms across the world, fuelling the peace movement's arguments that the Americans could never win the war.

The noodle shop was raided, and Ngo Van Toai was arrested and tortured for 20 days but he did not "open his mouth even half a word", the cleaner said. He was sentenced to life in the notorious Con Dao prison on Phu Quoc island, and released when the war ended in 1975. He died a few years later from ill health.

"I was not afraid of death," the old soldier explained in an interview after his release. "I had offered my home to the revolution. I cared nothing for myself. I was willing to sacrifice."

As I sat down, where US soldiers had slurped noodles four decades before, the cleaner handed me two books. One was filled with photos and press clippings of Ngo Van Toai and his noodle shop, and the other was a visitors' book, littered with observations that very little had changed in the last 40 years, and America was still involved in foreign conflicts far from its shores, this time in the name of crushing terrorism rather than communism.

The restaurant only offered two dishes – beef noodle soup and chicken noodle soup - just as it did when American forces ate there, not knowing they were just a few feet from the enemy. The cleaner pointed to the elderly man making my pho, and said he was Ngo Van Toai's son. I could see the facial resemblance, and the pride in his eyes, but there was sadness too, and not just the sadness of a man who clearly had a lot to live up to.

He was cutting up meat on a wooden board. Near to him were large joints of beef, covered in yellow fat that looked like melted candle wax. It was the same recipe and chopping board his father had used during the war.

The cleaner prepared my pho, carefully adding what he deemed to be the correct amount of hoisin sauce, chilli, and lime juice, and scattering herbs across the top of the steaming bowl, before mixing it all carefully with chopsticks. An American tourist walked in and sat down behind me.

"Chicken or beef?" the cleaner asked.

I passed her the two books, and warned her about the anti-US language in one of them. She had that slightly embarrassed look many American travellers seem to share these days when the subject of Uncle Sam's foreign policy comes up.

When I'd finished my meal, the cleaner showed me upstairs. There was an airy kitchen out the back with steps leading up to what he called the "classroom". It was a shrine to the Viet Cong guerrillas who'd launched the attacks. One photo showed the inner circle sitting around a small table, sipping tea, and planning their bloodshed. The table was still there – despite long pleas from the communist government for it to be housed in the nearby War Remnants Museum.

The cleaner said he often took pictures of tourists pretending to drink tea from the table, some of them American veterans who fought in the war, and wanted to make peace with their past. In the far corner were haunting mug shots of two women and two men, who had carried bombs into buildings and blown themselves up for the cause. He called them "heroes". In front of a cabinet containing war medals stood a photo of Ngo Van Toai in his military uniform.

"Police come many times, but they hide photo behind Buddha picture on wall, and they no look there," he chuckled.

He showed me the narrow alley at the back of the building – so narrow the police never bothered looking there. It offered the only escape route out of the restaurant – a 30ft drop. The rest of the three-floored building had served as sleeping quarters, but it was difficult to see how 160 people could have crammed in, even sleeping nose to foot.

As I sat there at the table, wondering at the fear they must have felt knowing the horrific tortures that awaited them should they be caught, I imagined Ngo Van Toai downstairs boiling beef for his pho. It was ironic that Vietnam's unofficial national dish, a meal created in the communist north, had played such a part in America's humiliating retreat from South Vietnam.

I WANTED to learn more about Ngo Van Toai. I was fascinated by the man's bravery. I thought about the megalomaniac head chefs I'd worked for in the UK, and their boasts about how tough cheffing is, and their feeble comparisons between the stresses of service and what "our boys" had endured during the Second World War.

And here was a cook who'd really suffered for what he believed in. Not to put food on the table for people to eat, but to rid his country of invaders. It put a huge amount of perspective on the prima donnas you meet in cheffing. Ngo Van Toai had never spoken about what he endured during his 20 days of relentless torture, let alone whined about having had a tough day in the kitchen, or why there wasn't clingfilm on one of the tubs in the fridge.

The next day, I got up early and then went back to bed again, and then eventually got up and caught a taxi to the War Remnants Museum to see the sort of conditions Ngo Van Toai was held in. Well, about a mile short of there. I got fed up sitting in traffic, so I walked the rest of the way with my T-shirt plastered to my back in the midday smog.

I got lost, and then there was a cloudburst, so I scurried for shelter under the porch of a posh-looking hotel. I asked a porter for directions, and was looking at my scrunched-up map when a loud, irritating Aussie, dressed in the international sex tourist kit of shorts, vest, and money belt, butted in. He was looking for the museum too. I tried to get rid of him, and sat on a step as the deluge continued, hoping he'd wander off. But he continued to strike up conversation.

"I was only going to the museum to shelter from the rain," he said, looking up at the sky. "What else can you do on a day like today?"

He was soon eyeing one of the club signs.

"Karaoke AND massage bar," he leered. "Wonder what happens in there..."

"Maybe you get a singing masseur?" I shrugged.

Thankfully, a receptionist with good English appeared and asked me where I wanted to go.

"I think that's a polite way of asking us to move on," said the Aussie.

Us? He'd definitely said "us".

I told him I'd head down to the museum later, and pretended to walk round the corner, and watched as he slouched off in the bucketing rain. I left it for 30 minutes, worried I'd bump into him in one of the torture exhibits.

THE FIRST thing you see when you go into the War Remnants Museum (it used to be called the Museum of Chinese and American War Crimes until officials finally got fed up with the complaint letters) are a collection of US helicopters, tanks, and planes. They'd polished them up so much, they gleamed like muscled beasts of the apocalypse. Round the side, past the bins, was the rusty North Vietnamese stuff – two tins connected by a piece of string, and a World War One starting pistol.

A Dutch couple walked past, smoking small cigars.

"Oh lovely," the woman said, pointing at an A-1 Skyraider that had been used to drop napalm and phosphorus bombs on starving villagers.

I'd read a lot about the museum's anti-US propaganda, but I was still surprised how blatant it was. One of the exhibit rooms was called "Historic Truths". There wasn't even an attempt to get any balance in there, but I suppose history is written by the victors.

When you compare it with the hundreds of war films America's Hollywood PR agency has pumped out, and the US still calling its invasion to this day "the Vietnam War" despite the fact that it engulfed all three countries – Laos, Cambodia, and Vietnam – that had formed French Indochina, it's a drop in the ocean. An all-enveloping, digital smog of an ocean that will no doubt leave Americans in 100 years thinking they single-handedly saved the world from speaking German, and helped Mel Gibson kick the English out of Scotland.

There was no mention of the atrocities carried out by the North Vietnamese Army, or the way it had backed the Khmer Rouge's autogenocide of up to two million people, or later its invasion of Cambodia – an invasion some saw as a greater evil than the Pol Pot regime it overthrew.

In every fact box, pie chart, and poster, Vietnam was portrayed as a victim of America's Goliath might. There were statistics about the number of aircraft and tanks the Americans had given to the "Saigon Puppet Government", together with the money the US had spent on the war compared with World War Two and the 1950-53 Korean War, but no mention of North Vietnam's capabilities, or the Soviet billions.

A large area was devoted to the tortures inflicted in Con Dao Prison on Phu Quoc island. I thought about Ngo Van Toai and what he would have endured in his years there. Burning in the relentless sun, day after day in a tiger cage. It was shocking and extremely depressing to read the victims' stories, and I left the place feeling strangely guilty that I had never been through similarly grotesque experiences. I'd never suffered true hunger, or seen my loved ones shot in front of me, let alone been guillotined, or had live snakes shoved down my trousers.

I felt dreadfully inadequate, and extremely lucky to be living in an age when I was more likely to be bitten to death by a bull shark in a duck pond than forced to sit under a drip with my scalp shaved, so that every drop of water soon felt like a hammer blow.

There was waterboarding too. Seeing it being used alongside seemingly far more mediaeval interrogation methods obviously shows how effective it is at breaking people, and why it is such a favourite at Guantanamo to this day. And it makes it even more bizarre to read how many US politicians still insist it shouldn't be classed as torture. I don't know where they stand on the use of live snakes.

There were brutal methods going on elsewhere in Vietnam, particularly with the US military's use of jungle-clearing Agent Orange. It was terrible to see photos of the mutations the toxic herbicide caused, particularly of infants and young children, and there were plenty of pictures of them. You couldn't help wonder at the crazed minds that decided on that appalling campaign, bombing and deforesting huge areas of Vietnam, eastern Laos, and parts of Cambodia just to flush out the Viet Cong they couldn't find.

On the way out, victims of Agent Orange - Vietnam claims up to one million of its people have died or been left with serious birth defects from its use - were singing to raise money for their charity. I left bloated with sound bites from defected US pilots, draft-burning students, and world figures critical of Washington's obsession with controlling tin and tungsten resources in SE Asia to underpin the manufacturing growth it so craved.

Anyway as I say, it got me thinking about the USA's napalming and bombing, and widespread use of chemical herbicides, and then I realised how hungry I was and stopped at a KFC on the way back. My Zinger meal was extremely dry. The burger had obviously been sitting there for a while, so I went back to the counter and ordered two pieces of hot and spicy chicken because they hadn't bothered to cook any of the original variety (no-one seems to buy it in Vietnam).

It came with proper cutlery - I couldn't see them dishing those out in Brixton. I glanced at my plate. It said "finger lickin' good". Not when the chicken is properly eaten with a knife and fork, I thought, and then went back to thinking about the atrocities of American imperialism again.

I SPENT a week writing in my hotel and researching the local street food, and then caught a tuk tuk to Saigon Race Track – one of the very few places in the country where the Vietnamese can legally gamble.

On the way, I thought about how I used to know a lot about horse racing, but never enough to make any money at it. I studied the form, and threw bricks into the dewy turf to test the going each morning, and unwrapped blankets around steaming Lancashire hotpots in the back of my beaten-up car in the hope of luring tips from passing insiders. At one point, I even found myself driving to King's Cross some evenings to buy the next day's racing papers. It was quite sad really.

And I was pretty sure I'd have even less chance of winning in Vietnam. But the one thing I did learn is that what you eat at the races says a lot about the food of the country you're in. I'm not talking about private dining tables and Royal enclosures; I'm talking about the soul food, the comfort food, the snacks of choice - the stuff eaten in the cheaper silver ring and grandstand enclosures, where 90% of punters go.

You say Kentucky Derby to race-goers, and they'll have the taste of yellow ketchup and fried onions in their mouths. Melbourne Cup, and it'll be the meaty gravy of that "proper Aussie pie". Fairyhouse, and it will no doubt be the fatty, breadcrumby taste of disturbingly pink Irish sausages, packed full of horse DNA. And Royal Ascot, and it'll be the tang of smoked salmon, moistening away nicely at the back of the throat with the heavily-buttered brown bread.

But given the overwhelming evidence at Saigon Race Track, the snack of choice was the sandwich. Alright, there were a couple of stands selling noodles - you can't go anywhere in Vietnam without falling over a fucking noodle stand - but it was definitely the sandwich. Or the banh mi, as it's known. A stumpy baguette filled with anything from tinned mackerel in tomato sauce to Laughing Cow cheese to fried eggs to a few cold cuts of pork belly and a smear of dubious pate (don't ask), and always with salad, herbs, sauces, pickles, and a generous scattering of chopped red chillies.

I apologise if I appear obsessive about sandwiches. I wrote an unpublished book on the weighty subject in my hopeful, naive 20s, and have always been fascinated by their history, and the cheerful, parcel-like comfort they offer ever since.

Sandwiches were obviously made well before a hungry John Montagu, the 4th Earl of Sandwich, was said to have ordered an idle butler to stick some meat between two slices, and to hurry up about it, because he didn't want to waste valuable gambling time leaving the table. Barbarians were no doubt chucking slabs of mammoth between unleavened, fire-baked bread thousands of years before that.

I mean it's hard to accept that mankind had invented the printing press before the complexities of the filled bap. But if you do go with it, and say it was Lord Sandwich who invented what we now regard as the sandwich in its modern form, then it makes an interesting journey from his stamping ground in Kent to Saigon Race Track 6,357 miles away in Ho Chi Minh City.

The British statesman made them fashionable, there were rosbif ripples in France, and then finally an uncomfortable acceptance of this entirely new food form that no-one had ever seen or heard of before (obviously with 'le' wedged before 'sandwich' in a Franco attempt to save pride, rather than a shoulder-shrugging, philosophical favor that it was just another nail in the coffin of the French language).

Parisians started filling baguettes with pate, and jambon and butter, perhaps with a few cornichons on the side for sharpness and colour, then came Brie and squished tomatoes with lots of pepper and sea salt, and then as happened in Britain's former colonies, France started disseminating sandwiches through its empire like rats from ships.

The French took their flour to Saigon and showed their Vietnamese servants how to make bread, and then finally – almost 120 years after the death of John Montagu, the 4th Earl of Sandwich - the banh mi was born. And it's amazing to think that no-one would have ever invented it, if it hadn't been for a British aristocrat, whose epitaph should have read "seldom has any man held so many offices and accomplished so little", according to his many critics. Apart from the sandwich, of course.

Yes, they embraced the sandwich in Vietnam. And some might say Lord Sandwich has a lot to answer for, because it shows in the diet. The Vietnamese tend to be much more rotund than their Cambodian and Thai neighbours. Men happily flop their guts out, and lounge around, scratching their balls, counting down the hours till their wives get home from work and they've got more money for sandwiches, fags, and beer.

And every restaurant menu has its own comprehensive sandwich section, sat awkwardly in a no-man's land between Western dishes and Vietnamese dishes, like some sort of oil-rich archipelago in the South China Sea, or Eastern Sea if you live in Vietnam, being fought over by two mutually-respecting, but diametrically-opposed culinary rivals.

At Saigon Race Track, they served banh mi the traditional way - a smear of pate, like home-made chicken liver pate but without the fuss, rolled pork belly slices, white sausage, and other things they produced from somewhere in the cart. And then came the salad - onion, lettuce, tomato, long strips of leathery cucumber, chopped red chillies, mayonnaise, and ketchup, and who knows what else, crammed in, pushed together, and wrapped in computer print-out paper fastened with elastic bands as though it's been handed over by a hopper in The Wire.

Or maybe a breakfast banh mi? Two eggs beaten in a bowl, with a little water - the key to any decent omelette. Not that they were making an omelette as such, as there was no gooeyness. Instead, they poured a little vegetable oil into a wok and fried the eggs until they had the texture and colour of a shammy leather.

It could have been a very ordinary dish, but they added a scattering of sliced onions to the oil before they put the eggs in, and this gave it that sort of big race, hotdog smell, except without the testacles and colouring, and you're back at that race course, anywhere in the world, screaming along with the crowd as the nags hit the 1,100-metre pole, and the hotdog or the burger or the taco or the kebab or the naan or the SANDWICH is falling out of your hands, and the mustard is already down your shirt, and it's neck and neck, and your horse finally comes in and the whole afternoon's saved, and you know you've got the money to buy another 10 hotdogs. Or 189 banh mi if you're in Vietnam.

MANY OF the experts I met in Saigon said the city makes you hard - and you have to be to survive. From the moment you wake up to the moment you go to bed, you're being hassled for money - and see poverty all around you.

Everyone has a good cause, everyone is an orphan, from the red-eyed street kids who are beaten and starved by their minders if they don't sell enough flowers, to the land mine victims sticking limbs in your face. I had sympathy for them, of course. But it was the thousands of other scavengers who wanted a piece of your wallet I grew to loathe.

Men sat around on mopeds on every street corner shouting: "Marijuana, charlie, boom boom, massage, charlie" at passing tourists. There were hustlers everywhere from the ladyboys on mopeds to the muggers and the druggers.

And one of the most predatory was a masseur called Hun who hung around in the bar I drank in most nights. He paid special attention to the white women. He would whisper in their ear, offering them sex for $5, and sometimes he was lucky, disappearing off with his client and then returning on his bicycle an hour later.

You couldn't help catching his eye. His dark pupils were everywhere, watching every scurry on his 20ft wide patch of pavement - his bitterly-defended hunting ground. His posture and instinct reminded me of a black mamba, poking its head above the shrub, forever looking.

One night, the pickings were desperately slim, and he wouldn't leave me alone. He kept creeping up on me, rolling his massage rubbers up and down my back. I kept telling him I already had a bad back and waved him off, and then on his third assault, I lost my temper.

He gave me a withering look and went off to sit on his bicycle, watching me from the street. Then he came back, sat down at my table, and demanded I buy him a drink. He walked off, mumbling curses, and came back as my Vietnamese chicken curry with a side order of red chillies arrived.

It was sweet and mild, with a delicious, bread-mopping quality - a nod to cornflour-thickened Chinese cooking. I was just soaking up the sauce with the rice when he sat down at my table again.

"I'm eating!" I said.

He just shrugged his shoulders, and started rubbing my arm aggressively. The food dropped from my fork and it became impossible to eat.

"No, you can't have a frigging drink!" I yelled at him.

He went back to his bicycle, eyeing the pavement with a reptile's instinctive cunning. I gazed out at the street, trying to avoid his glares.

A rat scurried in the gutter, the dark pupils were on it, the tongue flicking out to taste the air. The masseur grabbed his roller and sprang from his bike.

As I finished my meal, I thought about the events that had made him the man he was, and the many like him you meet in SE Asian cities. The struggle and hustle from childhood, the chilling ruthlessness. Night after night he was there, hassling tourists. How could he keep it up for so long? And if it wasn't an act, what sort of person had this street life crafted? A master of his trade with the skin of a rhino, exhibiting a peculiar mix of persuasion and mild threat, his patter varying in strength from insane tenacity to the hard sell.

Had I been too respectful in my initial responses? Had I shown him a weakness he'd quickly grown to exploit? Of course I had. I was worthless and weak compared to him, and he knew it. I hadn't lived on the street, begging at people's doors for food. What did I know of the world? As Adrian Gill once said, the older you get, and the more you travel, the less you know.

I looked at the same flower kids and beggars encamped in huddles on the pavement every night, cutting off all routes of escape. The bar owners, like those in Cambodia and Thailand, had a curious acceptance of them, and would only usher them out when too many descended.

Perhaps it was Buddhist culture, perhaps not. There were too many inconsistencies. As Thomas Fowler's voice-over begins in The Quiet American: "They say you come to Vietnam and you understand a lot in a few minutes, but the rest has got to be lived."

CHAPTER FIVE

IT WAS good fun being out on the road, roving about, living a nomadic life of cheap hotels and expensive Scotch, but I could feel the tropical tonto coming. The heat was stifling and the air smelled of rancid gutters, and news travelled slowly in a place where they steam the stamps off letters.

As I sat in that same bar night after night, drinking buckets of vodka limon with Saigon Green chasers, I knew I needed to get away for a bit – somewhere cooler with a breeze, where you might even have to wear long trousers in the evening. And about the only place you can get that in southern Vietnam is Dalat - a mountain resort famous for its flowers, fruit, vegetables, coffee, and endangered wild meat.

And I'm glad I did finally leave Saigon, because eating artichokes in the central market there was a major highlight of my trip through Vietnam. It immediately took me back to long summers in France, ripping off artichoke leaves and dipping them in vinaigrette, and watching the world go by from a cafe pew overlooking a dusty street.

I made do with one of those ubiquitous, ridiculously-low plastic chairs that surround every food stall in SE Asia, and leave anyone over 5ft 5in tall with their knees bent up around their chin like a flying yogic hopper who's just fallen off a bed. But I wouldn't have swapped it for the world.

Although there were thousands of beautiful artichokes in the market, lined up next to the massive avocadoes, bulging beetroot, cabbage, peas, and strawberries, there were none for sale in any of the restaurants, so I tried to persuade a stall owner to cook a couple for me and a Vietnamese woman called Qua, who I'd met on the bus on the way there.

I bought two fat specimens for 60,000 dong (£2) from a one-eyed woman, who'd stabbed her eye on an artichoke spear, leaving a bluey-white smear in its place, and handed them to the cook. We ordered a bottle of the awful local wine, and a plate of garlic prawns, and fried pork and rice to sweeten the transaction.

I had no idea what to expect. The stall specialised in "ancient hotpots" (lau thap cam) that combined everything from prawns to squid to beef to pork to vegetables in a simmering pot of spicy, herby goodness, so I imagined it would be something like that. But after five minutes I still wasn't sure if the cook knew what I'd meant, or whether she thought I was just giving them to her as part of some bizarre, foreign custom to ward off food poisoning.

Then a huge metal steamboat appeared with artichoke quarters sticking out. The cook put the dish between us and lit a paraffin burner underneath to get the water bubbling. The taste was incredible. Out of this world. I delved around in the pot with my chopsticks. It was just water, salt, sliced onion, fresh coriander, and a few chopped up artichoke stalks to flavour the broth. And the preparation was as rustic as the delivery. They hadn't bothered removing the fibrous choke – this was a stall in one of the best fruit and veg markets you'll find anywhere in the world, and it seemed fitting somehow that every part of the thistle should be cherished, or at least acknowledged. Every thorn has its rose, as it were.

As with all Vietnamese hotpots you get an intense boil for a few minutes, and then the dish just putters away for a bit, and the burner runs out. Not that I waited that long - the veg was so fresh it took barely 10 minutes to cook. And soon Qua and I were pulling off leaves and scraping the mushy goodness against our bottom teeth.

Somehow the haphazardness of the dish made it all the more appealing. There was the perfect amount of seasoning in the stock to give the artichokes a delicious, intense taste, while making a wonderful pea-green soup to drink afterwards.

The hearts were mouth-wateringly divine, and I soon got fed up with fishing out the fibres, and just bit into them to devour their succulence, and I still had a fibre stuck in my throat when I wrote up my notes two days later. They had a moreish, bitter aftertaste that massaged the roof of your mouth and screamed of Provence – from where they'd been introduced 100 years before.

The French turned Dalat into a tiny corner of France to escape the heat of Saigon, and revel in the produce of its incredible microclimate. Tropical fruit and vegetables were grown in the foothills, while further up, where the air was thinner, the soil lusher, and the temperature more reminiscent of the Med, it was the perfect growing spot for European produce.

As well as being the world's artichoke tea-producing hub, Dalat also has wonderful milk and it would have been churlish to say the dish needed butter – as it would have been served in France. But I'd hardly eaten butter in the five or so months I'd been in SE Asia, and I didn't miss it and nor did the dish. There was something in its simplicity that summed up Vietnam's skilled, pot-based cooking. It was the understanding of food, and the knowledge that smothering natural goodness is a crime.

When the bill came, Qua kicked up a fuss when they tried to charge us 50,000 dong (less than £2) for "cooking" the artichokes. She got quite upset about it. I was more than happy to pay, and pointed out how much a similar meal would have cost in the UK, and how if she hadn't been there they would have charged me double, and that I was happy to pay for the theatre and the occasion, and I did have some sympathy with the cook.

But to her it was an appalling rip-off.

"Fifty thousand dong for water, onions and a few bits of cilantro!" she kept saying. "FIFTY THOUSAND!"

"And they probably got the water from the lake," I added, trying to make light of it.

But she just glared at me and back at the stony-faced cook when she returned with my change, and the atmosphere quickly turned as spiky as those violet, thorny inner leaves that had taken that woman's eye out on the stall next door.

QUA LEFT a couple of days later, and I caught a bus eastwards through the mountains to the coastal resort of Nha Trang, and headed out to the beach just as the sun was going down. There was a faint orange hue over the coconut trees. The sky was turning purple and I could just make out a sail miles out to sea.

107

The beach boys were putting away the last of the Jet Skis, loading up pick-up trucks on the sand. The sea was now murky green and streaks of cloud were turning red. A young man, with a white scarf wrapped round his head, was standing knee-deep in water, holding a plastic bag. He wandered along slowly, occasionally turning stones over with his foot.

"You catch crab?" I asked.

"Only one," he said, showing me a tiny blue swimmer crab cowering in the corner of the bag. Its claws were tucked in, and it had given up all hope of escape.

"You have no friend?" he said, looking concerned.

"No, I have friend, but she's gone..."

"Oh," he said.

He looked truly sorry for me.

I stared out at the ocean, at the expensive yachts anchored a short dinghy ride away. For a second, I was lounging on one of them, munching lobster, looking back at the beach.

"How long you stay in Vietnam?"

It was the same stock question I'd been asked a thousand times, but this time it didn't annoy me. I realised they'd just all been trying to make conversation all along. It was my fault for not learning the language, however ridiculously difficult it was, and I felt anger at all the irritation and bitterness that had brewed up in Saigon.

"What do you do in England?"

"Job?" I asked.

He nodded eagerly. I thought for a moment, and then picked one.

"I'm a cook." I said "And you?"

His reply sounded like "forty but" and he made a swishing movement as though he was dealing cards. He repeated it again.

"In hotel," he added.

Was he a croupier? He repeated it again and it sounded less like "forty but".

"Oh, washing up!"

"Yes, yes!"

He looked delighted. I was envious of his happiness.

"You like it?"

"Yes, yes, very much!" he trilled.

There wasn't even the faintest lie in his eyes.

I WANDERED back along the beach and stopped at a stall to eat chicken noodle soup, but they hadn't got it. "Pork!" snapped the noodle cook, jabbing a finger at her spidery-scrawled sign. She didn't do anything else, and nor did her husband, who was crouched at the back, busy prepping a grimy tub of water spinach.

I perched on a stool, and my bowl arrived in seconds. There were a few slices of pork, tandoori red around the edges, a scattering of sliced spring onion greens, a few slivers of crisped garlic, angel hair noodles, and beansprouts. The nod to vitamins was the single piece of kale that had somehow found its way in on the back of a spoon.

Four pots of garnishes were thrust at me - pounded dried chillies with what looked disconcertingly like a pube sticking out from the top, an explosive chilli vinegar, sugar, and crushed peanuts. A bottle of fish sauce, toothpicks, and a plastic drum of napkins completed the street food decor.

Except I was wrong about the lack of greenery. As I delved deeper into the last loop of noodles, a piece of water spinach appeared in the bowl. I remembered the story the cleaner at Pho Binh had told me about how the Americans were literally hoist with their own petards when they bombed the vastly underequipped, but ruthlessly cunning Viet Cong making their way north to south through the mountain passes of the Ho Chi Minh Trail.

The passes were marked and American bombers flew over blowing holes in the mountainside. The men with their shoes made from old truck tyres were slowed, but still they came, clearing the rubble and finding other trails. And as the monsoon rains started, the bomb craters became pools.

Messages were passed and the next group of Viet Cong brought live fish with them and stocked the pools, and the fish slowly multiplied in their new mountain home. Then they planted water spinach cuttings, which quickly spread - long, hollow stalks with a few leaves at the top, delicious when fried with garlic and fish sauce. As each unit of National Liberation Front militia arrived, they found pools full of fish and swamp cabbage to feed them.

I bit into the tube and imagined those fighters sitting around a pot, sleeping off their evening feast provided by the bombs that were meant to kill them. I sipped away at my Saigon green label as the last of the light faded. The noodle cook sent a young boy to fetch more beer from a nearby store. Outside it was a newspaper stand packed full of American, German and British newspapers. At the bottom was the Sunday Sport. "Gordon Ramsay Sex Dwarf Eaten By Badger" was the headline. London seemed a long way away.

FOR SOME reason, I'd always been intrigued by Vietnamese Buddhist cooking (do chay). There is something in its cleanness and simplicity, and its 'mock meat' offerings that distract you from missing real meat - well for a day or two anyway. But it's not just that. It's the love they have for every humble ingredient, and the way it's eaten in such a communal manner, with people filling each other's rice bowls and ladling broth.

My first taster was at a weekend retreat run by Vietnamese monks at a convent they'd hired in the Chiltern Hills, west of London - an event attended by Wagamama founder and Asian food expert Alan Yau. During one meal, we were served something called "nine treasure soup", filled with seaweed, berries, mushrooms, and julienne vegetables, and I'll never forget it, and sadly have never come across it since.

Most of the meals at the retreat consisted of home-made tofu, formed into faux meat concoctions and cutlets, stir-fried vegetables, mushrooms, spring rolls, tempura, fried noodles, congee, sticky rice cakes (banh chung), steamed buns (banh bao), and always soup to wash it down. The workshops were led by a monk called Thong, whose brother helped run the famous Bat Nha monastery in Vietnam's central highlands province of Lam Dong.

The dishes came from there, and I'd always wanted to go, seeing pictures of how beautiful and peaceful the pagoda looked, perched on a misty hill-top in the middle of a tea plantation – the scene, incongruously, of some well-publicised violence between two rival Buddhist groups two years before.

I wasn't looking forward to the long trek back across the central highlands though, and had a few hours to kill before my bus set off. So I started my journey with a meal at the Long Son Pagoda with its huge white Buddha gazing down over Nha Trang.

I'd heard about the Buddhist food they served in the temple's restaurant. The signature dish was mi Quang, a noodle soup speciality from nearby Quang Ngai province, decorated with mushrooms, steamed tofu, and vegetarian 'pork chops' and 'ham'.

But I'd had more than my fill of noodles, so went for a selection of dishes to remind me of the different flavours that make up Vietnamese Buddhist cooking. The mushroom fried rice was excellent. The base was courgette brunoise, and the slivers of dried mushroom had the texture and colour of Bombay duck, and gave the dish a pleasant, earthy taste. It came with a sweet and sour tofu broth, deliciously seasoned in the traditional Vietnamese style with fresh tomato and pineapple, and a chunk of red chilli at the bottom spewing out heat.

The seaweed soup was thickened with corn flour, so it had a ham stock gloop that would be lost on most vegetarians, and there was a pleasant hint of sesame oil buried somewhere in the slices of baby sweetcorn, carrot, onion, coriander stalks, and seaweed. But the vegetarian spring rolls were a disappointment, and I folded them away in a plastic bag to give to the beggars who haunt the temple grounds.

I wandered around, and climbed the 152 stone steps to the giant Buddha, and saw the relief busts of Thich Quang Duc and six other monks who'd publicly burned themselves to death in 1963 in protest at the South Vietnamese government's regime.

Sitting in the shade, were a group of kids selling lottery tickets and chewing gum. I had scarcely reached for the spring rolls, when a fat little bloater appeared from the trees and snatched the bag off me. He was chased up the steps by the rest of the children, stuffing his face as he ran.

The pagoda hall was filled with ancient Buddhists, who'd travelled there from across the country. One of them looked at least 100-years-old. She held out her palm as I walked past, and I handed her $5. They would spend the next ten days sleeping and praying in their pyjamas on the stone floor, waiting for the next full moon. It certainly put my 10-hour ordeal across the rugged highlands into perspective.

Or at least that's what I thought at the time.

After an hour stuck on that "bus" – as the booking agent had described it – I'd have gladly swapped places with those doddery old Buddhists. There must have been 20 people crammed into that Ford Transit screaming through the hair-pin bends. Most of the time we were on the wrong-side of the road, the driver thumping the horn.

I was wedged between four women on a seat for three. But I was one of the lucky ones. Some people were compressed into L-shapes against the ceiling. They'd taken out the folding seats because you can cram more people in that way. And still we stopped to pick up more passengers.

The trucks and buses we'd overtaken on blind bends over forested gorges plunging hundreds of metres down to waterfalls, rocky streams, and certain death, clattered past us again. But we were soon on their tails, the horn blaring away, skimming mopeds by inches.

I had my lap-top pushed against my chest, and my money and passport stuffed into my pockets, but after a couple of hours of cramp and claustrophobia, my legs were so numb, I felt hands everywhere.

112

My bag was in the back, and all I could think about was the backseat rooting through my stuff, sharing out booty like jubilant thieves. Was that the sound of an electric razor? Not that I could hear anything above the whining from the spiteful toddler on the woman's lap next to me.

We missed another durian fruit moped by a whisker as we screeched out of the way of an oncoming truck. The pain in my knees was horrendous after another hour, and the brat was sticking his elbow in my ribs. After a few minutes, it appeared to be deliberate. He had more than enough room against the window. I mustered the last of my strength, and managed to free my arm enough to nudge him and get my arm back in time, and he started howling again.

Suddenly we screeched across the road, and pulled up for a pit stop outside a ramshackle bus station with parking space for about three mopeds. I thought the contents of my bag would be strewn across the backseat. But worse, I couldn't see it at all. I searched through the sacks of fruit, potatoes, and boxes of ducks, chickens, puppies, and no doubt live king cobras destined for Saigon's wild meat restaurants. Then I saw a soiled black backpack on the far side.

It couldn't be mine. There was a live bird attached to it. It was flapping around hysterically, opening its mouth at horribly-distorted angles. I looked again. It still had the green flight sticker on. It was definitely my backpack. The ribbon round its foot was tied to the zipper, and the fledgling had excreted foul juices all over the top. I thought about burning through the ribbon with my lighter, and demanding to know who'd tied a live bird to my bag.

But there was no point. No-one spoke a word of English, and I'd given up Vietnamese weeks ago after my hundredth attempt to order a hot, black coffee without having ice and sugar shovelled into it. Then a mean-looking rice farmer with a scarred face started feeding the greedy creature kernels from the steamed sweetcorn he'd just bought, and I realised it was probably his, and returned to my six inches of space at the front.

Eventually, the packed Transit pulled up in a one-horse town called Bao Lac - a place well off the tourist beat that only warranted two paragraphs in my travel guide. And one of those was to tell you about a waterfall 15 miles away.

I BOOKED into an empty guesthouse and got up early the next day. I had no idea how to get to the monastery. It was raining hard, and I didn't fancy hiring a moped and navigating the narrow, treacherous lanes. Not if there were nutters like that minibus driver on the road. Eventually I spotted a taxi, and we drove through the tea and coffee farms, up and down lush, green hills through tiny communes, until we got to Bat Nha monastery.

It was perched on a hill in the middle of a tea plantation, just like the pictures I'd seen, and the quiet was deafening. It was hard to imagine an armed mob smashing down doors and forcibly evicting 150 monks two summers ago in delicate negotiations between peace-loving Buddhists.

Those evicted were followers of Thich Nhat Hanh, the French-based Zen monk exiled from Vietnam because of his anti-war views in the 1960s, but allowed back 40 years later when Vietnam tried to get itself removed from a US list of countries violating religious freedom (a move which led to its admittance into the World Trade Organisation two years later).

They said they were beaten by an armed mob, enraged about their ideas on religious reform. The authorities at first denied that any incident had occurred. Later, the communist government described the matter as an internal dispute between two Buddhist groups, and pointed out that Nhat Hanh's supporters had organised religious courses without permission and failed to register their temporary residence at the monastery.

Human rights groups said it highlighted Vietnam's suppression of religious freedom, and attitude towards religious groups - particularly popular, radical ones it fears it can't control.

But there was no sign of any damage as I walked around the grounds. Everything was immaculate. The pagoda was set back behind grey stone columns inscribed with hieroglyphics. The garden in front looked like it had been manicured with a set square. Every part was tended and loved, and it was someone's job to patrol around and keep incense burning in every shrine.

To the left, a white statue rose out of garishly-pink petal leaves. A Hobbit bridge led over to the grotto in front. I strolled around the grounds, gazing at every perfectly-trimmed bush and shrub, struggling to think how that peaceful paradise had been engulfed in violence, and how depressing it was that the only religion I had ever had any notion of joining, however fleeting, could still be ridden with the same power struggles, intolerance, and hatred as every other religion.

I walked past more living quarters, and an old woman told me that an Englishman had been living there for the past ten days, but had left that morning.

"He English, but not fat you," she said.

I was sure it was 'less fat' she meant. I'd run out of belt holes what with the heat and the rice diet, and I'd only really been able to keep a respectable amount of flab on with the beer and baguettes. She'd definitely meant less fat. She pointed down the pathway and told me to go and look at the waterfall.

I climbed down in my flip-flops, and found a Buddha statue hidden in the trees. All I could make out was a patch of white sleeve to start with, until I cut through the coffee bushes, tripped over a tree root, and slid the rest of the way down the slope. I walked on round, past the snake and spider holes, to the pagoda at the waterfall, and then back up again, this time taking a route to the back of the grounds with less holes.

I couldn't have timed it better. They were just settling down for supper. Two long wooden tables – one for the men, and one for the women - were slowly being decorated with food. Suddenly the heavens opened and a monsoon thundered down on the tin roof. I looked out at the darkening grounds and my long walk back.

I sat down at the end of a bench, and began jotting notes in my journal, waiting for the torrent to stop. When I looked up, there were a dozen children standing around me, studying every pen stroke. They couldn't believe how small my writing was. They were from the poorest farms in the area, and had probably never used a mobile phone, let alone had their appreciation of life's humble pleasures trampled on by computer games. It wasn't an iPad – just a notebook and pen. Then more came.

The old woman I'd met asked me to join them for a meal. I hesitated at first, thinking about how it looked - a comparatively wealthy foreigner taking alms from impoverished monks. But I'd made a donation to the monastery, and a cheer went up from the children when I agreed. I'd never met people so easily pleased, and I was too, because I was desperate to try that food I'd heard so much about.

They sat me down at one end of the monks' table. No-one spoke any English. One of the older monks filled up my bowl with rice, and then pointed at the dishes – golden-fried tofu in tomato sauce, stir-fried pumpkin stems and leaves, deep-fried mushrooms in pakora-style batter, bitter melon soup, boiled jackfruit, and, of course, sticky rice.

The pumpkin greens reminded me of nettles slightly, but they had crunch and flavour, and were delicious. Just as meat-eaters savour every knobble of succulence, almost the same can be said for vegetarian food - from the slipperiness of the bitter melon to the crunch of the mushrooms.

The tofu dish was outstanding - the same flourishing skills when it comes to tomatoes as the best Italian cooks. I've always thought you can tell a chef's skill by how they make a good tomato sauce - what tomatoes they use, how long they cook them for, the amount of garlic, salt, sugar, and oil they put in. Put that in your sous video bucket, robot chefs.

I asked who'd made it, and they pointed to a small boy a few feet away. He could have only been 13. I knew it was pointless asking him the recipe, and I went through miming routines to guess at each cooking stage, but I could see he was confused. Either that or he was thinking: "Forty minutes for the fucking tomatoes? Thirty at most!"

I asked him to write down the ingredients, but he had even worse handwriting than his friend. It was full of Cs, Ts, and bent umlauts. I smeared through the paste with a chopstick. Just coils of tomato skin and delicious red sauce. I couldn't see anything but tomato. No suggestion of onion or garlic, nothing green, no real flavourings apart from salt, fish sauce, sugar, and perhaps some tomato puree, and the incredible blast of flavour you get from knowing how to cook tomatoes properly.

Then a stunning dish of boiled jackfruit appeared. You could have put down a roast chicken wafting of herbs, garlic, and bacon, and it would have had the same effect. Well, perhaps not. And certainly not a fiendishly-rare hunk of cow's buttock with horseradish and fondant potatoes cooked in duck stock, or green ham and boiled potatoes with English mustard, and a parsley and sage sauce.

But it was a knock-out punch all the same, and I immediately felt guilty for harbouring those carrion thoughts. They looked like lamb steaks. Straight through the leg. I could even see the bone and marrow. The flavour was amazing. The jackfruit had been marinated in lemon grass and soy sauce, and boiled until it was soft, but still meaty. In fact, it was so packed with umami, it smashed you round the head like an angry, rival Buddhist, it was so good. Again I got them to write it down. It was something like "qua mit kho".

"Like bo kho!" I kept saying, taking pride in the only Vietnamese phrase I can pronounce so they know what I'm saying after the fourth attempt. Then I realised I shouldn't be shouting about beef stew in a Buddhist temple. Not one with such previous anyway.

The rain had stopped and made way for lightning, and I promised I'd visit them the next day. I walked back through the grounds, feeling more sad than emotional. I'd been on the road for so long, I hadn't felt affection like that for months. I walked down the tiled steps, past the perfectly-aligned hedgerows facing east, and the taxi already had its lights on. All I knew was I needed to get hold of that recipe for the tofu in tomato sauce. I still couldn't work out if it was fresh tomatoes and tomato puree, or whether there were any tomatoes in it at all.

CHAPTER SIX

I HAD another week left on my tourist visa, but it was time to return to Cambodia to look for a restaurant. I couldn't afford a decent place in Vietnam, and the legal fees to get the required licences were far too expensive. Like in Thailand, the only easy, and relatively quick way to do it, was to put the business in a Vietnamese partner's name, and I'd heard far too many horror stories for that.

I caught a bus from Saigon and headed to Siem Reap, in north-west Cambodia, to see the temples in the ancient city of Angkor - once the centre of the Khmer Empire, then abandoned and overgrown by the jungle for centuries, and isolated by wars, and now one of Asia's top tourist attractions with 2.5 million visitors a year. If the rents were cheap enough, it sounded like a good place for a business.

On the way, I thought about the food in Vietnam, and the dishes I'd put on my menu. One thing that surprised me during the six weeks or so I spent there was how dismissive many tourists were of the food. When I was in Thailand and Cambodia, expats kept telling me that Vietnam was THE place for grub in SE Asia. Most of them had travelled throughout the sub-continent and knew their stuff. Some were chefs and food writers who'd been working here for years.

Perhaps it was the high expectations, but my first experiences of Vietnamese food hardly blew me away, and I kept bumping into people who said the same – that it didn't quite live up to the hype. I even met a rapper called DJ Shadow in Saigon, who had a bizarre theory that it was down to the fact that Vietnam had been at war for most of the 20th century, and its people had been too busy learning to fight than cook. He'd even written a rap about it.

I can't say I agreed with him, but it made for an interesting conversation from what I vaguely recall. After all, when the French colonised Cambodia, they tended to use Vietnamese chefs rather than Khmer ones, believing they were far more skilled cooks (which is praise indeed from the French).

But I did find some very good dishes during my travels in the country. And the best of the lot, for my money, were the breakfasts. I never thought I'd find a meal to rival the full English fry-up, but it was certainly true for banh mi op la (fried eggs cooked on a skillet with a freshly-made tomato sauce and a garlicky, mayonnaise-like emulsion, served with a crusty baguette) and bo kho (invariably translated on menus as "Vietnamese goulash").

And the latter is not an unfair comparison, because like a properly-made goulash, bo kho has that rich, meaty thickness to the stew that only comes from cooking cheaper cuts of cow for a long time, with root vegetables in towards the end.

There's nothing quite like mopping up a hearty stew with bread, and that's how it came in Vietnam, with a lovely fresh baguette to wipe up every smear of juice. But there was other stuff too: the ubiquitous plate of thorny coriander, Thai basil, and rice paddy herb for vitamins, and a saucer of tuk meric.

The meal is a sister of pho bo, and shares the same secrets in the stock – sugar, onions, cloves, star anise, cinnamon, ginger, and occasionally other spices, cooked to black. This gives it a deep, slightly bitter, sweet flavour that differentiates it from the hundreds of permutations of beef daubes, stews, and goulashes you'll find around the world from Paris to Prague to Phnom Penh.

The result after a few hours of simmering is an aromatic, velvety stew with lumps of falling-apart beef, potatoes, and carrots – the sliced onions long having been dissolved into the thick broth. The best place I had it was at Cafe 333, off De Tham, in Saigon, where it was only served on the breakfast menu, topped with a garnish of sliced fresh onion and spring onion greens.

I'd definitely put bo kho on the menu, along with some of Vietnam's delectable fish and shellfish dishes, when I opened my business, I thought as we changed buses in Phnom Penh. I'd already got some good Khmer recipes, but I knew I'd need more for the restaurant, and wanted to see what regional dishes I could steal in northern Cambodia. Then there were the pork pies to think about. I needed to find somewhere that sold lard...

THE SEVEN-HOUR bus journey from Phnom Penh to Siem Reap was a nightmare. I knew I'd hit the 'gap yar' trail soon enough, and be forced to listen to loud, tedious conversations. A couple of British students were sitting in the seats across from me. CC, as his adoring girlfriend kept calling him, had a deeply-affected, pompous voice and had obviously been listening to too many radio panel shows. His voice rose quickly at the start of each sentence, carried on at the same pitch, and then went down at the end.

He was as desperate in his attempts to grow a beard as he was in his determination to impress. He had either just finished, or just begun, a philosophy degree and went through a lengthy sermon about the existence, or otherwise, of "matter" from the early great minds, with repeated reference to Aristotle, to a lengthy diatribe about German philosophers in the 1700s. By the end, I wanted to throttle him as an ironic expression of the notion of self-evident intentionality.

On the way, we stopped at Skuon, a small market town in Kampong Cham Province, famous for a local delicacy - fried tarantula. The spiders live in holes in the jungle and are dug out and grabbed at the back of the neck to stop them biting before their jaws are snapped off with a machete.

They are then boiled in water for a couple of minutes and deep-fried until crispy. I bought one from a stall and bit into what is said to be the prized bit - the belly. My mouth was filled with an egg-filled, bitter sludge, and I fed the rest to a half-starved dog.

There was more gap year trauma to come as the bus eventually arrived in Siem Reap and I sat down for a meal at the Night Market. I flicked through the menu looking at the Khmer dishes and ordered samla kako ("stirring soup") made with kroeung, potatoes, snake beans, and bitter gourd, followed by deep-fried frog - three revolting, Gollum-like creatures, with patches of black skin still clinging to their bodies.

I took a couple of bites from a leg, which is about the only part on a frog with any meat, and then they started pushing tables together and three backpacking twats in Panama hats sat facing me, failing miserably to hide their grimaces. On my other side, a group of obese American girls were complaining about their meal, and demanding a discount.

"And the rice was cold," one of them moaned.

"It was nothing like last night's meal," her friend chipped in. "We had three pieces of chicken then, and less potatoes..."

I looked at the waiter as he smiled and nodded. They'd be given a big plate of rice with some meat for $1.50, and it still wasn't good enough.

I walked back to my hotel, through the Old Market, and saw a man crouched in despair. He had a baseball cap on, and no shoes, and was bent forward, staring at the ground. I'd never seen anyone look more miserable. Even the limbless land mine victim, who was wheeled around on a stretcher past the black Range Rovers and Lexi during rush hour in Phnom Penh.

He was like a human statue of The Scream - a snapshot of life's hopeless futility. I walked towards him. Was he dead? How could anyone crouch for so long in that tortured position without swaying? I stood next to him and said "bong" a few times. There was no answer. I spoke louder and eventually he looked up.

He had a goofy look and his eyes were crazed. He seemed to grin at me, but it was difficult to be sure. I took a note from my top pocket and handed it to him. His expression didn't change. There was no sense of surprise. He held the note gently and didn't look at it. I wandered off down the road and looked back a minute later. His silhouette was still in the same pose, the note still in his hand.

I WOKE early the next morning, hired a bicycle from the guesthouse next door, and followed the huge, green road signs to Angkor Wat. I passed a smart art deco building called Hotel de la Paix, and was just heading out of town when a fat, confident-looking Englishman with bulging calf muscles cycled past.

"I'll race you there," he said, looking over his shoulder and smiling smugly.

I tried to keep up, really I did, but the sun was beating down and my vest was soon a rag in the blistering heat. I carried on for a couple more miles and the buildings gave way to jungle shacks selling paintings of Angkor Wat and the massive beehive-like towers surrounding it.

The road straightened and I caught a glimpse of the reservoirs that had been built around the sacred city between the ninth and 14th centuries - a massive irrigation system that had provided water for its estimated one million-plus population, when the Khmer Empire was one of the greatest powers in SE Asia. There was a police box ahead. The fat Brit was there.

"I told you I'd beat you," he said.

I was too breathless to answer and he cycled off towards the ruins. A female officer was sat in the shade, scribbling a sketch of the temples.

"You have ticket?"

"How much?" I puffed.

She told me the ticket office was back where I'd cycled from. I pulled out some notes, but she just shook her head and pointed down the road. She was the first honest official I'd come across in Cambodia.

But it wasn't surprising, given the high-ranking snouts in the trough. The UNESCO World Heritage Site is run by Sok Kong, a business tycoon close to Prime Minister Hun Sen, who was granted a concession to collect the entrance fees in a hushed deal with no bidding, and the tickets are tightly controlled.

Opposition leaders claim much of the money flows into his pockets, and those of his cronies, rather than government coffers and Angkor's restoration. At $40 for a three-day ticket, and the hundreds of tuk tuks everywhere ferrying tourists back and forth to the ruins, not to mention the golf buggies and buses from the posh hotels, he must have been one of the richest men in SE Asia.

I cycled back and found the ticket office an hour later. It looked more like something you'd find in a Department of Homeland Security ferry terminal than a third-world country national park. They took my money, took a photo of me, and then printed out my pass, and I cycled over the bumps to the next police check and had to pull out my pass again. I rode back past the police box, and up to a huge car park as peasant girls descended, offering me drinks, ice cream, souvenirs, and demanding $1 to look after my bike.

Across the bridge was Angkor Wat - said to be the largest religious building in the world, and one of the most wondrous monuments created by man. And sure enough, the place was magnificent. I gasped at first sight of it, and am gasping still. Look it up. More than 200 acres. Every block of stone was immaculately engraved and the stones stretched as far as you could see.

It made me think about how first world countries pat themselves on the back when they put on a successful sports event with a few fireworks thrown in, and yet this was a feat that made modern endeavours petty by comparison, especially when you consider the absence of cranes and other technology.

I walked on to the sandstone causeway crossing the giant moat, with its naga, multi-headed serpents, rearing up from the balustrades, and looked beyond at the vast temple and its strange, rocket-shaped towers. Tony Bourdain was right - the place was so epic, it seemed to demand silence, "like a love affair you can never talk about". But there was no silence to be had, no vain attempts to assemble a private narrative, an explanation, a comfortable way to frame the experience.

There were tour guides and groups of sight-seers of all colours everywhere, all wearing matching T-shirts. For a moment, I could hear the history of the temples in Russian, Japanese, and French. One of the guides, a stocky Khmer man wearing sunglasses and a huge cowboy hat, suddenly broke out of French and bellowed at me.

"Put your shirt on please!" he said.

I pulled the sodden dish rag from my belt, and he turned back to his group, mumbled something, and they laughed. I wondered how many slaves had been wearing shirts when they'd built the fucking temples, breaking their backs on sandstone blocks, and toiling in the unbearable heat. Still enraged, I walked up behind the group as they stood on the bridge gazing at the moat, and thought about pushing the fat little cowboy in, then thought better of it.

I CYCLED around the sites, moving on from Angkor Wat to the temples around the fortified city of Angkor Thom, with their Apsara heavenly nymphs etched into every wall and column. Every face, every dance was different.

Then I got stuck at the top of Ta Keo - a stark, undecorated mountain temple, consisting of a central tower surrounded by four lower towers, and the first Angkorian monument to be built entirely of sandstone.

No-one knows why it was never finished. According to the travel-writer verbiage in my guidebook, some say it was the death of Cambodia's 'king-God' Jayavarman V, who was having it built as a state temple in his honour.

Others believe it was because the sandstone, quarried 30 miles away from the holy mountain of Phnom Kulen and floated down river on rafts, was too hard to carve and explains the lack of decoration, despite the many names of tourists scratched into nooks. And some say the work stopped years after Jayavarman V's death, when the temple was hit by lightning, and the resident high priests saw it as a bad omen.

It had been easy getting up, even though the steps were treacherously steep, 3ft high at times, and polished like bars of soap with all the traffic. And I hadn't given any thought to going down. People sat in quiet corners of the ruins and prayed, and I wandered round looking at the spectacular sunset views of the temples, trying to put the panic out of my mind.

How could a comparatively primitive race of people build something so magnificent? And why did they do it? The temples were originally Hindu, not Buddhist, with Angkor Wat being built in honour of the Hindu God Vishnu. Josh had a theory that a mystic sect of skilled and highly-educated people had been exiled from India, and had settled in the area, and taught the locals their secrets.

But I wasn't thinking about any of that as I looked for a place to climb down. I couldn't have cared if the place had been built by a mystical race of pig-faced aliens in space suits. The sun was dipping fast, and I walked round the edges, panicking at the drop. I'd had a terrible fear of heights ever since passing out on a bungee jump in Ecuador. I hadn't slept for three weeks after that. Every time I shut my eyes, I fell through the bed.

The pyramid-shaped temple had four levels, each smaller than the one below it. I walked to each of the four gates of steps and looked down as my guts tightened. They all looked as treacherous and steep as each other. One slip, and in my panicking state that was quite likely, and I'd fall at least 50ft, perhaps more if I bounced off the next narrow ledge. The vertigo was terrible. I kept walking around trying to calm myself, and wondering how the hell I was going to get down.

They would have to airlift me off. It was the only way. How much would Sok Kong's goons charge me for that - $500? My travel insurance wouldn't cover that - not that I had any. There was no way I could face those steps. My legs were shaking so much, my mind reeling in fear, that I couldn't trust myself to take the steps.

I'd have to go off one of the corners and climb down, clinging to the apparently uncarvable, yet crumbling, sandstone blocks. I dangled my feet off the ledge, and lowered myself down slowly, feeling for hand and foot holes, and trying not to think what might be inside those baking stones. A previously undiscovered, venomous tarantula the size of a human face? I got to the next level and looked at the drop, shutting my eyes and breathing deeply every time the fear got too much.

Suddenly I heard whistling. A small boy selling postcards was skipping down the steps like a billy goat. He wasn't even going down backwards. He could have been reading the bloody postcards as he did it. He waved as he skipped past.

Eventually I got to the bottom. I'd never felt more glad to feel earth below me, well not since that illegal bungee jump anyway. I looked back up at the temple. The boy with his postcards was on his way back up there.

I unlocked my bike, and was two miles from Siem Reap when the monsoon descended. It was so heavy, I couldn't see more than a few yards ahead. Soon I was cycling in a foot of water. Eventually I pulled over. A tuk tuk drew up beside me. We loaded my bike on, zipped up the tarpaulin, and then he hit me with the price.

"Fifteen dollars to go back to the old market!" I yelled, pointing out that it was normally $3 or $4 at most.

He looked out at the road, held his palm upwards, and smiled.

"It's raining," he said.

I yelled at him again, yanked my bike from his chariot, and kept venting curses as I cycled through the rising water. I thought about Dirty Derek, and his novel idea for dealing with what he called "the scourge of bloody tuk tuks in Cambodia".

"They should do what they do in Tunisia!" he'd told me. "Ban them from even talking to the tourists – they can only speak to you if you talk to them first. It's bloody brilliant, mate!"

It seemed pretty extreme to me at the time, even by Muslim country standards. But not with the rain thundering down and the tuk tuk drivers chuckling away in their rain coats as they passed me. I thought about how I'd once walked down Riverside in Phnom Penh and was bombarded by 17 "tuk tuk sirs" in the space of 50 yards. I know because I counted.

They could see I'd just been asked several times in the space of a few feet, but the next ones asked anyway. With the heat and the traffic, and the piled-up tuk tuks, mopeds, and Land Cruisers blocking every pavement, it was enough to test the patience of even the most modest and saintly person.

But Siem Reap was even worse, especially at night. There were hundreds of them around the Old Market area hissing "skunk, cocaine, massage, boom boom" and then giggling at your answers like a pack of hyenas. Sometime ago they'd banned tuk tuks from entering Pub Street - the main thoroughfare of bars and restaurants - at night. But although it meant it was about the only part of town you could walk without navigating your way through inch-wide gaps between prowling chariots, it made little difference.

They just parked their contraptions round the corner and clapped their hands at you as soon as you left – or looked as though you were about to leave – a restaurant. You only had to get up from your seat to go to the toilet, and they'd start clapping and whistling.

When you find out the prices the locals pay, it makes your blood boil. I spent the next afternoon in the outskirts of Siem Reap, travelling around on a tuk tuk with a hard-nosed Vietnamese estate agent. We must have driven 20km, stopping off to look at empty houses that could be turned into restaurants. At the end, her bill came to $5. So you can imagine my rage the following day when a tuk tuk driver demanded $5 for a fare that was barely a tenth of the distance.

They are only trying to feed their families, of course, and I should be more tolerant. But the simple truth is not every Cambodian man can be a tuk tuk driver – there are not enough fares to go round as it is. And as each new crop appears, the incessant badgering is just going to get worse.

There should be a limit on tuk tuk numbers, I raged, as yet another driver passed me grinning from beneath his hooded rain coat. It would be quite easy to police. You can't just buy a tuk tuk and set yourself up on a corner shouting "skunk" at tourists, and demanding extortionate fares for a short trip up the road.

Drivers have to pay $5 a year to the Government for a licence, and on top of that, depending on the allotted pitch, a fee of about $10 a month to the local tuk tuk guild – an amount that drivers can recoup by getting between $5 and $10 a month advertising a business on their back-board. I imagine if officials started putting limits on tuk tuk numbers, it would get strong support from existing drivers, not to mention the expats and tourists slowly being driven to madness.

It's no surprise to see nearly every tourist in Siem Reap riding a bicycle these days - and not just because it's illegal for foreigners to rent mopeds in the town. I'm surprised the tuk tuks aren't going round with screwdrivers bursting tyres, they must be so livid at the sight. But if they only charged a reasonable fare, and you weren't forced to go into a ridiculous haggling process every time you want a ride, they might get more trade.

As I say, I have to keep remembering to take a deep breath and remind myself that they're only trying to feed their families, and I shouldn't really blame them for trying it on - even if they do descend like a pack of starving wolves. But as I cycled back through that monsoon, I couldn't help wondering whether they'd gone far enough in Tunisia.

I'D BEEN told about the dingy, sticky-tabled cafe by an Australian expat chef called Steve, who ate lunch every day in an Indian restaurant near the Old Market. He said it was one of only three restaurants in Siem Reap that excelled in traditional Khmer food.

I found the place, and its sister restaurant a few yards away, opposite KFC. In the same 100-metre stretch of road, you have the two extremes of Cambodian cooking. A Khmer tasting menu at the $300-a-night Hotel de la Paix, boasting dishes like pan-fried broma fish with feroniella sauce, stir-fried frog with fresh ginger, and coconut heart and prawn salad. And the Khmer greasy spoon - offering meals like 'fried dry fish with watermelon' and the brilliantly-named 'farmer sour soup' - for a fraction of the price.

"It's a bloody great place," said Steve, tucking into his vegetable thali. "It's just a shame they use MSG – but then try finding a place that doesn't use the bloody stuff here! The Khmers swear they don't use it, but they all do! Go into any home, and you'll find a bag of the stuff next to the cooker, I bet you. They even put the stuff on their bloody fruit!"

He had a thing about MSG. Like most expats he rarely listened, and was an expert on everything. He could talk at length about how the Khmers had taken to flavour enhancers like bears to a honey vault after the country slowly opened up to the outside world after the civil war, and began readjusting itself to the modern world, and how the stuff absolutely ruined food, and was the complete antithesis to a cuisine based on fresh, seasonal ingredients.

He was right though, even if he did take hours to drone on about it in ever-ascending sentences, revealing perfect mastery of the moronic interrogative. Monosodium glutamate somehow rewires your taste buds so that everything tastes the same. The fresh vegetables and meat and carefully selected herbs so typical of traditional Cambodian food get lost in the mix, and instead you get an unwavering band of monotonous taste. When you try the same dishes without MSG, they're so much fresher and more defined.

Steve once worked at a Cambodian cooking school, where the Khmer cooks would drum it into tourists how important it was to put MSG in everything.

"What the hell are you telling them to use that bloody stuff for?" he asked on his first morning.

They just pointed at the packet.

"It Unilever – it good one," they said.

He said Khmers held all imported foods with the same reverence – particularly the dreadful bottled sauces fast making traditional Cambodian cooking a lost art. He told me he once gave his housekeeper money to buy fresh mushrooms from the market, but he gave her too much, so she bought a tin of mushrooms instead.

"What have you bought those bloody things for?" Steve asked her.

She pointed at the label.

"They from China," she said proudly.

I TRIED most of the dishes at the two cafes over a few days, and watched as they cooked them. They were all good. But my favourite was 'Siem Reap sour soup' It really was an explosion of tart flavours. The sourness of the tamarind and green tomatoes, together with the mild spices and careful use of fish sauce, made it uniquely Cambodian in character.

The only spice came from kroeung curry paste - the base for dozens of Cambodian dishes from amok to curries to creamy fish soup with noni leaves (chhou chhi) to stir-fried frog (kang-kep chha kroeung). It helped thicken the broth, and left a pleasing, golden rim on the bowl.

They made the paste by pounding chopped lemon grass stalks, kaffir lime leaves and zest, galangal, ginger, fingerroot, shallots, garlic, salt, and plenty of fresh turmeric in a huge wooden mortar for ten minutes, until it was a thick paste. The consistency is critical - if it's not pounded long enough, it can split when cooked, as Gordon Ramsay found to his cost in his celebrity travelogue flop, Gordon's Great Escape, during a highly-contrived, over-testosteroned scene cooking a banquet for members of Cambodia's Royal family.

You'll also find green and red kroeung in Cambodia. The green is essential to one of the country's best known dishes, rice noodles in green curry sauce (num banh-chok samla Khmer), and is made by using lemon grass leaves instead of stalks, and adding more lime leaves. The red version is made by adding soaked, drained, and finely chopped dried red chillies, and is the base for Cambodia's delicious, dun-coloured curry (samla kari Khmer) that you mop up with a crispy baguette.

Like many traditional Khmer dishes, the soup was incongruously delicate and fresh, and yet ferociously sour at the same time. Most Cambodian food is incredibly quick to make, and most restaurant dishes are made from scratch in minutes – even soups. Because of the speed of the cooking, each ingredient stands out, and adds its own character to the dish.

The addition of holy basil leaves (m'rah prov) a minute or so before the soup was finished gave it a refreshing, minty taste that hummed of cloves. It was a clever addition because it kept refreshing your palate, so you kept tasting the sourness of the soup again. Cambodians love holy basil – a sacred herb used to treat an endless list of illnesses from malaria to manic depression. It's different to sweet or Thai basil because it doesn't have an aniseed taste, and its spicy flavour intensifies with cooking.

Like the Vietnamese, it was noticeable how little oil Khmers use – even in stir-fried dishes. They pour about half a tablespoon of vegetable oil in a wok, tilt it around so it smears the sides, and then spoon the rest out. They are so sparing, you rarely see an oily glint to a dish – which is why some claim Cambodian cooking, with its heavy use of green and ripe fruit, vegetables, and dairy-free recipes, is one of the healthiest cuisines in the world.

Instead, they 'fry with water' by adding small splashes to give a fast bubble to meat, fish or vegetables cooking in a wok. It means you don't get the same singed, caramelised flavour to the meat, but vegetables cooked this way are far better.

In every restaurant garnish section I've worked on, spinach was always fried in clarified butter, almost as though that was the only way to cook it, and anything else was "wrong". But fry it the same way, substituting the fat for the same amount of water, and it's fresher-tasting and far less greasy. Purple sprouting broccoli and runner beans cooked that way are especially good.

To make the soup, the cook cut half a frozen chicken breast into cubes, and then sliced some onion, green pepper, green tomato, and fresh pineapple, and put them in a bowl with the chicken. She heated a wok, poured in a little oil, smeared the sides, and spooned the rest back into an old paint tin. When the oil was beginning to smoke, she added two teaspoons of kroeung, and stir-fried it for 30 seconds.

She then added the chicken, and fried it for a minute until it was sealed but not browned. She poured in a little water, and then tossed in the green tomato, green pepper, onion, and pineapple, and continued to stir.

She added half a pint of water, and boiled the soup rapidly before adding a splash of tamarind juice - made by pouring hot water on ripe tamarind fruit and soaking overnight - and a dessert spoon of fish sauce. She then added a little salt and sugar, and a liberal sprinkling of MSG before I could stop her. She let it boil for a couple of minutes, always topping up with a little more water, and then tossed in a handful of holy basil leaves, which quickly wilted like spinach.

The old woman stepped back suddenly as the head cook appeared at the stove. He dipped a spoon in and sipped. He looked thoughtful for a second, and then nodded his head, turned to the grimy table of condiments and sauces behind him, and reached for the MSG.

131

The head cook then showed me how to make his signature dish - pork fried with hot basil, lemon grass, and chillies. It shared similarities with other dishes I'd tried during my travels in SE Asia, but still had a taste of its own - encapsulating the fast, fresh, and fragrant hallmarks of Cambodian cooking. It also helped destroy the myth that Khmer food is never spicy. I've tasted the meal in many restaurants since, and it's always eye-watering - just like the green mango, papaya, and cured beef salads they serve.

While it's true that with the vast majority of Cambodian recipes, little or no chilli is used, and when heat is needed, cooks often turn to green Kampot peppercorns or ground black pepper, it doesn't mean Cambodians don't like chilli. They just serve it separately - usually sliced, red bird eye chillies in a saucer, pickled green chillies in jars, and a relish of sliced red chillies and garlic - so people can heap on as much or little as they want.

But that dish, simply called "hot of pork" in that wonderful cafe, was a meal aimed squarely at chilli aficionados. It needed no accompaniment, other than a soup, a bowl of sticky rice, and a kettle of champagne-pink tea poured into a mug of ice and drunk through a straw.

To make it, the head cook finely sliced a little frozen pork fillet, and then bruised and finely chopped some lemon grass stalk. He fried the lemon grass for 20 seconds, and then tossed in the pork, stirred it for a second, and then added a splash of water, and stirred again. He then added half a tablespoon of fish sauce, the same of soy sauce, and a sprinkle of sugar and salt. He was about to reach for the MSG, but this time I was ahead of him, and said I'd have it without.

He cooked the meat for another minute, topping up with splashes of water all the time, but not too much to lose the fast bubble. He then threw in two handfuls of holy basil leaves and a finely chopped red bird eye chilli, and the kitchen was quickly filled with the acrid fumes of singed chilli seeds. But he didn't stop there. He added a splash of bottled chilli sauce, and a teaspoon of ferociously-hot fried chilli paste. Chilli three ways. He added a little more water, to get the right gloop to the sauce, and then served it up.

132

FOR A country so rife with corruption, and so full of human rights abuses, it was a crying shame there was not more printed about Cambodia. Much of it had to do with the media's ever-growing obsession with celebrities and soft news.

It hammered it home one night when I typed "Cambodia" in a Google news search, and most of the stories that came up were about how Angelina Jolie's kids love eating crickets and munch them "like Doritos" - as she revealed in an interview during a visit to an impoverished village in Siem Reap Province to plug a £7,000 handbag for Louis Vuitton.

Light-hearted yarns about child labour, mass faintings in sweat shops knocking out goods for Tesco and Marks & Spencer, and foreign conglomerates, largely from China and Vietnam, driving out villagers from their homes to make way for rubber plantations and shopping malls, don't stand much of a chance against what an A-list celebrity's adopted brood like to scoff while playing video games.

But in the unlikely event that Jolie's kids ever find themselves on skid row, they could always try this novel way of catching crickets I came across on a tour of the floating villages lining the massive Tonle Sap lake, just south of Siem Reap.

It really was shocking to witness the extremes of wealth in Cambodia, where there was little or no state help. Siem Reap was so developed, with its $800-a-night hotel suites and world-class golf courses, and yet an hour's bike ride away there were villagers earning just $500 a year.

When the lake is down, they pretty much survive on snakehead fish - ugly looking things with dark reptilian eyes that glint angrily as they're pulled from nets, and are about the only fish that can survive the dry season buried in muddy puddles, pretty much like the people who live on them.

As I cycled there, one side of the road was lined with plastic bowls with what looked like giant hankies hanging over them. I'd seen them on the bus to Siem Reap, but still couldn't figure out what they were for. I'd seen calves drinking from them, and initially thought they were just water tubs, but why so many? And what about the netting

133

and the electrical cables and fluorescent bulbs dodgily hooked up to the overhanging power lines?

A dead frog was floating in one. Was it a frog trap? That didn't explain the electrics. Or did it? A group of young Khmer men emerged from a karaoke hammock bar. They were working for an English school and offered me a $5-an-hour job on the spot after discovering I was a native speaker - which helps explain why there are so many unqualified English teachers working in the country. Some say the only qualification you need is to have a pulse.

It turned out the splat-smeared netting was to catch flying crickets, so they plunge down and drown in the slimy green ooze. I looked closer as one of the bolder Khmers began fiddling with the fizzing electrics to demonstrate how it worked. A cable ran from the overhead power line to a plastic water bottle with two connections, providing some sort of switch so the bulb dangling perilously over the water could be switched on at night to attract insects.

The crickets were then collected in the morning and cooked for breakfast, or sold to street vendors. One recipe I came across was deep-fried crickets (charet bampong). The crickets are caught alive and fed grated coconut for a couple of days. Their heads are ripped off and a peanut is pushed inside their bodies, before they are marinated in salt and sugar, and then deep-fried until golden and crunchy.

As I was cycling up to one of the poorest villages, several policemen lounging in hammocks by the side of a muddy track called me over and told me I had to pay $2 to go in. I was directed back to the ticket office at Chong Kneas, where tourists are charged $20 to go on a short boat tour of the floating villages and schools.

At first, the touts denied it was possible to buy a ticket for the village and kept pointing at the boat, and then they said it was $4, and finally agreed it was $2. It wasn't the money that bothered me. It was knowing that none of it would go to those villagers trying to scrape a living in the mud.

I cycled through the floating village, and the tin shacks and wooden houses on impressively high stilts became even more ramshackle, until there were families of 14 living in single room shelters with reed-stitched roofs. The people looked content with their lot, and I was reminded of the Cambodian saying "mien tuk, mien trey" (have water, have fish) - but the poverty was appalling.

Children were playing in the mud, and everywhere I went there were choruses of "allo!" It was obvious they got few foreign visitors. The only tourists they saw were the boat loads of holidaymakers who floated past on organised tours of SE Asia's largest lake, which during the rainy season swells up so water comes through the floorboards, and the only way to go shopping is by boat. It's these monsoon rains that are the secret to the regeneration of the area, bringing a wealth of young fish and freshwater shrimps that feed off the vegetation as the surrounding fields are flooded.

It was an existence of mud, fish, and water. I passed a boat yard, and the smell of the wood oils enveloped the air with a fresh, musky, aftershave smell that for a few seconds overpowered the relentless stench of fish. It was a tough life - the dreadful poverty meant the average life expectancy was just 54, 50% of children were malnourished, and 12% died before the age of five, according to the NGOs that raised cash for the villagers.

Some of the wooden shacks were bought for families by foreign visitors, and had the sponsors' names plastered on boards outside like 'for sale' signs. The whole economy was based on fishing. And I was glad the Cambodian government had finally announced action to restore fish stocks in the Tonle Sap by removing the commercial licences of fishermen who'd been pouring toxic chemicals into the water to drive fish towards their nets.

The 35 lot-holders, who had been paying the government a total of $2m a year for the privilege of overfishing and poisoning the lake, had been banned from operating for at least three years to allow fish stocks to recover. Locals were still able to fish the lake to feed their families, however - which was lucky considering there was very little else for them to eat.

But there was another threat too - hydroelectric dams planned for the Mekong River, which were set to dramatically decrease water flow into the lake and the number of fish and snakes for the locals to eat. When I wrote this, the river's fast-flowing currents, which run more than 2,700 miles from its source on the Tibetan plateau to the vast delta in Vietnam, had only been dammed across its upper reaches in China.

But campaigners warn that if the Xayaburi Dam in northern Laos - the first of 11 dams proposed for the Lower Mekong mainstream - goes ahead, it will devastate fish stocks in Cambodia and Vietnam by blocking migration routes, and may lead to the extinction of critical species like the giant Mekong catfish and Irrawaddy dolphin.

Work is already being carried out on the dam - including land clearing and road building - and some of the local population have been forced to relocate despite regional agreements that no work should take place until more environmental research is carried out.

NGOs fear that if Xayaburi is built, the other 10 (eight in Laos, and two in Cambodia) - will also be built. They say the dams will have a "catastrophic impact" on Cambodia's impoverished villagers, who scratch a living in the world's largest inland fishery. Yet again it would be voiceless villagers and their future generations that would suffer.

ON THE dusty road back to Siem Reap, a tuk tuk full of lycra-clad tourists, clutching beer bottles, stopped in front of me. They got out and disappeared down a slope to a lotus flower farm with a 1,000 riel ($0.25) honesty box outside for visitors. They started clambering around in the middle of the flowers, taking pictures of each other.

I watched for a bit wondering whether the entrance fee would pay for the damage to the plants, and then there was lightning over the hill and soon the full strength of a monsoon. I was drenched in seconds. The potholes and craters quickly filled with muddy, red water and it was impossible to know which would lead down into a crunching chasm, and which was older and filled with stones.

I stopped outside one of the hammock bars lining the road. A family welcomed me in and sat me down with a tray of beers and a bucket of ice. I drank the Anchors in quick succession, staring out at the lush green rice fields that would soon become a lake again. I could have been in Wales, except the rain was stronger, the heat left breath trails in the air, and there wasn't a curried chip or shell-suit in sight.

The rain gathered strength, and soon poured through every hole in the roof. They moved me to a room at the back with a sturdier roof made of rusty corrugated iron, and I drank a few more beers as I waited for my sour chicken soup (s'ngao chruok moan). A steaming bowl big enough to feed a brigade of hungry soldiers arrived. There was so much there, I shared it with the family.

The chicken was the gloopy, gelatinous parts of the bird – feet and wing tips mainly – as well as offal and gizzards, and with the sourness of the tamarind and lime juice, flavoured the stock brilliantly. It came with rice, bean sprouts, chopped spring onions greens, and a bowl of Kampot pepper. Every time the liquid level fell below five gallons, an old woman would arrive with a cauldron of bubbling chicken stock to top it up. It was absolutely divine.

I sat in my hammock and gazed out at the paddy fields that now resembled a patched quilt with squares of brown in the afternoon haze. I looked down at the water-filled trench below and the goat and her mewing kid. The top of a reed fish trap was poking out from the water. There was movement inside and I could see a snake's head squeezing out through the bars.

It tried one side and then the other, each time looking for a bigger gap. Finally it pushed half its body through and dangled unsteadily in mid-air. I felt slightly guilty, but did it anyway. I walked out to the front of the restaurant to tell the family they were about to lose a snake.

They had no idea what I was talking about so I got them to follow me. They squinted for a bit as I pointed. The snake had gone still all of a sudden and you could hardly tell it was there. Then it gave a final lunge and vanished into the brown water. I gestured again, but the woman just shrugged.

"You want me go and get and cook for you?" she asked.

"No, no, I not like," I said quickly.

They wandered back to their hammocks, and then the woman returned with a stick in her hand. Her silhouette got closer. When she was a few yards away, the stick bent upwards and I realised it was a snake.

"I cook for you?" she said.

"No, no," I said, panicking, and wondering how I could jump out of the hammock without falling over the low banister into the snake-filled trench 20ft below. She grinned in a slightly disturbing manner, and I thought she was going to throw it at me. But she walked off and chucked the serpent back into a large, foul-smelling vase to rejoin its friends and live for a few more hours. I staggered to my feet, paid the bill, and got back on my bike to brave the rain.

AS I cycled back, dodging the craters, I thought about that delicious soup, and how the defining characteristic of this mysterious cuisine had to be its sourness. It embraced tart flavours like no other country I'd been to before. Diners screwed up their mouths and smarted their faces in a gesture that in most countries would be seen as a look of utter disgust, a confirmation that the dish was truly awful, and a look so solidly damning in appraisal, it would no doubt test the breaking point of even the thickest-skinned chef.

But in Cambodia, it was a sign of sheer gastronomic delight. As lip-puckeringly unripe as possible, as citrus as you can make it, as zesty as it comes. The tartness was as much treasured as the buttery softness of freshly-boiled lobster or the earthy richness of truffles in more glamorous cuisines. There was no call for cream sauces. And certainly no meatballs in veloute sauce soups, followed by a kilo of flown-in caviar, sandwiched between sour cream-strewn, warm potatoes, as one extremely rich French man liked to make for his dinner parties in Sihanoukville.

It really was a land of sour pickles and green fruit. Lime juice, zest and leaves, lemon grass, tamarind, rice vinegar, unripe fruit, mysteriously bitter herbs and leaves foraged from the hedgerows and rice paddies (it was hard to find a direct English translation for some of them), were used to bring sour notes to food.

Another was preserved, salted limes, used in Cambodia's ngam nguv soup. The limes were dried in the sun for a day, and then soaked in brine, and a few quarters in a soup, stew, or stir-fry gave a soapy, citrus tang immediately evocative of Moroccan cooking.

I'd tried it in a Khmer-owned happy pizza joint the day before. They made it for me with chicken, but said "Cambodia's number one style" was made with duck, when it was traditionally served at weddings. A whole duck is chopped up with a machete, deep-fried and then boiled, and the bones are sucked from the lemony broth to toast the happy couple.

The smallest globules of oil glinted away on the surface. There was no fat in the broth itself, it was from the browned garlic sprinkled on top. It came with culantro (chi bon la), a coriander-tasting, jagged-toothed herb originally from the Caribbean, where it's widely used in sofrito recipes.

I thought about the way the soup glorified zesty flavours – first, fragrant lime leaves infusing the stock in the same way that European cooks would use bay leaves, and then the all-powerful addition of salty, bitter lime.

But just when it got too much, there was a tickle of warmth from the chilli, and then a strong blast of coriander from the culantro, and then finally a deep taste of fried garlic. It was easy to see why some hailed it as the king of Cambodia's many sour soups - even though the preserved limes themselves were of Chinese origin.

I'd watched as an old woman, who was clearly in charge and wouldn't let anyone near the stove, poured a small bottle of drinking water into a wok, lit the hob, and then threw in three kaffir lime leaves and waited for the liquid to boil. She diced half a small, frozen chicken breast, and then chopped up a preserved lime, pips and all. A man, who was no doubt the owner because he asked me twice if I was going to pay for the meal, bashed three garlic cloves with the end of a rolling pin to remove the skins, and then chopped them.

The old woman added the chicken breast to the bubbling water, then the preserved lime, a few diagonal slivers of red chilli, and a sprinkle of salt, sugar, and half a tablespoon of fish sauce. She let the soup bubble away for a few minutes, topping up with a splash of water from time to time, as she made the garnish.

She heated a smear of oil in a frying pan, added the chopped garlic, and fried it until it was brown, and then tilted the pan to let the oil drain off. She let the soup boil for another minute, and then ladled it into a bowl, garnishing the top with nutty garlic and chopped culantro. A soup made from scratch in five minutes – the perfect healthy fast food.

CHAPTER SEVEN

MY ATTEMPT to learn how to cook Cambodian food hadn't been an easy one. There were only a few decent cookbooks on the subject, and even they were filled with contradictions, making it even harder to get to the bottom of what was undoubtedly one of the world's most overlooked cuisines.

Take lok lak, for instance. It's easily the second most famous Cambodian dish after amok. It's on every menu, even in places that do actually serve proper traditional Khmer dishes. But it's undoubtedly Vietnamese - even the name is Vietnamese. And calling it 'English lok lak' with the courtesy of a fried egg on top is just ridiculous - and shows how unconfident Cambodians are about their food, and how reluctantly they reveal the real, pongy, delicious stuff they hide near the ruins at Angkor Wat.

You can still find traditional Khmer dishes in the countryside, passed from mother to daughter in homes and a few restaurants and street stalls. But I knew my quest wouldn't be complete without visiting Joannès Rivière - a chef widely seen as one of the world's leading experts on Cambodian cuisine.

The Frenchman, who worked as a food consultant for Rick Stein when he visited the country, had been shining the path in Siem Reap for the past nine years. Chefs and food writers kept telling me that what he doesn't know about Cambodian food can be written on a 100 riel note.

I was convinced Rivière was the man to talk to, even if he was only going to dispel a few of my theories, and even more so when celebrity chef Raymond Blanc heaped huge praise on him during a visit to Rivière's restaurant, Cuisine Wat Damnak, a week before I got there.

"Oh mon Dieu, this man can cook, he is blessed!" Blanc wrote on his blog after trying his Cambodian tasting menu.

The menu certainly sounded interesting - an amuse bouche of green mango salad; fresh rice flake pancake with prawn, smoked fish, and aubergine puree; pan-fried chlang (an eel-like fish from the Tonle Sap lake) with crisp vegetables and hyacinth blossom; quail curry with pumpkin and long beans; and a sticky rice crème brûlée.

"Those moments are rare when you know that you are in the presence of a very gifted craftsman," added Blanc. "Remember this name: Joannès Rivière."

That was it - I had to meet the man. I rang and he told me to come round the next day. I walked along the dusty, crater-filled side streets near Wat Damnak temple, a mile or so from town, and then spotted the restaurant's blue logo. The place had been converted from a traditional Khmer house, with a large kitchen extension at the back, and was set in a beautiful garden.

Rivière emerged from the kitchen with fat beads of sweat rolling down his forehead. He gestured me to a seat flanked by herb pots and we shared two bottles of water as the midday sun beat down.

He was good company, and very self-effacing given his credentials. He grew up working in his family's small restaurant in Roanne, in the Loire region of France, and then went to chef school for three years before working as a pastry chef in Nantucket and Philadelphia.

He then decided he needed a change and moved to Cambodia, working as a volunteer for two years teaching impoverished kids cooking and hospitality skills at the French NGO-run Sala Bai Hotel School in Siem Reap. But savings don't last forever, however much Buddha's on your side, and he spent the next five years as executive chef of Hotel de la Paix, launching its Cambodian degustation menu.

In April 2011, during Cambodia's hottest month, and at the beginning of the low season, he and his wife Carole opened Cuisine Wat Damnak "with the aim of serving delicious and imaginative Cambodian food to locals, expats and travellers alike," according to their website. They also had a baby.

"It wasn't a very clever idea," chuckled Rivière, rubbing his eyes. "I wouldn't recommend to have a baby and open a restaurant at the same time. It's extremely tiring! You finish work at midnight and then you have to wake up at 6am, and it's like this every single day!"

It wasn't the most auspicious start. Business was slow, and then he was hit by the country's worst floods for ten years, and had to close for two months. But the word slowly got round as foodie tourists and expats and rich Khmers from Phnom Penh flocked to see a Frenchman showcasing traditional Cambodian recipes using seasonal fish, fruit, and vegetables that are nearly impossible to source.

"I wanted to open a restaurant like you would in France or England by focusing on the products, which is actually very rarely the case in Cambodia. So I base all the recipes on that. If I find a good fish then we change the menu, and put the fish on the menu," he said.

Rivière built up a network of local suppliers, getting fish from the Tonle Sap and pigs from farms near Angkor Wat.

"The two good meats in Cambodia are fish and pork," he explained. "If you can get Cambodian pork - because 70% of the pork here is imported from Vietnam, and is industrially farmed."

The beautifully-white local pig meat was showcased in dishes like braised pork shank with star anis, caramelised palm sugar, fresh bamboo shoots, and crispy trotter. But it was the freshwater fish he was most proud of - a food that he said truly defined Cambodian cuisine.

"There are very, very good freshwater fish here. The Tonle Sap is actually the second biggest source of freshwater fish in the world after the Amazon, and because the ecosystem is so unique there is a variety of fish of all types," he told me.

There were two fish on that day. Kay, which is originally from the Danube, but was introduced to Cambodia to help boost fish stocks. "They're very, very bad in Europe - they taste like shit. But here they're very good. They're one of the best fish from the lake," he said. It was served as a fillet with tamarind reduction and pounded ambarella (golden apple).

The other was sanday (butter catfish), a big, torpedo-shaped predator with a large mouth and small tail that migrates between the Mekong and Tonle Sap. He served that in a yellow curry sauce with green jackfruit.

Both fish are highly prized by Cambodians, and fetch high prices at the market, where the 32-year-old cook followed the French tradition of shopping every morning for that night's menu. With some foods only available for a month or two every year, he created a new menu every week. But he had given up describing his food as "local and seasonal", cringing at the Noma-fuelled cliché it's become.

"Everyone says that now," he chuckled. "Now we say we choose premium products that happen to be seasonal..."

His food dashed any preconceptions about Cambodian food - or at least what most people think is Cambodian food - being bland. It was piquantly flavoured with herbs, fish paste, fish sauce, and fermented soy beans.

He was a big fan of bold flavours like prahok, and its more expensive sister maam, which is milder and more refined, if you can describe rotten fish that way, because it's made using a different fermentation process. He ran off to the kitchen and brought back a plastic box full of maam, which he said he would bake that night with minced pork and egg, and serve with herbs, flowers, and crudités.

"I always get it from the same supplier. She makes it for me without colour or MSG. The fish is salted for 24 hours then stacked in a jar with salted rice and galangal, and stored for one month until it becomes sour," he said. "I don't invent anything, I just use local products, and use quite traditional combinations, and then the technique and the presentation are definitely French."

Another thing that differentiated his food was coriander. He didn't use it. It was hard to find, because like carrots, potatoes, and onions, it doesn't grow well in Cambodia. Instead, most restaurants use culantro. But he didn't use that either because he said it was brought there by Chinese immigrants, and you generally don't find it in traditional Khmer dishes.

Confusingly though, he did use 'local thyme' (chi slokkrahs, or pig's ear), even though it was another herb from the Caribbean. It's a common fragrance often used in traditional Cambodian beef and tripe recipes, he explained. I didn't push the point any further.

He showed me the kitchen, pointing out the foot-high flood mark on the wooden door frame. It was a lovely, airy space built on to the back of the house. When I mentioned how much it must have cost him, he just shrugged: "I have to spend 14 hours a day in here, so I want it to be a nice place."

He led me into a side chamber where a girl was prepping frogs for his pan-fried frog meat on a dry Vietnamese soup dish. Hang on - Vietnamese? I was confused already. They had a short conversation in Khmer. From what I could tell she wasn't happy because the frogs weren't as big as the last batch.

He led me back into the main kitchen and proudly showed me the chicken stock simmering on the stove. He starts by frying prahok paste, and then adds water, barbecued chicken, plenty of lemon grass stalks, lime leaves, and several heads of garlic, which are carefully peeled and used as a garnish. The sour soup is then served with straw mushrooms, holy basil, and local thyme on the $17 five-course tasting menu.

Next to it was a tray of aubergines grilled to black. They were to be made into a paste with ground smoked fish to go with the fresh rice flake pancake. In the fridge was a bowl of chocolate and holy basil ganache, served on the second tasting menu, a six-courser for $24, with rice praline and salted caramel sheet.

I could tell from his passion, the presentation of the dishes, the quality of the ingredients, and the incredible smells why Blanc was so impressed - the fellow Frenchman describing his food as having "supreme command in the spicing, warm in the mouth, long flavours so perfect, complex but no sophistication: simply delicious."

I asked him about the TV chef's visit and his high praise, but Rivière just shrugged and said Blanc had had a few glasses of wine.

"I knew his name but I wasn't very familiar with his restaurant or anything. The chef from La Residence called me and said I want to book a table for Raymond Blanc - and I was fully booked. And he said: 'Oh come on, it's Raymond Blanc!' So we found him a table at the back in a dark corner of the terrace so he wouldn't see too much," he laughed.

Afterwards, Blanc asked for a tour of the kitchen and shook hands with the staff. He was intrigued by one of the dishes - 'soup outside the pot' - a vibrant, green dish of raw herbs and vegetables which at the last minute has broth made from dried fish and spices poured over it.

"He said I've never had such a thing before, this is genius! But it's not something I invented, it's very, very, traditional. Cambodians will put grated boiled eggs in it to thicken it up, but we don't because it looks quite ugly..."

I asked whether it was possible that Cambodia might be on its way to its first big restaurant award, given Blanc's hyperbole, and the painfully-trendy vogue for locally-picked weeds, but Rivière just laughed in his usual modest manner.

"It's not me who's going to decide that," he said.

Then I asked if I could do a day in his kitchen. He looked less surprised than reluctant. Then he told me to meet him at 7.45am at a cafe next to the Old Market the next morning and we'd take it from there.

But he wasn't there. He'd already begun shopping for that night's ingredients. He appeared from the sweaty cauldron after a few minutes, shouting my name from across the street. You could see the stress in his eyes - he'd got to come up with six new seasonal dishes in the next nine hours.

"I had to crack on," he explained.

I looked at my Rolex and tapped it a few times. I knew I should have bought the one for $15. We necked a napalm-strength espresso, and then headed into the covered market. I was hit in the face by the smell of freshly-slaughtered pig and gasping fish. The place smelled like a blood-filled swamp.

Rivière pointed at the different stalls as we pressed on. Everyone knew him. A chef from a luxury hotel walked past with a group of Asian tourists wearing masks as we were picking through hyacinth plants for that night's garnishes. The cooks met like two old boxers, slapping each other on the back.

"He does tours round the market every morning for the guests. He hates it!" Rivière laughed afterwards.

As we headed to each stall, he bantered away with the women in their hats and pyjamas. What impressed me most, even more than his knowledge of the local ingredients, was his Khmer. He cracked a few jokes with the women at the next stall, and then the next, and I was left carrying the bags.

He showed me the freshwater fish and shellfish from the Tonle Sap, pointing out the ones that were perfectly in season. There was a splendid display of catfish, snakehead fish, Mekong langoustine, chlung, clams, and croaker fish. He described the latter as tasting like sea bream, and said he was putting it on that night's menu.

"What defines Cambodian food for me is freshwater fish and the products that are used to keep them - the smoked fish, the dried fish, the fish paste," he said.

We passed more stalls and he talked about the wide range of preserved fish Cambodia has to offer, from smoked minnows to prahok to maam to sun-dried fillets to the most pungent of all, a thick, black paste made from tiny fish and shrimps. I pointed to a bowl of minced, raw fish sweating in the river-fed furnace.

"They don't quite have the same hygiene - and with the heat!" he threw his hands up into the air. "That will probably be there all day - I wouldn't recommend that for anyone."

He chatted away about the need to pickle, spice, or brine fish and meat to stop it turning putrid in a region as hot as Siem Reap. I thought about how labourers building Angkor would have sat among the sun-baked stones, seasoning their vegetables and rice with the rich, salty, delicious taste of rotten fish.

It reminded me of the Romans, another great civilisation that had thrived on a similar fermented fish sauce to flavour food - and for some reason I thought about Keith Floyd, when he was filming at

Hadrian's Wall, recreating a traditional Centurion recipe while cooking in a gale and berating the crew and assembled historians sheltering under a tarpaulin behind the camera.

Floyd was making pork stew flavoured with carrot, onion, garlic, red wine, parsley, cumin, ginger, marjoram, thyme, and dill. And then the crucial ingredient came - an addition that plunged it back 2,000 years to when the Romans finally tired of the dreadful weather in Britain - a few glugs of what Floyd called his "Centurion's Worcestershire sauce".

It had taken him three weeks to make, he said proudly, waving the bottle at the camera. Anchovies, sprats, marjoram, red wine, and salt had been boiled up and left to ferment before being strained and bottled.

The Cambodians generally just use salt and freshwater fish to make prahok, mashed under foot like the French crush grapes for wine. They leave the bloody mush to go off in the sun for a day, then bung in more salt and leave it to ferment for months, depending on the desired taste.

Just as the Khmers add sugar to cut the taste of prahok, the Romans added honey (they didn't have sugar in those days). It reminded me of the first time I'd ordered a prahok dish. It was so sweet I could hardly eat it. When I asked them to skip the sugar the next time I went in, I threw the restaurant into chaos. Even the owner emerged from her hammock near the kitchen to quiz me.

"No sugar? But it very salt!" she said.

I told her no sugar, and she cracked a joke in Khmer to the policemen playing cards in the corner. It was probably along the lines of: "What the fuck does the long nose know?"

We bought some pork, and then headed to the chicken woman for a bag of wings for staff food. Then we stopped at the frog woman. She dug through blooded plastic bags in the bottom of her ice box. It was a messy task. Rivière sniffed the frogs before taking them.

"They sometimes don't smell too good," he whispered to me, "then I don't buy them..."

We sat down and ate grilled pork, rice, and pickles at a stall in the middle of the market. When I arrived in Cambodia, it had quickly become one of my favourite breakfasts, and I was pleased Rivière held it in similar esteem. There is something incredible in the way the pickled vegetables, chewy slices of grilled pork, and the pork and chicken broth work together with pickled chillies from the condiment trays to make something amazing.

The pork is marinated for hours and then slowly grilled, giving it a deliciously salty flavour and intense red colour. You pour spoonfuls of the clear broth over the rice and pork and then dig in. The pickle is usually made from carrot, cucumber, and daikon. They are cut on a mandoline into julienne strips and then salted. The water produced is drained off and then they are soused in a pickling mixture of water, white vinegar, sugar, salt, and spices. Think kimchi without all the PR.

Rivière downed two iced coffees, and then picked up a small bowl of sweet chilli sauce and poured it over his pork and rice and began mixing it all together.

"When I first came to Cambodia nine years ago, I didn't eat anything with MSG. Now I realise you can't get away from it. Sometimes I now think I can't taste anything without it," he laughed.

He waved at an old woman drinking coffee.

"She's the best cook in Siem Reap - believe me!" he said.

I wrote down the name of her restaurant - Bopha Leak Khluon, tucked down an unmade road 200 yards or so from Hotel de la Paix - and went there later. The walls were made from green Heineken bottles. One of her specialities was prahok ling (fried prahok), translated on the menu as "fried rotten fish with egg and pork". It was the best meal I'd tasted so far in Cambodia.

As Rivière sipped away at his third iced coffee, we talked about Cambodian food again. He told me how important it was to differentiate between traditional, ethnic Khmer dishes and

149

Cambodian cuisine, with its heavy influences from Indian, Thai, Vietnamese, and perhaps most of all, Chinese cooking.

"People will tell you Khmer cuisine disappeared during the Khmer Rouge, but it's actually not true. Phnom Penh cuisine from the 60s may have disappeared, but Khmer food from the countryside has always existed," he said.

"You can still find those dishes - but people just cook them in their homes. When I was working at Hotel de la Paix people would come in and say: 'Oh you're rediscovering Cambodian food.' But that's bullshit, it's always been here - you just have to find it and rip it off, and use it for you and claim it."

We talked about the balance of salty, sour, bitter, and sweet shared dishes making a whole rather than mixing the flavours in one dish - a practice popular in every cuisine that hasn't been refined, he pointed out. I asked him what he thinks every time he reads how Cambodian food is touted to be the next big thing. He agreed that it was "definitely on the up" - but had a long way to go.

"To make a food famous is quite complicated, because people have to be familiar with it. Laos food is virtually impossible to find in France, for instance. I know one Laotian restaurant in Paris, which is excellent," he added. "But Laos food is very unknown, and is actually quite similar to Cambodian. People will tend to talk about it if they know about it. I'm sure it wasn't easy for David Thompson when he started with Thai food in the 80s..."

He met the Michelin-starred chef when he first visited Cambodia, and gave him a tour of the restaurants and street stalls in Siem Reap.

"It was very interesting to see Cambodian cuisine with a very objective eye, not 'I'm coming from Thailand, I'm going to compare it with Thai food' - but more 'is there any similarity?'"

Thompson told him that Cambodian cooking was almost the same as Thai food 20 or 30 years ago, before it became more refined, and far sweeter and spicier. Rivière said the biggest obstacle facing Cambodian cuisine was the lack of confidence the locals have in promoting it, and how "some restaurants are doing a very poor job of it".

I quizzed him about Cambodia's unofficial national dish amok, and said I still hadn't had a good one. I just hoped he hadn't got amok on that night's menu. I was relieved when he agreed.

"I'm still trying to figure out why amok. I think the first guy who wrote Lonely Planet must have put it in. I have no idea why it's amok because amok is done exactly the same as it is Thailand - and it's called the same!"

I asked him what dishes really sum up Cambodian cuisine. He thought for a while, and then said kha trey - river fish braised in a mildly-spiced palm sugar sauce with grated green mango on top. I'd had the dish a few times and it was wonderful.

"What's interesting about Cambodia food is it's still quite rustic. It's a matter of contrast - it's not a matter of how balanced it is. You have the very sweet fish and then the very sour green mango on top with the herbs."

I asked him for others, but he took even longer to answer - kha trey, he added again, prahok, maam, eels "if they're well done", and num banh-chok. I wanted to question him further, but there was no time and we were off to the next stall. I was handed bags of fish and meat, and a crate of eggs which were then haphazardly stacked on to a waiting moped to be delivered to the restaurant.

I reminded him about working in his kitchen, and he looked thoughtful for a second, and then told me it would be better if I worked there the following afternoon, given all the new dishes he had to create that day. I could see he was going off the idea.

I walked home, thinking about the 14-hour day Rivière had in front of him. Cheffing was hard enough anyway, but working in that heat was unbearable.

CHAPTER EIGHT

I SPENT another week in Siem Reap looking for bars and restaurants to buy. I couldn't afford any in Pub Street or the surrounding area. Some were $50,000 just for a three-year lease. There were a couple on the outskirts of town I could just about afford, but the rents were almost as high as Phnom Penh, and double those in Sihanoukville. I'd have to sell mountains of food to pay $800 a month rent, especially at the prices I'd be able to charge.

I thought about what Rivière had said about opening his restaurant. He was originally going to buy a business in the sleepy river town of Kampot, but then changed his mind when the house in Siem Reap came on to the market.

"I'm glad it was Siem Reap, and not Kampot," he said.

When I mentioned Sihanoukville, he just laughed. Others said I should look at Cambodia's second largest city Battambang - a place nicknamed the rice bowl for its excellent rice-growing climate, and famous for its green oranges. I bought a bus ticket and headed there the next day.

I CYCLED through the hot, dusty streets of Battambang for a few hours looking for the old Pepsi factory, when I realised I was looking straight at it. I'd sat down at a road-side stall selling green mango salad, and was ferreting through the ice box for a second cola, when I turned round and saw the same logo, but this time faded and sorry-looking and without the "Max", on a disused building across the road.

The place was massive. I pushed open a side door and an old caretaker waved me away. I offered him some dollars, but still he wouldn't let me in. So I took a long shot of some old Pepsi bottles that had survived the plant's sudden closure when the Khmer Rouge seized power in 1975, and walked back out into the yard.

A Pepsi plant was never going to get an easy ride from Pol Pot's thugs, who'd thought nothing of destroying their own temples, libraries, and schools to cleanse the country of its perceived political enemies, let alone a brand so strongly associated with American capitalism. It stood out like a bucket of KFC at an anti-vivisectionists' meeting.

I was amazed how much of it was still standing. I went round the back, but there was nothing to see apart from a couple of cement water tanks, so I returned to the old man, and handed him another note, and this time he relented. I couldn't go into the dusty office block, but he opened a gate and let me into the warehouse.

"But no machine," he kept saying, as he stuffed the note into his back pocket.

It looked like a film set from an Armageddon B-movie, with shell damage and bullet holes letting in shards of sunlight. The place had stopped in time like an old watch. There was the odd broken Pepsi bottle buried in the rubble and debris. But other than that, a series of switches was pretty much all that remained of the 1960s machinery.

Back then, Coca Cola had signed a deal with Bangkok to only allow its cola to be manufactured in Thailand, so Pepsi set up the bottling plant on a ferry point in Battambang, near the Thai border, so that it wouldn't miss out on the lucrative Thai market. I took a few more photos, and had a last stroll around the rubble, watching my step for coiled vipers, and then returned to the old man. He was padlocking the door to the office block. I tried another bribe, but he just shook his head and smiled.

I rode back out and stopped at the stall for another drink. I ordered a green mango and smoked fish salad (nhoam svay trey chha-ae), and chatted away to the woman as she made it. She told me the old man and his family were paid to sleep in the factory grounds to keep out visitors. She said the government was planning to turn the whole thing into a huge fresh water-producing plant at some point, but they'd been saying that for years.

She began breaking off pieces of smoked fish and pounding them in a large, wooden pestle and mortar. The fish was from the prahok market, a few miles up river, that I planned to go to the next day. It was hard and chewy and full of bones, and had a strong but pleasant taste of that magical, hot-smoked combination of salt and burned wood.

She added three whole red chillies and three peeled garlic cloves and continued pounding away for another minute. And then she suddenly stopped, and frowned at me.

"But this one we only eat with rice, and you eat only alone? It's very sharp! It's very hot, and maybe you get diarrhoea?" she said.

She was right - it was hot. And sharp. Heat-wise, it was as spicy as any som tam papaya salad I'd had in Thailand, even in the notoriously fire-eating Isaan area. But my word it was good.

She continued pounding, and then sprinkled in half a teaspoon of salt, a teaspoon of sugar, and about the same again of MSG. She worked away with a hand-sized mandoline shredding long strips of green mango into the mortar, then mixed it together and pounded the salad lightly. She spooned it on to a small plate and garnished it with three roughly-chopped culantro leaves.

"We can use the green mango, but very sour, but when we put the grilled fish, not," she said, reminding me again of the Cambodian custom of balancing flavours.

I've made the recipe since, and it really is good, but very hot, so lessen it to just one red bird eye chilli if you don't like the heat. You could always brine and then barbecue the fish yourself over smouldering wood, but Rick Stein recommends the far quicker method of skinning a couple of smoked mackerel fillets, flaking the meat, and deep-frying them in a skillet filled with an inch of oil for a minute or so, until the fish is golden-brown and crisp. You then scoop out the fish pieces and let them drain on a piece of kitchen paper to soak up the oil before pounding them to begin the salad.

In my version, I missed out the sugar and MSG, and instead balanced the sweetness and chemicals with a splash of Pepsi at the end. It was a fitting reminder of that old soda plant and the day I spent cycling to the pre-Angkor ruins at Ek Phnom and Phnom Banan that had also survived the Khmer Rouge's rule.

THE NEXT day I went in search of what I'd been told was one of the smelliest places in the world - Cambodia's prahok-making hub, Phsar Prahok (fish paste market), on the banks of the Sangker river, a few miles from Battambang, where hundreds of tons of freshwater fish are bought and sold each year.

How anyone could ever know it was one of the smelliest places in the world, I have no idea, and I'd been to a few. But mention the name and even Cambodians hold their nose. I kept cycling up and down a mud track lined with stalls, and stopped to ask people for directions. But no-one knew what I was going on about.

The smell of rotten fish was definitely getting stronger though. There was just a gentle breeze in the hot midday sun, but sometimes with the wind on my face as I cycled, there was the distant whiff of Cambodia's infamously smelly fermented fish paste.

I kept cycling, and then stopped to ask an old woman for directions. She was selling boiled duck foetuses at the side of the road. She had five chairs outside her stall, and her cats took up two of them. I didn't want to push them off. They looked vicious. The sort of cats used to keep snakes away.

I thought about dark, hooded encounters with monocled cobras hissing like garage tyre inflators. One of the cats yawned at me and stretched out its claws. It licked its lips, and we both looked round in the same direction. The wind had definitely changed. The smell of rotten fish was coming from somewhere behind those trees to the north-east.

I asked the woman again and she kept shaking her head when I said Phsar Prahok. Then she asked if I could speak French. She started to babble and slowly a few words came to me, and before I knew it she was shouting Phsar Prahok exactly the way I'd said it to her, and I'd gone through a number of possibilities.

She slapped me on the chest, as if to say 'why didn't you say so all along', and then pointed to where the ginger cat was drooling. A mile later, the stench of fermented fish was breathtaking. It smelled worse than the Siem Reap crocodile farm I'd been forced to spend two days in for a story about whooping tourists hurling live chickens and ducks into crocodile pens.

It's so strong if you get some on your hands while dipping chunks of barbecued veal and raw vegetables in prahok sauce, you soon know about it. Even bleach doesn't get rid of the smell. Or as some wit on a travel forum put it: "To describe prahok as pungent is being too charitable. It smells like it should be buried with corn seed."

There was a huge fish processing plant hidden behind iron gates and then further on, where the boats were moored on the Sangker, a long line of huts filled with people covered in fish guts. Men were offloading fish they'd netted from the river, and the locals were sorting them into plastic barrels and crates before the real process of prahok fermentation would begin, exactly the way their ancient ancestors had done to preserve fish and guarantee a year-round supply of protein.

The fish are cleaned and then salted and mashed underfoot in barrels before being left to rot in the sun for a day - which helps kick off the fermentation process. More salt is added. Then they are weighted and left in huge barrels for months, depending on the desired taste or price, with prices rising in the rainy season when the paste becomes scarce.

The taste and smell varies largely from batch to batch, depending on the type of fish used, how carefully they've been prepped, and the time, skill, and methods used to ferment them. The cheapest stuff is filled with bones, fins, and scales like the bag of prahok I'd bought from a street stall in Sihanoukville. It looked like it had been made from crab bait, and had a disconcerting ripeness.

In some of the other huts they were smoking and curing fish. Racks of fish no bigger than sticklebacks were being slowly grilled over charcoal coals until deep bronze and rigid. Some of the larger fish were being turned into maam.

I remembered what Rivière had told me about fermented fish products defining traditional Khmer food. Many countries use fermented pastes and sauces, of course, to add the savoury, meaty 'fifth taste' of umami to food. China and Japan have soy sauce and miso made from fermented soy beans, wheat flour, water, and salt. Vietnam and Thailand have fish sauce, drained from salted and fermented anchovies, prawns, or squid. Malaysia has its blocks of shrimp paste, or belacan, and there are many other varieties around the world.

But none of them I've tasted have the peculiar, cheesy punch of prahok. Most people agree it tastes of blue cheese. But it's more the harshness and saltiness of Danish blue rather than the creamier, more refined flavour of say Roquefort or Stilton. And always there on the palate and in the nose is the smack of rotten fish, as though you've been cutting skata with the cheese knife.

For that reason, you don't see it on restaurant menus much, especially in places where tourists go. Sadly, many Khmers talk about how it's now looked down on by Cambodia's emerging middle class as a reminder of the bad old days. They say it's the smell of poverty - a remembrance of their tough, previous lives working on the farm.

It's certainly true of Cambodia's aspirational brand pop videos, which always seem to feature affluent, pale-skinned Khmer couples with silly haircuts posing around in shiny SUVs that would keep a whole village in food for a year. You never see them munching prahok at a street stall. It's always pizza or fried chicken in soulless, chain-style restaurants.

It breaks my heart more than the appalling car crash, which is how most Khmer music videos seem to end, with a girl crying hysterically, holding the lifeless body of her boyfriend in her arms, and screaming "WHY!" at the sky. Which is not the best viewing when you're being forced to watch it on a bus clattering away on tyres with less grip than a pickled egg.

After an hour, I could take no more and cycled across the bridge to the old woman's stall. The cats were still there, but this time there was a seat free. The ginger cat sniffed the air again and looked at me. The smell had suddenly got a lot stronger.

I SPENT a few days walking around the centre of Battambang. I liked the place - if you sat by the river and squinted your eyes at the mustard-yellow colonial mansions, it almost looked like the Mediterranean. But it was far too quiet to run a business.

There were a handful of expat-owned restaurants and bars, but that was reflected in the tiny number of tourists. Whenever I walked past one of them, the owner would be sat desolately, surrounded by empty tables, and leap to his feet when he saw me. It was tragic to see the forlorn hope and then gloom on their faces.

I imagined myself sitting there, doing the same, worrying about the rent money and electricity each month. If I was going to do that, I might as well be by the sea. I decided I'd head back to Phnom Penh and then have one last look at Sihanoukville.

But before I left, I wanted to see Battambang's famous bamboo trains - wooden beds resting on two sets of wheels that shoot along battered, broken rails at speeds of up to 25mph. Even though I'm normally sceptical about any "must see" attractions in guide books, it turned out to be a brilliant, quirky – and bone-shaking - experience.

It had taken hours to find the trains - or "norries" as the locals call them. I'd set off on my bicycle in the wrong direction from Battambang. But eventually I cut through a trail running alongside a river, where JCBs were carving huge chunks of earth from the jungle, and found a rusty, broken track. I waited for 30 minutes, and eventually a bamboo train appeared with waving passengers.

I cycled along the track, and found a small ramshackle station that served as a pool hall. As I chatted away to the well-fed tourist police, who were there to explain and oversee the non-negotiable fare of $5 a passenger, or $10 a norrie, whichever was greater, groups of holidaymakers arrived in tuk tuks to take the 12km train trip to O'Sralau village and back.

I got on, and soon we were off on our white-knuckle journey – well, it would have been if there was anything to hold on to. It wasn't that fast, of course, but the incredible noise and the fact you were only a couple of inches off the ground, and only occasionally in full contact with the buckled rails, made the train seem as hairy as a souped-up go-kart.

Sometimes, you'll meet a bamboo train coming in the other direction (the protocol is the lighter-laden norrie gives way) and then the platform, axles, and heavy Kawasaki engine are lifted off the track to let the train pass.

We stopped at O'Sralau, and I sat with a local family drinking iced tea under a tamarind tree. They were eating the green fruit straight from the lower branches, dipping the pods in a bag of mashed green chilli, salt, and sugar.

An ancient Cambodian man introduced himself. He spoke perfect English and said he had fled the country when the Khmer Rouge took over, and worked in London and Paris before moving back to live with his family. He sighed as he pointed at the tracks, and said the villagers had been warned they only had a year left at most – and then the wooden contraptions would be taken off the tracks to make way for fast trains linking Pursat with Phnom Penh.

He said Cambodia badly needed infrastructure as it slowly emerged from the aftermath of Pol Pot's brutal, agrarian-based regime, but it was always the poor that lose out. The brilliantly-efficient norries they'd been using to carry people, medicine, livestock, timber, and rice between impoverished villages for the past three decades were to make way for shiny locomotives run by Toll Royal Railway, an Australian-Cambodian joint venture, funded by AusAID and the Asian Development Bank, that they wouldn't be able to afford to use.

The 50mph trains wouldn't stop at their tiny village shacks selling cold drinks and scarves – they'd be in far too much of a hurry to deliver goods to and from the capital. And the farm boys who drive the norries would no longer get their $1 per trip (the rest of the $10 fare goes to the station owner – which is why there is so much pressure for tips).

But far worse was what was happening in other parts of the Kingdom, where residents were being booted out of their homes to make way for the new railway, and a long list of other foreign money-backed land grabs. Locals living along one disused section of track near Phnom Penh had been offered a few hundred dollars compensation to move – and were threatened with having their homes bulldozed if they refused.

He then showed me around the old rice mill next to the track. I wondered how many more mills would be left standing idle with the hundreds of thousands of hectares of paddy fields that had been hit by flooding, driving up rice prices, and making the Khmer staple diet less and less of a staple.

And, according to a climate change study for US Aid, food shortages were only going to get worse in Cambodia with temperatures expected to soar by between 4C and 6C by 2050, and rainfall set to increase 20% or more in some areas, reducing the growth of rice and other crops, and leading to a surge in the number of malnourished children.

The last thing they needed was for the tiny trickle of revenue they got from passing tourists to disappear as well.

I WAS back in a guesthouse in Phnom Penh, writing every day in the cafe downstairs, and occasionally making forays into the sweltering streets to look for restaurants to buy. It was a relaxing place, filled with backpackers all tapping away on their computers and updating their Facebook statuses as modern day travellers seem to do these days.

It appeared a lap-top, iPad, or at the very least a smart phone, were up there on the trusty travellers' check list with sunscreen, sandals, and bug dope, which was very definitely needed in that mosquito-filled, thatched roof canteen.

Every hour a bus or a packed tuk tuk would arrive with more tourists, some old, some young, some hauling monstrous backpacks that a small elephant would turn its trunk up to. Some were on their way north to Laos, some down to the coast to Sihanoukville or Kep, some were heading east to Vietnam, or west to Thailand, and some were just killing a day until their plane took them back to their normal lives again, and the drudgery of a 9 to 5.

It was like sitting at a crossroads watching the world go by. Other times, I felt like that bloke who lived in a French airport for six years. I felt mildly jealous of their energy and meticulously-planned itineraries, but all most of them seemed interested in was ticking off places they'd been to.

None of them stayed anywhere long enough to find out what a place was really like. How anyone can "see" India, Thailand, Cambodia, and then Laos in two weeks - as Raymond Blanc had done before losing all his luggage and "Zen" on the flight home - is beyond me.

Day after day, I scribbled away in the corner of the room, eating the same two dishes every day - chicken porridge soup for breakfast or lunch, and prahok ling for supper. The owner, a fellow prahok addict, cooked the latter for me one day after I told her I was planning to open a restaurant selling Cambodian food.

I ate so much of it, she even started calling me 'Prahok Ling', and threatened to make me up a T-shirt with "I Love Prahok" on the back, which admittedly was a lot more original than the jaded "Same, Same, But Different" and "No Money, No Honey" T-shirts that men of a certain age wear over here.

But I couldn't stop myself - it wasn't as good as the one at Bopha Leak Khluon in Siem Reap - but was still a splendid dish. And whenever I thought I was being odd, or noses were wrinkled when my rotten fish arrived, I just looked round at the backpackers munching their cheeseburgers and garlic bread, and wondered what the hell the point was of travelling 6,000 miles to eat horrendous attempts at Western food every day.

Prahok ling is fish paste fried with hand-chopped pork, onion, garlic, egg, and chilli. And it's so strong there are strict government laws in place to ensure you only get a small saucer of the stuff, which you eat with boiled jasmine rice and a plate of raw vegetables to take the edge off the extremely pungent taste.

You start by hand-chopping about 500g of pork shoulder until it is minced but still has texture, and then thinly slice two onions, and chop four cloves of garlic, and two red bird eye chillies. You heat a little oil in a wok and fry the pork for a few minutes before setting it aside.

You add a little more oil to the wok, and then fry the onions for a couple of minutes until soft, and then throw in the garlic and chillies. You cook it for another few minutes before adding the pork, two tablespoons of prahok paste, and lime juice. You then stir-fry the brownish mixture for 10 minutes, and keep it in a tub in the fridge ready for service.

When an order comes in (i.e. me), you heat a little oil in a wok, and then add an egg. You stir away furiously until the yolk has just cooked, and then add about 100g of the pork and prahok mixture, and one or two whole red chillies, and fry it over a medium flame for three or four minutes. You serve it on a saucer with rice and a plate of raw vegetables - usually cabbage, aubergines, onion, and cucumber.

I decided that if I ever did open a restaurant in Cambodia, or hold Cambodian pop-up nights when I got back to the UK, or ran a barbecued calf street stall, or opened a cafe in Croydon doing the odd Khmer special, or indeed pursued any other of my half-baked plans that seemed to change daily with the breeze blowing in from the Tonle Sap River, then prahok ling would definitely be on the menu.

I WENT to see a couple more restaurants for sale on Riverside that were far too expensive, then strolled past the shrine, near the Royal Palace, where police would escort high-ranking Cambodians who went there to pray, and bought a huge, grapefruit-like fruit that had seeds the size of pumpkin seeds, and thick, leathery skin. It was a pomelo – a fruit that tastes slightly less bitter than the smaller, common grapefruit (which is actually a cross between a pomelo and a sweet orange) but gives up its pearls much more easily.

As I sat there on the riverbank, unpeeling the fruit and looking at the small green islands of vegetation floating past, and the anglers pulling tiny, glinting fish from the water, it made me think of the time I'd spent at the Fat Duck, and all those pointless hours of slavery, prepping endless grapefruit pearls to garnish the salmon poached in liquorice gel dish.

But there was none of that as I sat there on the riverbank, easily separating the pomelo into segments, and seeing the pearls fall unbroken into the bag, without the need for wads of towelling to soften their fall. I realised that all that finger-numbing torture could have been saved if they'd only used pomelos instead of pink grapefruits from Waitrose. Even with my rusty shovels, the pearls were falling away into such bundles that it would have caused envy in

162

even the most skilled, starry-eyed Fat Duck stagier. One cook could have done a whole day's worth in minutes, saving his colleagues from hours of unspeakable drudgery.

I was still experimenting with the unbruised pearls, and hadn't really eaten any of the pomelo, when a man in a wheelchair, pushed by an older man, approached me for the second time that morning. I'd given them money 20 minutes earlier, but they obviously didn't recognise me. I mumbled a few words, patting my pockets, and pointing at them, but the man in the wheelchair just pointed at my pomelo and then his mouth. I handed the fruit over, and they smiled, then slowly headed northwards along the river in search of the next barang.

I wandered over to the plush tourist information centre, which had a plaque outside saying the toilet facilities had been donated by someone called Mr Toilet, whose mission in life had been to improve toilet sanitation across the world, starting with Cambodia presumably, which is probably as good a place to start as any. The plush lavatories – donated by the late Mr Toilet's South Korean-based World Toilet Association - certainly were a shiny affair, looking more like something you'd get in an upmarket casino than a tourist office. Not that I'd seen toilets in a tourist office before.

Compared with some of the more basic powder rooms I'd come across on my travels, including those at my favourite Cambodian restaurant, Pot Pot, which after midnight were covered in vomit from jug-swilling Khmer men determined to drink more, it was certainly a welcome change. But it did seem an odd choice of mission, making sure visiting South Koreans have decent toilets to perch on, given the widespread, grinding poverty in Cambodia, where many villagers struggle to get by on $2 a day. What did they expect travelling to a third world country?

It seemed as absurd as the noticeboard outside the North Korean embassy, adorned with pictures of their late, Elvis-loving leader Kim Jong II. In one, he was standing in a factory wearing sunglasses, pointing at an egg with a confused look on his face. The caption said: "The leader Kim Jong II provides on-the-spot guidance at the 927 Chicken Farm."

163

I wandered back north and soon caught up with the man in the wheelchair, who was sitting in the shade munching my pomelo. I smiled at him but he didn't recognise me. Buddhists were queuing outside the shrine to receive a blessing from a white-clad monk. Three pensioners emerged with small cups of sacred water and headed towards a group of women holding cages full of tiny birds.

They said a few words as they sprinkled the birds with water. The birds thought it was raining again, and huddled down on their perches. Then the worshippers opened the cages and let them free in batches, saying a prayer to Buddha as they did so.

One of the pensioners then stood on the concrete wall lining the riverbank and gazed down into the murky water. For a moment I thought he might topple. Overcome with emotion, he said another prayer and wiped his brow with the last of the water.

Then they handed bundles of riel to the women holding the empty cages and wandered off with their police escort. I sat there for a while, as the birds slowly returned to their cages, ready for the next customers, and thought again about the stagiers locked away day after day in that prep room in Bray.

THAT NIGHT, I went to the night market to eat with a few Cambodian friends at Pot Pot. The place specialised in huge bowls of beef soup that you cooked on burners on the table. It was a great dish and one of the best communal meals I've ever had.

Cambodians love eating - they graze all day - and are very passionate about food. And I loved watching the arguments that developed about whether, or when, the noodles should go in, whether the thinly-sliced raw beef fillet should be mixed with beaten egg first. And how long it should be poached for. Forty seconds? There are few finer things in life than friends sitting around a table squabbling about food, while topping themselves up with endless jugs of beer.

It begins as a bubbling bowl of beef stock containing chunks of tougher cuts that have been cooked until they dissolve in your mouth in a pleasing squelch of fat and gristle. The bowl is put on a gas burner on the table and so many side plates appear that there is hardly room for the beer jugs.

164

There are plates of ice-strewn vegetables, fresh herbs like mint, holy basil, and culantro, a couple of raw eggs, beef fillet, yellow balls of egg noodles, white balls of rice noodles, chillies, prahok sauce, lemongrass, salt, and always Kampot pepper. So many in fact that you could probably order the dish 100 times and never have it the same way twice - depending on who's doing the cooking that is.

The place was filled with middle class Cambodians, mostly of Chinese and Vietnamese descent. Chubby men in football shirts, women checking their smartphones, and groups of young men with Korean haircuts and designer glasses. All forever reaching for more ladles from the bubbling cauldron.

As I gazed out at the street, a desperately-skinny woman of about 18, with a krama holding a sleeping baby across her chest, looked sheepishly at a just-cleared table and then came a few steps closer. The waitress stacked the plates, and the girl gestured towards her. She held out a plastic bag and the waitress poured the half-full soup cauldron into the bag. The transaction barely took a second.

The girl twisted the top, holding in the warmth, and walked off. Not a word was spoken. She still had the same expression, but the fear in her eyes had sunk back somehow, the resignation to misery ebbed away for a second, and she knew she had enough food to see her through the night. Just another day in Cambodia. Now all she had was the morning to worry about.

CHAPTER NINE

IT WAS the expat characters and their stories I loved most about Phnom Penh. The old hands left you in no doubt that Cambodia isn't the place it was a few years ago. It had become more sanitised and wrapped in cotton wool like most places.

But where else would you meet the sort of frazzled expat bar owner who hands $1,200 rent to the wrong man? The owner and his mate were sitting outside their bar, the monthly rent a few days overdue. "Hey, isn't that the landlord?" said his pal, pointing to a Cambodian strutting towards them. The owner rushed off to the safe and came back with $1,200 and stuffed it in the bloke's hand. He looked surprised and then handed it back. It wasn't the owner, just a very honest man who looked like him, or a man who didn't think quickly enough to carry it off. He must be kicking himself now.

Or the old Etonian, who'd spent a lifetime barking orders and being waited on hand and foot, now working for $150 a month and free food as a bar manager in a sleazy guesthouse. Or the drunk Australian chasing girls around a bar with his penis hanging out. He knocked into a huge Nigerian, who floored him with one punch. "I didn't come here to see your cock," he said as the owner thanked him and the tuk tuks dragged out the Aussie. Or the expats on ice, stumbling around like zombies, four years over on their visas and facing weeks in an immigration cell until the police finally realised they hadn't got any money and put them on a flight to Bangkok.

Then amongst the flotsam, you'd find some great foreigners in Cambodia – some of the best people you'll ever meet. But the losers and sexpats were two a penny, and it wasn't just the ones on holiday. Far from it – they still had money. For now anyway, assuming they leave.

Cambodia might have cleaned up its act, but the distractions were still there by the score. It was probably still as easy as it ever was to end up like one of the washed-up bums. Like the German in his cheap jewellery who wandered from bar to bar, and then returned four hours later claiming one of the girls had stolen his ring in the hope of getting a free beer, or the Russian who bought a couple of drinks in each bar and then presented them with a $100 note, and when they said they hadn't got change, promised to settle his bill tomorrow.

But the strangest of them all was a man I met at an American-themed bar who claimed to be an ex-forces agent, waded through swamps with king cobra serum in a holster on one leg, and viper serum on the other, and had "fired every Goddamn weapon on this earth".

Ned had been living in SE Asia for 40 years, helped run a charity clearing land mines, and was a partner in a security firm transporting millions of dollars of payroll cash to garment factories across Cambodia. Or so he claimed. The last time I saw him, he was wearing a grimy bandana and eating cold chicken out of a plastic bag in a supermarket canteen.

It was only later I found out that everyone in that bar claimed to work for the CIA. The one Brit who drank there told me he'd worked for MI6 and had been given a mission to pose as a drunk Australian in Poland during the Cold War. He said he lined his stomach with bread and milk every night and would then get so drunk he vomited.

"I was shit scared for three months living in this horrible tiny room, waiting for the KGB to come in every night. The number one rule is don't let them take you alive," he said, forming a gun with two fingers and prodding his temple.

The first night I met Ned, he lectured me about how vitally important vitamin C is in the tropics. As we drank a few beers, he kept devouring lime quarters, and was horrified when I told him I hardly ate fruit.

"You gotta eat fruit buddy. You ain't got a rat's chance out here without the fucking fruit, man" he said. "It's the vitamin C - you're body can't store it. You need to keep stocking the shit up."

He told me fruit was the only way to prevent serious stomach problems and other infections in Asia, and that lime juice and fresh coconut juice were the best. His basis for the healing powers of the latter seemed to be based on the fact he can't drink rum without it. He said he'd always been allergic to rum, but a Thai billionaire business contact persuaded him to drink it with fresh coconut milk one afternoon, and he was able to down six daiquiris.

Ever since that conversation, I'd been squeezing lime juice into my beer, and eating those bitter little oranges, and starting the day with a mango and passion fruit smoothie. I was put on to them by a woman who ran a fruit stall at the end of the narrow alley that led into the muggy catacomb where my guesthouse was regularly hidden.

There was something nice about sitting on a plastic chair in the gutter, watching the world go by as I waited for my smoothie. It brought back memories of Cartagena in Colombia. There were dozens of jugo sellers near the harbour, and it was quite an event to sit at a bar and pick your fruit from big glass jars and see them whizzed into delicious shakes.

My favourite was banana con leche, and it was so thick I didn't need much else to eat for the rest of the day. There was always an old ship hand, dressed in rags, hanging round the stands, hustling tourists. "Banana, or...marijuana?" he'd whisper at me before laughing maniacally.

In SE Asia, they just blitzed fruit with ice, sugar, and condensed milk. But if you're going for the passion fruit and mango you don't need the milk and sugar – they're creamy and sweet enough already. You peel a sweet mango by shaving the skin off away from you with a sharp knife, and then sit the fruit so the widest part is in your palm, score it into cubes, and run the blade tight against the stone to remove the flesh.

You cut two passion fruit in half, and spoon out the pips and juice. You put the fruit in a blender with crushed ice and a splash of condensed milk, and blitz for at least one minute to make sure it's properly smooth, then wander round hot, steamy streets and drink it through a straw.

ANOTHER NIGHT, Ned was lecturing me about how physically strong Khmer men are, and that's when he told me about the Coconut Man. He took a swig of beer and put his grubby baseball cap back over his glass. He sounded like Bill Hicks, but more angry.

"This dude can climb trees and rip coconuts open with his fucking teeth man," he said. "Can you do that? I know I'm goddamn sure I can't!"

I told him I didn't think I could either.

"Damn right, you can't! The Khmers are the toughest people on Earth! Pound for pound I'd put them up against any other nationality."

He told me the Coconut Man lived in the jungle, somewhere along the Mekong River - a river that stretches 300 miles across Cambodia. When I pressed him further on the location, he admitted he hadn't actually seen the Coconut Man, but had read about him some time ago in one of the local newspapers.

"Were there pictures?" I asked.

"Damn right there were pictures! The man was ripping coconuts open with his freaking TEETH!"

The next morning, I did a few internet searches, and eventually found a feature in the Phnom Penh Post about a man called Sai Song, who, according to the copy, lived in Preak Anh Chanh village, near the Kampong Cham border in Kandal Province.

It was miles away, but I thought the story might make a few dollars. I found a Khmer taxi driver, who for some reason called himself Keith, and claimed to know the village. In fact, he said he was born in a village a few miles away.

He was shifty looking but spoke decent enough English, and said he sometimes worked as a driver and translator for foreign journalists visiting the country. Only the week before, he'd escorted two Swedish photographers taking pictures of the children who worked at the city's biggest rubbish dump, he said.

He met me at my hotel the next morning and drove me in his old Toyota saloon into the flooded provinces along the Mekong River. We crawled down muddy tracks, built for oxen, with the worn suspension thumping away. But there was no sign of the village, let alone the Coconut Man.

Keith kept getting out to ask for directions. I could make out a few words. Occasionally someone would point up the road, or across rice paddies now flooded to the size of Lake Windermere, but with trees sticking out from the water. There seemed to be a lot of men who could rip open coconuts with their teeth in that part of Cambodia. But no-one had heard of the village.

Eventually, I phoned the paper to try to get hold of the reporter who'd written the story. It took her a few minutes to remember the tale, and a few more to admit she'd probably written down the wrong Preak Anh Chanh village, and that it was nowhere near the Kampong Cham border. We headed back towards Phnom Penh, with Keith moaning much of the way about the "waste of gasoline".

"Near Kampong Cham border!" he kept tutting.

We stopped at more communes, and I was about to suggest we head back to Phnom Penh and forget all about the elusive Coconut Man and his self-proclaimed "special powers" - invisibility clearly being one of them - when three young children fishing in a tiny trench pointed excitedly down the road.

From the slightly terrified look in their eyes, it was obvious we weren't the only ones who'd heard about the Coconut Man's incredible feats. We drove down the dirt track and asked more villagers, and they pointed at a wooden house with palm trees at the front. An old woman was sitting on the front steps with a baby on her lap. She was apparently the Coconut Man's mother-in-law.

She pointed behind the house and we walked down an overgrown path, lined with ducks, chickens, and half-wild dogs, and stopped at the last barn. After a few minutes, a hugely-muscled rice farmer appeared. It turned out he wasn't the Coconut Man - he was just there to check us out. I began wondering about what they were growing in the barn. Then the Coconut Man appeared. He was much shyer and smaller than I'd expected, but his arms looked like they'd been made from smelted iron.

He took us out to the front of the house as word quickly spread round the village that a barang with a camera had appeared. Soon there were dozens of villagers crowded round the car waiting for the Coconut Man to work his magic. But Cambodians are a suspicious lot, and none of them were standing too close.

I began filming as he scaled a 40ft tree in just 15 seconds and then climbed back down carrying five heavy coconuts. He then ripped open two coconuts with his teeth – taking barely 40 seconds to remove the fibrous, brown husk of the first. And then just 50 seconds to shell the far tougher, green husk of the second.

His other stunts included flexing his neck muscles out like an angry, hooded cobra and ripping rope apart with his hands. I interviewed him through the taxi driver afterwards, but he was a man of few words.

"I knew when I was 12 that I was strong, and decided to start climbing trees and bringing coconuts down for my family and friends to eat. Then I trained myself to rip them open," he eventually muttered.

I turned to the rest of the family in hope. Anything to break through his steely silence. His five-year-old daughter Yisoung simply said she was proud of her father. I asked the Coconut Man whether she had special powers too. He gestured at her, and she held her hands to her eyes and turned her eyelids inside out.

There was more silence, and then his wife Seap appeared from the back of the house. She said she was too scared to watch his stunts.

"I tell him not to do them because I'm afraid he will fall from the tree or break his teeth on the coconuts, but he does not listen to me," she sighed.

A huddle of villagers were standing well away from the others. They said they were scared he was using "Khmer black magic". "We worry he may bring evil spirits to the area," said an old woman.

But when I talked to the monks in the local pagoda, they just laughed. They said his skills come in handy every year for the Pchum Ben festival of the dead, when they get him to climb trees in the grounds of the commune to collect coconuts, which are then left with rice and wads of fake $100 notes as offerings to the ghosts of dead ancestors. I climbed back into the taxi, not knowing whether we had a story or not.

I WAS sitting in a cafe, drinking a shake and watching the world go by, or at least two frail French pensioners ambling up the road for their next pastis, when an American in his late 20s sat down at a table next to me.

He was loud and confident and was soon drawn into a conversation with a lonely Brit expat, who always wore the same vest and sad expression. The American - whose name I would later learn was Brendan - lit up a joint and the usual questions followed.

"How long have you been out here?"

"About two years."

"Do you work here?

"No, I've retired," said Brendan.

He was 29-years-old and lived on the rent from a lake-side house he'd inherited in California. He told me he had a home in Mondulkiri, a province in the remote north-east of the country, and was heading there with his girlfriend So Pheakj the next morning. We chatted for a few hours and then he asked if I wanted to go up there with them. He sold it to me on the fact you don't need air con or a fan at night - rather than the gruelling nine-hour bus ride.

"It's the only place you can live in Cambodia," Brendan grinned.

I'd heard a lot about the food in Mondulkiri. People kept telling me it was the best Khmer cooking they'd eaten in Cambodia, and it was worth going just to try the cured goat salad. They made it by slicing seared goat steak and marinating it with finely chopped lemon grass, lime juice, and a few shakes of fish sauce. Then they made a dressing with shrimp paste, fish sauce, palm sugar, and enough water to form a fudgy paste. They tossed the goat with bean sprouts, peanuts, chilli, and coarsely chopped mint and basil leaves, and then covered it with the dressing.

I'd also heard Wayne, the bad-tempered Australian with the huge nose I'd met in Sihanoukville, had just moved up from the coast. He'd rented a five-bedroom house for $300 a month on a two-year lease, and turned it into the province's first Western bar.

I wanted to see if there would be enough trade for a restaurant there. Everywhere else I'd been to in Cambodia - especially the three tourist hot spots of Phnom Penh, Siem Reap, and Sihanoukville - had too many bars and restaurants and not enough customers. And I liked the sound of the cool temperatures.

TWO DAYS later, I was sitting in a restaurant, listening to backpackers haggling over elephant rides - "That one's a very bullshit operation for the elephants...Yeah, but we got offered two bucks cheaper from the other guy" - when Brendan finally called: "Hey, So Pheakj forgot to wake me again. Do you fancy going to the waterfall?"

He hired two moto drivers and we headed off through the windswept valleys surrounding the one-horse town of Sen Monorom, the provincial capital. Children waved at us as we crawled past trying to avoid craters in the red dust roads. We climbed higher, the engine screaming, and arrived in a jungle clearing with an elephant tethered by one ear to a shack. Just out of reach were 100 green bananas, and the beast was eyeing them morosely while batting away flies with his ears.

Brendan looked at the waterfall jump. It was usually about 10 metres high, but he said the water level was much lower than last month, because of the new dam up river. The Elephant Man threw a stone into the water indicating where he claimed it was deep enough to jump. But as he was not jumping himself, I was taking no chances.

We climbed down through the jungle and bathed in the pool. Something was nibbling away at my feet. I swam to the other side and foam thundered down around me. The sound was deafening and for a moment I forgot all about what the locals call "anacondas". A little boy scampered across the rocks, picking up beer cans. We climbed back up and the Elephant Man took a photo of us and printed it out on a contraption hooked up to a car battery.

We got back on the motos and stopped off at a karaoke bar specialising in wild boar meat. A line of drunk highlanders were taking it in turns with the microphone. One of them staggered over and slurred a few words. He had cruel eyes but I think he was trying to make friends. Brendan's girlfriend So Pheakj sang a few songs, but the only tune they had in English was Jingle Bells.

We watched the last of the sun dip behind the hills and then headed back to the jungle shack - one of the few places in town that stays open after dark. It was traditional to cook a communal meal there a couple of nights a week. Grella, who owned the place, was moaning about her husband's cooking. He'd bought a snake from the market and his friend was chopping the meat and bones into paste with a large machete.

"I say to them cook it in steaks so you can take the meat from the bones. You might as well have it so everyone can eat - not just two people," she grumbled.

It smelled unpleasant, like frogs that have been sitting in the sun too long. He fried it in a wok with lemon grass and lime leaves and it came out as a brown mush filled with tiny, sharp bones. Even So Pheakj didn't eat it.

The next day I woke early. A monk was announcing to the village, and everyone in a 100-mile radius judging by the size of the PA system, that a young couple were getting married. Grella said that in the Bunong tribes, it was traditional for the bride's father to kill a buffalo - the village's most precious beast - for the feast. She said they fermented the beast's blood for two years and then cooked with it.

She drove us through the hills in her battered Toyota and we stopped off at the Sea Forest. The sun was behind us, and when you stared out to the horizon, the tree-top mist flattened into a dark grey strip, and for a second I thought I saw a distant ship. I thought about land grabs and illegal logging in Cambodia, and how much of that stunning forest would still be left in 20 years.

We passed more wooden shacks filled with Bunong people dressed in filthy rags. Over them loomed a huge mansion on a hill. "It's owned by Hun Sen's nephew," said Grella. "He never uses it. He only comes once a year and then lights fireworks to let everyone know he's here." It sums up everything about Cambodia, she added.

We headed down to the market to buy food for that night's meal. The place was a muddy, fly-ridden sweat bath. I bought two kilos of pork from a stall that seemed to have less flies, then vegetables, spices, prahok, and kroeung curry paste. We got back to the shack and started a fire.

The dogs were eating out of the biggest saucepan and Grella went away to clean it as I got to work on the carrots and onions. I put more wood on and the meat sizzled away. Backpackers had started to gather. One of them, a loud, fat American woman with a black dragon tattoo poking out from her vest, gestured at So Pheakj as she crouched over the pot stirring away with a ladle.

"You wouldn't get that in America," she bellowed, "a girl cooking for you in high heels. I don't think women's rights have caught on here."

More budget backpackers arrived. There was a middle-aged Spaniard and his wife who'd spent the previous night scrounging drinks. I know things are tight in Spain, but I had no idea people like that existed. They stuck to 1,000 riel rice wine and their bill for the night had come to $0.75 - and like all the backpackers there, they wanted to know the cost of everything and were forever haggling over prices.

I put the pot of pork stew on the table and everyone dug in. The backpackers had two bowls each and then wandered off into the dark, clutching their laptops and expensive cameras. Not one of them had paid a single cent for the food, bought anyone a drink, or left a tip for their hosts. It was an idyllic setting with its warm days, and cool, star-strewn nights. But I felt sorry for Grella and her husband running a business, dealing with those mean bastards all day - and there was no way I was going to open a restaurant there and do the same.

"Those backpackers are arseholes man," slurred Brendan as the last one left. "That American woman didn't buy a single drink all night - she just came to use the free WIFI."

175

THE NEXT night we were at Wayne's bar. He'd kicked out the locals for "hogging the pool table" and they were quietly plotting to kill him. When rumours circulated that he was turning it into a lady bar they were furious - they'd already worked themselves up about the thin strip of flashing lights he'd put up outside the door.

Most nights, Wayne sat at the end of the bar, picking his gigantinormous nose and exchanging messages on Asian dating websites, and occasionally filling the glass of the one customer in his bar.

As we walked in, a drunk Khmer woman staggered towards us, told us it was her birthday and demanded we drink with her. There were two bottles of Stolichnaya vodka on the table and soon she was ordering a bottle of Malibu for $20. She became aggressive and started shouting at So Pheakj, claiming she'd said something about her in English.

"She can't speak English," Brendan kept saying.

We walked out, staring up at the stars and the bright glow of the Milky Way, as we wandered back to the jungle shack. We bought a few cans of ABC - a hideously-strong Cambodian stout - and Brendan told me a story about how So Pheakj's parents had died when she was a child and she'd grown up on her uncle's farm looking after water buffalo.

When she was 12, two men had tried to rape her. Her uncle heard her screams from the next field and killed one of the men with an axe.

"Imagine that - she went through that," he said.

I'D RETURNED to Phnom Penh when I read a news report on an expat forum about an Australian who'd crashed his Mitsubishi four-wheel drive returning from Mondulkiri. It could only be one person.

Wayne had been complaining about not being able to shake off a cold for months. He was driving back in his Pajero - which one of the trolls on the forum had pointed out was a car that couldn't be marketed in Spain because it meant 'wanker' - and blacked out, according to police.

His car ended up upside down in a lake. Several locals had managed to pull him out, and spent 30 minutes pumping water from his lungs. Wayne refused hospital treatment, his Pajero was impounded, and he caught a taxi the rest of the way to Phnom Penh.

A day later, he was in hospital with water on the brain, shivering like a child in a snowstorm. His friends gave him two days. They tried to persuade him to fly home to Australia to get medical treatment. But Wayne wouldn't listen. The lonely old man was loving the attention.

His friends phoned Brendan, who eventually hacked through the padlock on Wayne's bar to get his passport, and caught the bus down the next day. But still Wayne wouldn't fly home. The next night, Wayne pulled up at the bar we were in at 2am in a tuk tuk.

He was delirious, and telling stories about how he'd been visited by ghosts in the hospital, and said the place was haunted by the slaughtered souls from the Khmer Rouge era. His friends yelled at him, and drove him back to the hospital, but still he refused to fly home. I wondered what it would really take for Wayne - and the many expats like him I'd met - to finally leave Cambodia. Clearly many of them had come here to die.

CHAPTER TEN

I HADN'T been to Victory Hill for months, and was shocked at how run-down the place had become. The bars were empty, and most had changed hands. I dropped off my bags at a guesthouse and then strolled down the high street.

There were still a few of the old characters there, but many of the old faces had gone. Rodney's bar was now called the Moscow Bar, but still had the original lights up. I got to the top of the broken road and was about to turn back when I saw Josh speeding towards me with no shoes on. He had a cigarette in his mouth and was mumbling away angrily at the ground.

"Cambodians are the laziest fucking people on the planet. They won't fucking walk! They won't fucking walk! It's only around the corner, and she wants to get a tuk tuk..."

He sped past in a waft of blue smoke, and then stopped suddenly to check his pockets, and spotted me.

"Pork Pie!" he said, spitting out his cigarette. "Where the fuck have you been?"

A DAY later, I was working at his restaurant. It was good fun getting back into the kitchen, despite the heat. But I'd forgotten just how irritatingly tight-fisted some customers could be, especially the sort of drinkers and loners that wash up on Cambodia's beaches. I knew it was a third world country, but it was astounding how many expats wanted something for nothing. And it wasn't just thrill-seeking pensioners stretching out their money each month - the worst were the ones with money.

Take Dirty Derek, for instance, a man with a huge apartment overlooking Sydney Harbour. He'd been known to buy a draft beer from one bar for $0.50, and then wander over the road to drink it in another bar, where it was $1 a glass. He ate in our restaurant some nights, but always brought his own bottle of wine and asked for a glass.

When Josh got fed up with it, and said he was going to start charging him a $1 corkage fee, the wealthy, bronzed pensioner got quite upset. One night he complained that the lasagne was too big.

"Next time, I think I'll just ask for half," he said.

"Well, you're still paying $5!" Josh snapped.

Dirty Derek told me he was friends with a wealthy British couple who "got their kicks by doing runners from restaurants in England". They had done it dozens of times, and kept little notebooks detailing their crimes. They would scout out their next target and then head off to a charity shop. The husband would buy himself a smart sports jacket, and his wife an expensive-looking handbag.

They would go to the restaurant, order bottles of wine and food, and then the husband would leave his jacket on the back of his chair, saying he was "popping outside for a ciggie". His wife would then leave her handbag on the table and go off to look for him, and then they'd disappear into the street. All the restaurant got was an empty handbag and a jacket, and no tip. A £10 outlay for a £200 meal.

"They could afford to eat there," said Dirty Derek. "But they wouldn't have got the thrill. It was how they got their kicks. Well, that and the car keys..."

But the worst of the lot was a railway contractor called Ray, who regularly boasted about how he was getting $160,000 a year in a country where the average annual income was less than $1,000, and shelled out just $5 a night for our delicious, slaved-over food – and picked fault with everything.

Every night he came in with a new request. It started off with cauliflower. He said he wanted a few florets with his next meal, and then it was pumpkin, and then he started dictating orders into the kitchen.

"Can you prick the sausages before you cook them," he asked.

"I can do more than that," I muttered.

179

The next night, Ray ordered the spaghetti bolognese I'd put on the specials board and I nearly exploded. I counted to ten in my head and bit my lip, but still the bile was rising.

I knew how to make bolognese. I'd spent 15 months of my life I'd never get back making bucket load after bucket load of the stuff in a kitchen supplying very demanding Italian clients who'd scream down the phone if there was ever the slightest deviation.

The recipe – which had been handed down by the chef-owner's grandmother and mentor - was perfect. There'd even been an oil painting of the old crone glaring down at us as we chopped the precise amounts of garlic, pancetta, and plum tomatoes to make "Grandma's Bolognese".

I hadn't skimped on anything, and it took me three trawls of the local markets just to find celery. There was so much red wine in it, we were barely making a dollar on the dish. I'd even cured the pancetta myself with salt, sugar, and Kampot pepper.

But the trouble was I couldn't get saltpetre anywhere, which although isn't essential, stops the bacon going grey when cooked. The closest I got was a packet of "powder for fermenting pork" imported from Thailand, which contained sodium nitrite, and worked fairly well to keep it pink.

But it was all lost on Ray. And it didn't help knowing that he'd earned far more that day than I would in a whole month cooking bespoke meals for him.

"I don't like it when the meat is runny, you know what I mean?" he said. "Can you cut up the spaghetti into small pieces and then mix it with the sauce – you know how Heinz does it?"

I fought the urge to ask whether he wanted me to fetch him a little bib to eat it in. The next day he ordered pizza and threw the Khmer staff into chaos when he asked for "the crust to be turned inwards to keep the cheese in". Then he asked if we could make him rissoles the next night.

"But they've got to have onion in. Chopped up small and everything, know what I mean?"

Later, I was showing the Khmer staff how to cook a half-pound steak burger, made from fillet steak I'd aged in the fridge and then minced. Khmer beef was so cheap - you could buy a whole fillet for $9 a kilo down at the market. Chuck and shin was $8 a kilo.

They didn't really understand cuts. Meat was just meat, although head and offal were cheaper. When I went down to the market with one of the Khmer cooks to buy three kilos of tenderloin, and they charged us $27 instead of the normal $24, she began screaming at the butcher because she thought he was trying to rip us off.

I'd made a sauce from mayonnaise, mustard, and a little ketchup, chilli sauce, and finely chopped gherkins, and had given the girl who strolled the streets selling cakes and samosas some sesame seeds to make me some buns, and it was all going well until Ray stuck his head into the kitchen.

"Yeah, that's it. Nice and crispy on the outside like that," he said.

He honestly thought we were practising his fucking rissoles. He'd been in Asia for far too long.

"This is a burger," I told him, but he wasn't listening.

"Oh good, you've got the onions in already...can't make rissoles without them."

THEN THERE was the Sunday roast. I did roast chicken with all the trimmings - stuffing, cauliflower cheese, bread sauce, steamed vegetables, pigs in blankets, roast spuds et al. I'd made stock from bones and the off-cuts I'd got from trimming the eye fillets, and the gravy was pretty good. It must have been, because the only complaint I got was from a miserable old American hippy called Malcolm, who moaned that it wasn't as thick as the lumpy, Bisto gravy granules version he normally had with his pies.

He was the one who'd complained about my Cornish pasties. The Khmer cooks had been putting gravy in the pasties until I stopped

181

them. I got them to make them the proper way, using chopped raw beef, onion, potato, and a type of sweet potato that tasted a bit like swede, but didn't stay firm like swede when cooked.

Malcolm ordered a pasty for lunch every day, as I was to find out, and was pretty much the only person who ate them. When the next one arrived at his room, he cut it open, complained it was too dry because there was no gravy inside, and threw it back at the delivery boy. He didn't even try it.

The roast must have gone down quite well though because we were the busiest restaurant on the street, and we even got a few of the more sniffy French customers eager to find fault with a 'rosbif' cook. But there was still the usual list of bizarre requests. A party of English publicans phoned up to say they wouldn't come over unless there was Yorkshire pudding, which I had to hurriedly knock out because they were relatively big spenders, and some idiot asked whether we had any mint sauce for the chicken.

The plates came back empty. But there was no praise or appreciation. No understanding of all the hard work and expense that had gone into their meals. Just a cold, clinical evaluation of whether it was worth $5 - and what else that could have bought on the Hill. The only feedback I got was from one regular, who said the meal was so big he could barely finish it, and suggested we gave people the option of buying a smaller one for $4 next time.

AFTER TWO weeks, I'd had enough and walked out. I realised that the only way to cook there was to run my own place. Then I could serve the customers I liked, and be able to tell Ray exactly what he could do with the pumpkin he'd requested for next week's roast.

So instead of spending the next Sunday in a cramped sauna, I spent the day lazing on the beach at a restaurant shack, talking to the owner Colin - a retired police officer from Yorkshire. I was doing a bit of homework because the hut next to him was for rent for $350 a month – and I was toying with the idea of turning it into a seafood shack, building up the business, and then selling it on.

Alright, I knew I wasn't going to make any money running a restaurant in Sihanoukville, especially with its long rainy season, but that wasn't the point. I gazed out at the waves and the peaceful, soon-to-be-developed, mist-shrouded islands. Where else in the world could you own a lease on a restaurant on a white-sand beach just 20 yards from the sea?

Forget the money. As the British writer Alan Watts, who popularised Eastern philosophy in the West, said: "Surely it's better to live a short life full of what you like doing than a long life spent in a miserable way? Why spend your time doing things you don't like doing in order to go on doing things you don't like doing?"

Later that night, I was sat at a bar when Ray walked past.

"They missed you in the kitchen with the Sunday roast today," he said.

I put my head in my hands briefly, and waited for it.

"Why, what was wrong this time?" I said.

"Well...there wasn't one...they said they couldn't remember how to cook roast potatoes."

I WALKED down the steep, broken road to the beach and had another look at the restaurant. It would make the perfect spot for my seafood shack.

I could imagine shopping for fish and shellfish each morning from the boats arriving at the docks a mile away. Then boiling them up in sea water, and serving them plateau de fruits de mer-style with proper mayonnaise and shallot vinegar. I'd get the old fisherman, who went out every night on his washing-tub squid skiff, to carve me some 2ft-long boats to serve them on, nestled on ice. People would drive down from Phnom Penh just to eat there.

The restaurant was about 50ft long and 20ft wide, and there was a small kitchen at the back. There were no toilets - just the block you shared with the seven neighbouring shacks. There was no keyhole money either. The landlady, a rich Khmer woman from Phnom Penh who owned all the shacks, wanted a year's rent in advance for a two-year lease.

I stared at the water buffalo statue, knee-deep in water, next to the pier, and imagined what life would be like cooking there every day, washing away the sweat of the kitchen with a dip in the waves. I'd have a couple of Cambodian staff to do the serving, and a guard to sleep there at night. I strolled along the beach and had another look back at the shack.

The massage ladies and fruit sellers were sitting in a huddle under the coconut trees.

"Business no good, no customer," they moaned.

It was the same thing they said every day, even during the four months of the high season when the beach shacks would just scrape enough rent to get through the long monsoon.

It was the worst year for a decade, the bar owners whined. They couldn't just blame the floods – the end of the rains hadn't brought the usual tide of tourists. There was trouble in the US and Europe - the financial meltdown. That was what was keeping people away. Not that the fruit hawkers knew much about it. The holidaymakers were being extra careful with their cash. The expats were always careful.

I lay on one of the sun loungers, and started jotting down a list of equipment I'd need for the kitchen. I still had $3,000 left of my savings, and $2,000 due from the crocodile and Coconut Man stories. It was enough to pay the year's rent up front with $800 left for fittings and the top shelf. It would be tight alright.

Kieron, a thin, red-faced man in a grubby Panama hat, was walking the stretch of beach for the third time that day. It was too late to pretend to be asleep.

"Pork Pie! How the devil are you?" he said, sitting down on my sunbed, and helping himself to a cigarette.

Kieron had sold everything he owned in Dublin, apart from his Martin guitar, and then flown to Cambodia. He'd spent the first two months drinking solidly, often for days at a time, and then was barred by all the bars on the Hill for not paying his tabs.

He'd got himself a job doing the graveyard shift at Sandswept Bungalows – a 24-hour bar filled with alcoholics that was even avoided by the hard drinkers on the Hill. Kieron began his story again about how his house had been burgled when he first got there - and that was what had got him "smashed into a spin".

"But I don't like to say too much about it," he said, "because the Khmers are lovely, beautiful people, and it could easily happen anywhere – even in Dublin."

He glanced at my scribblings, paying particular attention to the numbers, and I was forced to tell him about my plans to open a restaurant.

"Oh, that seems like a lot of stress," he said. "Better to work for someone else and let them deal with all the headaches - that way you won't lose what you put in..."

"How's life at the bungalows?" I asked, hoping he'd go away.

"No, that only lasted a week. They wanted me to work seven days a week. It all blew up when I took my first day off. You know they were paying me $150 a month! I tell you I didn't come to Cambodia to work as a slave..."

He was now working in a guesthouse, tucked away on a mud track next to a pig farm, for free beer and a hammock to sleep in, but was hoping to get a job on one of the islands.

"I tell you that'll be fucking paradise," he said. "Anyway, I'll continue my stroll – just catching the last hour of sunlight before my shift begins..."

I'd scribbled another page of notes, when a gnarled man in his 60s sat down. He opened a bottle of green tea, and handed it to me. It had "no artificial colourings, no preservatives" on the label.

"Will you have a drink with a former Royal Marine?" he asked, introducing himself as McKenny. "That's not my first name, it's my surname. But it's what everyone calls me..."

I took a sip of the cheap Mekong rum, grimaced, and handed it back to the old sailor, who'd got into an argument with two women in the next shack.

I wandered up the beach and up the hill, past Sandswept Bungalows. There was the usual gang of tuk tuk drivers outside. The first time I'd been in the bar, everyone had been out of their heads, but drinking Coke. I couldn't work it out until I realised they were buying heroin from the tuk tuk drivers across the street.

I passed the two-room wooden shack where Akara, Rodney's old bar manager, lived with six members of her family. She was sitting on the steps, a black and white puppy dancing at her feet, as her mother and father gambled with a few cronies in the shade.

Akara had a few minutes left before she took her usual walk up the hill to work all night and earn the few dollars that would go straight to her parents. It was the Asian pension system. When they were old enough, your children looked after you. You'd paid to bring them up, and now it was your turn.

That was why Cambodians had so many children. It wasn't just the high infant mortality rates. The more children you had, the better off you'd be. But it was still a strange sight. Akara was 19, and her parents were in their late 30s. She'd be supporting them for the next 30 years, and then at some point it would be her turn, if she ever met a man and had children.

I went back to my guesthouse to wash off the sand and then walked to the Ruby Bar to talk to Victor, the Wallock who managed the place. I wanted his thoughts on the beach shack. He knew everything that was happening on the Hill - nearly as much as the motodup spies the bar girls paid to keep tabs on their customers.

Victor was holding court in the corner as usual, making occasional pipes from the contents of his tupperware box. Bob Dylan's Like A Rolling Stone came on. Rolling Stone magazine had just rated it top of their chart of 500 best ever songs. I Can't Get No Satisfaction was second. There was definitely a theme. I sat there listening to the customers and then the place thinned out and Victor lurched over.

"Down the beach there's a beach hut, in fact there are about eight of them..." I began.

"And they want one year of rent up front, and 475 beers of rent a month," Victor said.

"What?"

"They want 475 beers of rent a month!"

"Beers?"

"Yes...sir!"

"Alright, forget the figures..." I said.

I was depressed already.

"No, they want 475 beers of rent a month! Meaning that you have to sell 475 beers to be able to pay a rent of $350, plus you're going to have the electricity, plus you're going to have the staff. That means you have to sell 600 beers..."

"Look, I'm not talking about selling beer. I'm talking about food..."

"Go upstairs!"

"What?"

"Go upstairs! You can make food here for 200 bucks. You will not make no fucking money over there. Talk to Colin! He's making fucking rat shit! Open it upstairs..."

He showed me the bar upstairs. The stairway bent round and ended in a lounge with a balcony area, with a side room that could be turned into a kitchen.

"There is plenty of space. Perfect for a kitchen. You have sea view, you have balcony. You can put 20 people here, and you have a hot shower here and toilets."

He flicked a switch.

"Fans - working. Fifty square metres..."

"You could do a lot with this," I said, craning my neck to catch a glimpse of the sea.

"And you are in the street, and you're going to save $150. But you don't start big - because a small stream makes big rivers..."

I staggered home, thinking about all the kitchen equipment I'd need to buy. It would be over $2,000 at least - nearly half a year's rent at the beach shack. I was already going off the idea. I knew Victor would just be waiting for me to go bust so he could buy all the equipment at a reduced rate.

I WENT back to cooking at the restaurant for a few days to help Josh out. He was in a sorry state. He was heading up to a province near Phnom Penh with his Cambodian wife Loung to see how badly their house had been hit by the country's worst floods for 10 years.

"The stilts are leaning but just about holding," he said. "Yep, they're leaning alright. Is it going to fall down? The answer's I don't know. I don't know if it's going to fall down. I haven't got a CLUE if it's going to fall down..."

The day before he left, a dodgy-looking man called Too Jee appeared. It turned out he was some sort of relative of Loung, could speak no English, and wanted to move south - and stay in Josh's house for free like the rest of the growing family - while he found a job.

In fact, it didn't take him any time at all. He had a job the moment Josh left town. Too Jee's cousin, Wee, who also worked at the restaurant, had obviously decided an extra member of staff was needed to make the rainy season staff-to-customer ratio look even more ridiculous.

I went in the next day, and saw him skulking near the cash till. Wee pointed at me as I walked in, and muttered something to her cousin, or nephew or husband, or whatever he really was. I don't know what she said, but it was nothing good. From the look in his eyes, I wouldn't have even wanted him drinking in the restaurant, let alone working there.

I decided enough was enough, and spent the next few days looking at other restaurants to buy, but none of them were suitable. The woman who owned the beach shack wouldn't budge on the rent, and I kept thinking about the 475 beers I'd need to sell each month.

Josh phoned a few days later and insisted Too Jee would no longer be working there, but I could tell he'd long lost control of the business to the family. It was obvious they were trying to scalp him. And I'd just been seen as a thorn in their side, or worse. And in a country where you can remove problems for as little as $150 - probably even less in the rainy season - I was taking no chances.

RODNEY HAD sold his tiny wooden bar to a Russian for $20,000 and moved down to Ochheuteal Beach, the town's main backpacker area.

"I had to get out. I couldn't stay there anymore. The Hill was doing my fucking nut in," he said when I arrived.

But all he could talk about for the rest of the night was the Hill, and how it was dying and would soon turn into the Chicken Farm. There had been no keyhole money for his new bar, but he quickly spent most of the $20,000 on fittings, booze, and paying off debts. On the day he picked up the money, he took a tuk tuk around town and handed bundles of cash to everyone he owed.

His bar had been open for three months, but he was already struggling. He was away from the main drag, with no footfall, and was reliant on his old regulars from Victory Hill for business. But as the return trip cost $8 - or 16 beers - in a tuk tuk, most of them soon stopped coming. Most nights he'd be lucky to take $30.

Rodney was talking to an old Alaskan wearing a black cowboy hat. I'd met him in Rodney's old bar. Jake was slow speaking and told us about how he'd spent time in prison in the US for growing marijuana. He knew everything about the plant, and could bore you for hours on the subject.

189

"I came out of the University of Georgia with a stack of papers about this high, and we went right into growing it," he drawled. "The fertilising stuff is very similar to corn - high nitrogen - and at the end you can give it a shot of potassium and it helps it flower somewhat.

"We grew some amazing crops there, but every frigging time I got caught, so they put me in jail a couple of times. I could grow it in Cambodia and find myself in a very similar situation - and I really don't want to go to a Cambodian jail.

"But I suppose you can pay your way out. Last year, some limey, some Aussie, or somebody, was driving a car and on the console he had a pretty big bag of weed, an ounce or more. He got stopped by the cops, and they see that and they say: 'Oh, you're in big trouble. Very big trouble.'"

He began chuckling: "It cost him $17 to get out of it. But that doesn't mean that counts every time..."

Rodney came back from the bar with three shots from the huge glass container on the bar he'd been throwing sticks into.

"But honestly, smoke here is legal, it's the heavy drugs they want - the yabba, the ice, the meth, all this," said Rodney. "Smoking? That'll come eventually, but not yet - because the fucking policemen are selling it themselves!"

Jake then told us about life back in Alaska - the caribou hunts, and the coho salmon and crabs he caught by drilling holes through metres of ice, and the Huskies he'd had to shoot for not being tough enough. It was the "medium-sized dogs" that were best, he kept saying.

Rodney butted in: "My sister had a half-Husky and a half-Alsatian dog, and I tell you what it was one of the most vicious dogs I've ever met! I wouldn't go out the house. They had to get rid of it. Wild dog! Red eyes, fucking evil! Lovely, beautiful pure black fur, but fucking evil. I said have you tied that dog up when I'm coming out the house? Yes. Right in the car!

"I got locked in the fucking greenhouse all night once. I was sitting there having a drink and they'd forgotten to tie the dog up, and the dog's running round the fucking farm. Big fucker, right up here! When I was in the kitchen he used to look in at you through the window.

"They got a dog trainer in, and it bit the fucking trainer. He wouldn't go back. 'I'm not going anywhere near that dog - he's fucking mental!' he said. When he was a baby he was spot on. It's the genes - you're not meant to mix those two together..."

Then we were in Mexico, and they were both talking at once.

"I tell you, talk about wild dogs!" said Rodney. "Packs of them - about 30. They used to come out with guns from the disco to take you home."

"Chihuahuas! Chihuahuas!" said Jake. "Like bees, swarms or something. They're too little, you cannot kill them..."

"Once you're in the bar, fucking stay there until the morning," added Rodney.

"Chihuahuas are little dogs right, but when they're riled, they're very strong little dogs, right. And they come on like a herd. Little bitty dogs that bite the fuck out of you. Birdshot or a snakeshot, you know a pistol with small pellets. Bham! Bham! Bham! He killed four, five, ten! Hurry up! That's the only way to get out of there..."

TWO DAYS later, there was a knock at my hotel door. It was Josh – he'd returned from the province. He walked straight in and lit a cigarette, and then another one off the butt. He was so angry he could hardly get the words out.

"I'm so angry...I'm so angry," he kept saying.

It turned out that Too Jee was hooked on ice, and had stolen Josh's motorbike, all his antiques, jewellery, and cash and disappeared to Vietnam. Josh asked me to come back, but I was dead set against it. Then he reminded me it was his birthday at the weekend and I'd promised to do the barbecue. Before I knew it, I'd somehow agreed to do the Sunday lunch as well.

I BUTCHERED half a small pig into ribs and chops and then got Dee and the rest of the Khmer cooks to help me prep some chicken kebabs and wings. We bought six kilos of fillet steak and made 60 or so burgers, and then knocked up potato salad, coleslaw, and a few plates of nibbles.

The place was soon packed, but it was hardly surprising given the mealy-mouthed expats that lived there. They were probably just disappointed that the drinks weren't free as well. Trays of grilled meats went round, and then Ray appeared and sat on a stall nearest to the barbecue, and stuck his nose into everything.

"You want to get some burgers on there," he said.

The grill was covered in ribs and wings. There wasn't an inch of free grill space – that's why the burgers were being cooked in the kitchen. But still he knew best.

"Hot enough for you?" he chuckled as I continued to ignore him.

He could see the streams of sweat flowing down my front as I charged between the kitchen and the BBQ, but still he thought I had time for conversation with a man sporting the personality of a stuffed frog.

I kept biting my tongue as he offered unwanted cooking tips. I was desperate to move him on to something he might actually know something about. Railways, for instance. But I wasn't too hopeful. He'd somehow invited himself on to our quiz team the week before, and had hardly said a word. The only time he did was to describe to the waiter in painstaking detail how he wanted his pizza cooked – this time he wanted "a thick base, but thin round the edges".

He hadn't known a single one of the 50 questions. When the only railway-related question came up, we all turned to him, but he just started drawing maps in the air and mumbling names of US states, and it was obvious he hadn't got a clue, especially when the answer turned out to be Reykjavik.

When he asked about the Sunday roast, and whether we were doing cauliflower cheese, and whether I'd be pre-boiling the roast spuds, and how I was going to cook the pumpkin he'd requested, I started asking him about Cambodia's new $142m railway system he was working on, and when it would be finished.

He stopped for a moment, and in an apparent attempt at humour, dipped his head slightly and looked out at the night sky.

"Jeez! Christ knows," he said. "Have you got a crystal ball?"

I don't know what he was looking for. There was nothing but a monsoon out there.

I thought about Battambang's bamboo trains, and asked Ray how long they had left, but he just looked confused.

"They've already kicked them off haven't they?" he said matter-of-factly.

CHAPTER ELEVEN

GEORGE ORWELL said pepper was good at getting rid of bed bugs, pointing out that it was worth putting up with the sneezing just to rid himself of the terrible, itching bites. But it didn't work for me, despite living two hours from Kampot, with the best pepper in the world for $9 a kilo.

To save money, I'd moved into a very cheap room on the Hill, even by Cambodian standards, so you could say I'd asked for it. But Buddha did I pay. I suppose the moment I put my head down, I was aware from the smell of the mattress and pillow, and general state of the room, that I probably wasn't sleeping alone.

There were telltale piles, as I know now having researched the subject at length on the internet, of pepper-like dust (not just from the grindings I'd put down) that are said to be the blood-sucking bugs' droppings. The sheets were scattered with them. But there were two much larger, darker piles under the bed frame.

At first I thought something had burrowed upwards through the tiles. They looked like the sort of mounds ants make, and the ramshackle joint was filled with ants. You only had to leave a piece of fruit out, or a half-drunk can of Pepsi, to find thousands of aggressive fire ants marching across the walls.

But after sweeping up the mounds, there were no holes in the tiles, no cavern entrances to what would become a hellish ordeal of mandibles and eternal, fiery itching. I checked the bed frame and a chunk of rotten wood came away in my hand, leaving a few maggot-like creatures squirming on the floor.

They didn't look like the pictures I'd found on the many bed bug forums devoted to these tiny barbaric vampires, which I quickly learnt can produce 10,000 babies in three months, and drink three times their own body weight of blood in a single troughing.

But I couldn't help wondering what else was in there, hidden away in the wooden tunnels, waiting for the long hours before dawn when they're said to strike. But whatever they were - and you can only wonder at the horribleness of the creatures that had left such huge, itching, red welts across my arms and back - they almost ate me alive.

Bed bugs strike in threes, apparently. Three bites in a line - breakfast, lunch and dinner, according to the feverish accounts on the bed bug sites. But they'd clearly run out of space, and had just bitten wherever was in reach. There were bites upon bites, and always a horrible yellow, itching crust. My forearms took the worst of it. It felt like I'd been hog-tied with poison ivy. The burning only gets worse if you finally cave in and scratch - and then there is the risk of infection, especially in a country like Cambodia.

But then I still wasn't sure whether it was bed bugs, or whatever had been eating the bed frame, or whether the mattress was just a big red herring. After Josh found a small cobra wriggling across his lounge carpet, and a bright green snake wrapped round the shower head, I was beginning to think anything was possible in Cambodia, even armies of tiny, but extremely vicious, hawk-headed death scorpions.

I'd been finding a few striped, territorial, and much larger than normal, mosquitoes in the room of late and wondered whether it was them. But the bites were much more savage and had developed into a welter of full-blown hives. Always with a red hole in the middle - much wider than a mosquito straw. It was more the sort of bite from something that could gnaw through heavily-varnished teak.

I had a disturbing thought as I switched off the lights, and waited for the interminable itching and soft scurry, or would it be squirm, and gentle parting of hair, then bite, that they might have tunnelled inside me, and found a new lair. But I put the thought out of my mind as best I could, remembering how psychological trauma and obsession were listed as common afflictions on the BB forums.

The next morning, I complained to the French owner, a strange, heavyset man with uncertain eyes, who'd recently bought the grimy guesthouse and over weeks of early morning hammering, drilling, and tile cutting had slowly been turning it into a restaurant. He didn't seem too bothered when I told him.

The guestrooms were the last place that would get attention - he was far too busy painting the concrete floor outside the restaurant.

Perhaps bed bugs were more common in France? But eventually he agreed to swap my bed for the one in the empty room next door, exposing a large, grey rectangle of dust, hair, condom wrappers, and lofty peaks of drilled wood.

There were far more of them than I'd feared. Some of the holes in the wood were the width of a small pencil. I stood there itching at the sight. But the bed was soon gone, and the floor half-heartedly mopped. The new bed looked in far better shape. There were a few holes here and there, but the frame looked far less crumbly. And although the mattress still had a grimy look, it certainly smelt a lot fresher.

I got the woman in the hut next door to wash all the bed sheets and pillow cases to get rid of any lasting traces of the burrowing beasts, and settled down for a good night's sleep. But there were more belters in the morning. It couldn't have been the mosquitoes because whatever it was had broken through my liberally-sprayed shield of "F-Off!" insect repellent.

There was so much Deet, it burned your eyes if you'd forgotten to turn off the fan. I'd long given up chasing mosquitoes around the room, and instead just napalmed the general area I'd last seen them in, and they'd quickly be writhing on the floor waiting to give up their last squirts of my blood as I splattered them.

But Deet didn't trouble these hardened parasites. Curse them! It tied in with the apocalyptic warnings on the forums about how they were forever evolving into more monstrous creations as they developed unique resistance to insecticides like deltamethrin and beta-cyfluthrin, until pesticides and other powerful chemicals normally used outdoors no longer had any effect on them – and beware therefore! They'd soon be a pestilence on every hotel around the world. Aum. Ha.

"I am telling you these bugs don't care what your income, race or habits are," wrote a woman from Connecticut who'd burned all her furniture and was now sleeping in the shed on a trampoline. "They want blood and carbon dioxide. I have made my home hostile to them until I can afford fumigation."

196

For a while, the accepted wisdom was to douse an infested mattress with turps – something that would obviously increase the dangers of smoking in bed – or coat the bed legs with lethal radioactive waste to stop the evil creatures climbing upwards.

But evolution and fiendish arthropodic intelligence struck once again, and they somehow communicated with each other that it would be a good idea if they emerged from their cracks and crannies at a synchronised time as normal, but this time, rather than taking the usual short cut up the bed legs, they would scurry in lines across the tiles, up the wall, and then back on themselves over the ceiling, and then drop somewhere near the sleeping prey.

There was also a lot of talk about how bed bugs were good hitchhikers, most efficiently it seems in hotel luggage, and once they were inside, would quickly emigrate like conquering tribes, so I had no way of knowing whether the bites were from creatures connected with the old bed or the new one.

I talked to an old Parisian called Albert in the bar that evening, and he just shrugged and told me to lay the mattress in the sun, and turn it over from time to time. He said he got the guard to do his every six months.

"You have to," he said. "This...is Cambodia."

The affected pause, shrugging, and way he strangled the vowels in Cambodia made it sound like it was a philosophical point about asceticism, an experience that should be embraced as much as any other. I felt better, and chided myself for worrying too much and being a product of a system that had distanced itself so much from nature, but still the burning itches continued.

It hadn't helped that I was reading Into The Wild, a book about human endurance and suffering, and being eaten alive by mosquitoes in Alaska. What were a few bed bugs, if that's what they were – and I'd still failed to get conclusive proof - next to starvation and a lonely, painful death?

We clinked pastis glasses and I itched my arms again. I climbed off my bar stool and suddenly felt faint. It wasn't just the drink, the flu I'd had for the past two weeks seemed to be getting stronger, and was turning again into another sore throat. I had no idea at the time that it might have been something to do with those bites. All I knew was the last person I'd chatted to, who'd had similar symptoms, had been diagnosed with dengue fever.

The next day, after more bites, I told the owner about Albert's mattress trick. I could see he was losing patience, but continued to wear his stretched smile. It was the same cartoon grin he'd used when I rang the bell repeatedly at 3am, thinking it wasn't working.

The mattress lay there all day in the blazing sun, flipped over whenever the guard remembered to rouse himself from his hammock. When I got back, the owner had obviously had a change of heart. Had he been itching too?

He'd painted over the holes in the bed frame with white paint, and pointed at the label. It had a picture of a badly-drawn, furry, green worm with a red cross through it. He'd even bought a couple of new pillows. But he said he couldn't buy a new mattress because he'd only had the guesthouse for a month. I also noticed he hadn't bothered to paint the underside of the bed.

I slept tight and tried not to let the bed bugs bite, but woke at first light with more lesions. A couple of evil-looking, black creatures were writhing on the floor. They'd either just flipped on their backs or had more likely been winkled out of their holes by the paint. There were bites this time on my legs, and my fever seemed to be getting worse. I told the owner I could stand no more, and was moving out, even if I had paid for the next month upfront.

"No-one else is complaining about the small animals," he sniffed.

I moved in to the new Khmer hotel up the street – it was a hundred times cleaner, and ten times more expensive. I knew I'd soon get through my dwindling cash. But I needed to get some proper sleep in a clean bed for a few days, without the thought of marauding insects. I filled the sink with water and washed the black vest and shorts I was wearing – the last things that hadn't been through the laundry.

I let the vest sink back into the water, and then my stomach turned and I felt that crawling itch as three red bugs scurried towards the side of the sink. I had proof at last. They were definitely the bed bugs I'd seen on the forums. They were so fast and confident, it was no wonder I hadn't spotted them.

The nausea, cough, and fever I'd been suffering fitted in with some of the more extreme symptoms other BB victims had complained about. I didn't have dengue fever – it was some sort of allergic reaction to the bites.

I STAGGERED down to the Khmer restaurant, where I ate most afternoons, and almost collapsed as I walked in. None of the pills the doctor had given me had worked, but then, as I found out later, he wasn't a real doctor anyway, just a nurse in the army.

I was desperate, and threw myself on the mercy of that happy, peaceful family. I told Sophie, the cook-owner who'd been teaching me some traditional Cambodian dishes, about my symptoms and bites, and she said she was pretty sure it wasn't malaria because I wasn't getting cold shivers.

She told me I should drink fresh coconut juice and get some sleep. I drank three that day, two the next, and the following day felt stronger. There was no sign I'd transported any more bugs from the room, and it was the first time in days I'd woken without fresh bites. But the fever was still there, as was the cough and itching.

I lurched back down the hill to the restaurant to thank Sophie. I was getting my appetite back and ordered her delicious chicken and aubergine soup (samla kov pet), remembering how good chicken broth is for flu and restoring the spirits. She said she wanted me to show her how to make beef stroganoff for the Russians who stayed at her guesthouse. She also wanted to learn something called "key-kerr salad".

Was it Russian? Maybe a Moldovian peasant dish? Or a Lithuanian speciality, no doubt comprising of potatoes? I'd never been much good on Slavic cuisine. Let alone Baltic. Or any wok-based curry dishes for that matter.

But as an old Singaporean cook had told me as he served hokkien mee – thick noodles with pork, prawns, and squid in a soy gravy made from pig hock - it was impossible to know everything about food; it was far too big a subject. She'd definitely said 'key-kerr'.

"Oh, Caesar salad!" I said suddenly.

She asked me to show her the next day, and I stumbled back up the unmade road, wondering how she was going to make any money on Caesar salad given the price of tinned anchovies, let alone parmesan, and the ridiculously low prices she was forced to charge in that stretch of identical Khmer restaurants.

I COLLAPSED on my bed, trying not to think about the bugs, and woke with no fresh wounds. I drank three coconuts at the stall and then wandered down to Sophie's, and rather than having the double egg and chips with sea salt and rice vinegar I'd been planning, had a delicious meal of fish and water spinach soup (samla m'chou tra-koun).

The family were about to sit down to eat their Sunday lunch, and I didn't want to disturb them, so asked if I could have the same. It was so different from the fatty roasts the expat restaurants served.

"Is it in here?" I said, flicking through the menu.

"No, it's Khmer food..." Sophie's daughter laughed, almost apologetically.

There were a number of Cambodian and Chinese-Cambodian dishes on the menu, and I'd tried them all. But what she meant was proper Khmer food – the magical, prahok-flavoured stuff the locals eat, but are afraid to give to the tourists.

She looked surprised and anxious when I ordered it. I finished the dish, eating it the Cambodian way by pouring spoonfuls of soup on to my rice. Some might say that as a Sunday lunch, it doesn't quite measure up to the finest roast salt marsh lamb with samphire, or a bloody slice of bone-in rib with a freshly-grated horseradish sauce, but I felt a lot lighter than I usually do after eating Yorkshire pudding with all the trimmings.

200

Normally after a roast, cheese, and a few ports, I can barely manage a few turns in the garden, but after that clear, simple fish soup I felt ready to run a marathon – or at least get on my bike and cycle up the road in search of egg and chips.

After I'd finished, Sophie showed me how to make it. She put a saucepan of water on to boil, and then took one of the small prahok fish she'd bought from the market, and soaked it for a minute in hot water. She mashed the fish, removing the bones, and poured the liquid, skin, and flesh into the boiling water.

She soaked some tamarind in hot water, removed the seeds, and added the pulp and liquid to the pot. Then she added small rectangles of barracuda steak and a handful of water spinach, cooked it for a couple of minutes or so, and then added salt and sugar to taste.

And that was that delightful Khmer family's Sunday lunch, and they looked just as grateful and pleased to be served it as if it was roast turkey stuffed with prunes, duck flamed in cherry brandy, or spit-roast suckling pig with apple sauce. And after I'd got my shameful egg and chip cravings out of my head, and allowed myself to bathe in the simplicity of that wonderful lunch, served in the traditional Cambodian manner of making a small bit of protein go a long way, so did I.

IT ALSO hammered home how soup seems to be the most important meal in Cambodia. Look at a lot of Khmer literature, and if there's mention of food, it will often be soup – whether it's a shared steamboat of choa horn, or just a humble vegetable soup at a family gathering.

I'd read somewhere that soup is so integral to the Cambodian diet that women often greet each other with the phrase: "What soup will you cook today?" I'd never heard them say it, but I'd never come across a cuisine so full of broths and liquors. There must have been hundreds of varieties across the country. And just when I thought I'd tasted all the soups worth trying, along came another one I'd never seen before – and not just a cannibalisation of a previous one, but a dish in its own right.

Like the one I tried when I was cycling down near Sihanoukville's deep-water port a few days later, and stopped at a fish restaurant where most of the local senior police officers seemed to be lunching. There were a couple of US Navy ships in, so there was more security presence than normal. But whatever the occasion, seeing police officers at a restaurant was always a good sign in Cambodia.

They seemed to have more time and money to spend lounging around in restaurants than the rest of the work force, so given the amount of research they put in, it was always worth following them to their favourite whisky holes, as it was a good indication of the food served there.

The soup they were slurping was quite a sight. The bowl was packed full of tiny sea shrimps, no more than a couple of millimetres wide and a centimetre long - not much bigger than the freshwater shrimps you find in watercress beds.

They'd been cooked whole in a pinky broth, flavoured with tamarind and dried shrimp paste, with thick slices of onion, a few fresh anchovies from the shoals you can catch here with a fine-gauged fishing net within feet of the shore, and holy basil leaves in at the end.

The liquor smacked of fresh, briny goodness, made even better by the sharpness from the tamarind. I sat there crunching through the prawn heads, feelers and shells, and microscopic pieces of meat, thickening the broth from time to time with a spoon of rice.

I cycled back along the harbour, and looked out at the two US Navy boats. The Cougar Bar had been full of American servicemen the night before. The owner had got his girls to give out flyers when they got off the boats. If they had an American accent, it was $50. All the girls kept to the same price.

Albert, the old Parisian, who looked in his 50s, but was actually 74, was walking along the beach, wearing a tall yellow hat that made him look like something out of a Cervantes novel. He swam in the sea every day to keep his shape, but that was his only real concession to health. You could find him in the bar at any time of the morning, either beginning or about to end a two or three-day binge.

Then he'd stay in his room for a night or two, and then emerge to do it again. He had travelled around the world, and spent much of his life living off beaches in the Caribbean, spear-fishing for a living. I wondered why a man who had travelled so extensively had ended up in Sihanoukville. I often asked myself the same question.

"I like it here because I like hearing the stories of the people who end up here – there are some real stories, some real characters here," he'd always say.

The first day I met him, he was wearing his conical hat, but his face was painted green, blue, and red. He'd drawn a huge red moustache on his face and wrinkles in black paint. Under his arm was a huge bundle of fireworks. At various stages in the street, he would light a powerful firework, sometimes getting someone to hold the tube as it spouted fire. He let a firework off every hour. They must have cost him $100. It turned out he was celebrating the autumn equinox.

"No-one does here, so this is my celebration to remember," he'd said. "It is to celebrate the time when there is exactly 12 hours of light and 12 hours of dark."

Albert and I strolled back along the beach and then we sat on the sand drinking beer. I looked at the palm-thatched shack where I'd planned to open my seafood restaurant. A Lithuanian family had bought it, and put up a large white rabbit sign where my scallop shell should have been. Why hadn't I bought it when I still had the money? What was it that made me so indecisive? Was it just common sense or a fear of commitment?

Colin, in the next bar, was arguing with a fat Russian in tiny Speedos, who was sprawled across a sunbed, but refusing to buy food or drink.

"Well if you're not going to order anything, it's $1 for the sunbed," said Colin.

"I'm not paying you $1!"

Colin lifted the end of the sunbed and began shaking it.

"I'm Russian!" the man said, before collapsing into a sausagey heap on the sand.

As we waited for sunset, Albert told me about his miserable life back in France, and the man he'd met who'd completely changed his life - and spurred him into his Grand Tour.

"That was the person I learned the most from," he said. "I was sharing this apartment because I had very little money, and I had two rooms, so I put an ad and only one guy came and he knocked at the door and there is this little guy. He was maybe only 5ft 5in, maybe 5ft 4in, and I opened the door and right away he passed me and went into the room, looked, and he said: 'Oh I prefer a television here and something here...'

"I said okay, but of course I didn't know he came to my village with nothing. I didn't know he had no money. He couldn't pay me, but I let him stay. And then one day I was sleeping in my room, okay, and I felt something like a butterfly. I woke up and he was putting money on my bed. Bills everywhere! He said merci, and I never see him again..."

"How much money?" I asked.

"That's not the point," snapped Albert, irritated by the detail. "One day before he went, he got a little bit of money from somebody else, I don't know, and invited me in the restaurant to have anything I wanted. The best restaurant in the south of France, okay. So we had fresh fish with herbs, a little salt. And then suddenly in the conversation he said something like this: 'Well you know Albert, there have been other stages in my life a long time before. There were people, they were very frightened...'

"And then I heard what I knew already about his own life, because all his brothers were in the Legion, his father was in the Legion, the brothers of the father, and the grandfather were also in the Legion. He was a killer!

"So he told me one day he had a big property in the south of France, okay, and then his wife liked a fur coat and went out of the big house, and they had a big garden here, and she said it would be very nice to have a swimming pool here. And he said 'no problem'.

"So he got a mission to Suriname against the guerrillas. Of course, a socialist community who wanted to change the Government like all the countries in central and south America. So someone paid him a lot of money and he came back and he had a swimming pool made in the garden, okay, and bring his wife with him to look.

"Then he said to his wife: 'You like this swimming pool? You want a swim?' 'Yes,' she said. So he said to his wife: 'You know, see the water here? That is not water. It is blood.' That's how he offered the swimming pool to his wife. That's what I call an extreme guy..."

He said what he'd learned from the mercenary had inspired him to write a book about some sort of epiphany moment he'd had at the Golden Triangle - a notoriously lawless area bordering Thailand, Laos, and Burma. He said he'd translated it into English, and asked me to take a look. He left the beautifully-illustrated book, and translation, with Aidan at the Irish bar the next day.

The two files were carefully tucked into a brown envelope. It looked like he'd entrusted me with his life's work. I took it straight back to my hotel and opened it carefully. It was all about confronting your past experiences in order to find happiness, and was structured as a journey along the three sides of the Golden Triangle – the first side was the "attainment of cognition" by embracing your experiences, the second was the "discovery of the rainbow within", and the third was finding your "personal temple".

It was written in a flowery style, and there were touches of poetic beauty. It took me two nights to type it out on my computer, and then I printed out my translation and left it in Aidan's bar with his manuscripts. I didn't see Albert for a couple of days, and was surprised by his reaction. He thanked me half-heartedly, and then mentioned there were a few mistakes in the translation.

I looked at him, wondering where the hell these people on the Hill had come from, what they had become. What was it in that tiny stretch of red light bars and hazy drinking dens, perched on a hilltop on the south coast of Cambodia?

The selfishness among the expats was something else, and I thought Albert was one of the better ones. It was a place full of misfits and loners. Expats escaping from something, or looking for something, and nearly always reinventing themselves in the process.

I knew why Rodney had needed to get out. It wasn't just the smashed ashtrays on his head he got removing freelances from his bar. I'd been on the Hill too long as well. I was drowning with the rest of them.

I looked at Albert as he lit a cigarette and took a sip from his Jagermeister. Mistakes! Had he any idea how much work had gone into it? Did he have any concept of how bad his handwriting was? I smiled and gritted my teeth and stared at him in disbelief, and told him I could make any changes and print a new version for him.

"I didn't realise you would have a script," he said.

We stared at each other. Not even a thank you.

"Now you have a copy?" he added suspiciously.

He honestly thought I was going to flog his book to Walt Disney. I shook my head, and made an excuse about needing to eat, and walked off. I didn't talk to him again after that.

BUT IT wasn't just the expats getting me down, it was the continual reminder of how cheap life is in Cambodia. Even when you thought you knew something about the Khmers' quirky customs - about how the bar girls believed they could cast bad spells on each other, and would only let the barang boss tend the Buddhist shrine in the bar because they'd be too scared of bad karma if another girl did it, and how they'd throw sweets on the floor for baby ghosts - you saw something that would hit you for six, and leave you pondering the mysteries of these shy, spiritual, but at times incredibly brutal people.

One night, I saw a woman wandering along the bars, trying to sell her baby for $1,000.

"That's the downside of this place," said a retired bus driver from Canada before quickly getting back to his beer.

On another night, bars emptied and tourists and Khmer staff descended into the street, attracted by the primordial sound of someone or something in pain. There were screams and boozy shrieks all the time on the Hill. But it was different somehow. They were in a tone that made the hairs stand up on the backs of our necks, and brought a fearful animal instinct into each and everyone one of us.

A boy in his late teens was being viciously beaten by his mother and father. His father was screaming at him and punching him in the face. His mother was whipping his bare legs with a length of knotted rope.

The boy was hysterical, but for some reason barely flinched from the pain, which only spurred his parents on to more vicious assaults. The father kept grabbing him by the neck, screaming hate-filled words into his face, and then delivering spiteful, well-aimed jabs at the boy's mouth and nose.

The crowd watched in a horrified, confused, but oddly fascinated silence. The boy kept shouting back the same words as he was hit. I asked Annie, the Khmer manager of Aidan's Irish bar, what he was saying.

"I don't know," she said. "He's crazy." She listened again. "He say something like you my mother and father, I cannot fight you..."

The boy stood there shouting and sobbing, holding his arms as far behind his back as the blows would allow. His mother whipped his legs again, leaving more red marks across his thighs. Not to be outdone, her husband throttled the boy and then punched him a few times in the face and stomach in quick succession.

Suddenly, a Swiss expat called Eric – who was flying home the next morning after running a restaurant for five years in Cambodia, and had been drinking pastis since 11am - brushed past us.

"I can't see this," he said.

He strolled across the road and put himself in front of the boy to protect him. The mother backed off slightly, but the father lunged again. Eric held his arms out to push the man back, and then gently nudged him up the street, shouting at him to stop.

There was movement from the house, and their largest son – a fat, acne-ridden manboy who must have weighed 120kg – sprinted towards the pair. He yelled as he ran towards them. It was like a war cry – high-pitched and filled with hate and evil intent, and a furious urge to restore the family's loss of face at not being able to inflict more punishment on his younger brother.

He turned slightly, and I could see he was gripping a wooden truncheon, almost the width of a rolling pin. With the boy's weight behind it, it was heavy enough to cave in a man's skull and leave brain and foam on the gravel.

The crowd gasped in shock and utter horror at what they feared was about to happen. Well-thumbed phrases about time stopping still and slow motion replays don't really do justice to terrible, stomach-gripping moments like that. The boy was now just a few yards from the back of Eric's skull. It would be a horrible, cowardly blow. He raised the club and then stopped suddenly at the last second. The Belgian owner of the bar next door stepped forward, his hands clenched together as if praying.

"Eric, don't get involved," he pleaded. "This is Khmer..."

The father and son returned to the boy, who was still being whipped by his mother. Seeing them coming, he made a break for it and was chased into the house by his parents who looked hell-bent on inflicting further injury, but this time without prying eyes. The street fell silent, and the crowds eventually wandered back to their chairs to discuss what they'd seen.

"Only in Cambodia," Aidan was muttering.

Only the Khmer staff seemed unruffled by it. Annie said he was beaten in the street as a public humiliation so that everyone could see his punishment and to let people know his family had taken action over his undisclosed crimes.

But whatever he'd done, it was a dreadful thing to witness. I felt a sickness in my stomach, and a hollow feeling descended as I thought again about how violent human beings can be to each other. I'll never know what the boy had done to deserve such punishment, and his family refused to discuss it, but his terror as he was being whipped and beaten by his own flesh and blood was awful to see.

Eric sat down at his bar stool, looking shocked and agitated, and slightly annoyed that no-one had helped him. I don't think he had any real notion how near he'd come to never leaving Cambodia.

The strength with which the son gripped that club a second before contact, and the madness in his eyes as he sought to restore the family honour, made me realise how easily Eric could have been killed, and the further bloodshed it would have sparked.

Whatever the rights and wrongs of physical punishment, let alone public punishment, there was something vile in the bullying savagery they inflicted on that boy, and the sheer terror they put in his heart. But for some reason, it felt less terrible than the violence that so nearly came from stopping it.

CHAPTER TWELVE

JOSH'S WIFE Loung had returned from her province after seeing a witchdoctor. He'd read her palm and told her she was being plagued by evil spirits. The madness had begun four weeks ago and left her unable to walk.

"Sure. I speak sure," she told us that night in Josh's restaurant. "I sleep and I see many, many people come to kill me with knife, you know. I go to see teacher in province..."

Josh was nodding his head, a fag end burning smoke in his eyes.

"She did, she went mad. She didn't even know who I was. She went off her tree - majorly one day."

The witchdoctor told Loung she needed to sell her share in the karaoke bar Josh had just bought her to get rid of the evil spirits. Her sister owned the other half. She claimed she didn't have any money, so Josh gave her his half for free. The entire charade had cost him $800 for the witchdoctor, and $1,500 for the bar.

"She sold it to her sister - the witchdoctor said if she didn't sell it, she would die," said Josh, before quickly tailing off and lighting another cigarette. He still had one burning in the ashtray.

Loung limped back from the bar unsteadily on her stick after helping herself to another beer.

"You want me to die?"

"No, I don't want you to die - that's why we sold the bar..."

Josh was slowly losing everything he'd worked for. He'd met Loung during a holiday in Cambodia four years ago and stayed in touch when he went back to New Zealand. She told him she was pregnant and he quit his job at the bank, and returned to help bring up the child.

She told him she had lost the baby six weeks later. Then there were more made-up pregnancies. Josh was a clever man, but an alcoholic, and I feared he would one day return home with nothing - if he lived that long, of course.

THE PAINS in my liver were getting worse. I was feeling seedy, and getting quite nervous about it. The giddy spells were getting worse too, and I was losing all grip on reality. Joseph Conrad wrote in Heart of Darkness: "In the tropics one must before everything keep calm..." But I'd long lost any feeling of peace. Even the slightest knock sent me into a fit of considerable bitterness, reminding me of the wretched circus we call someone's life.

But it wasn't just me - the madness was everywhere. I'd once walked out of my room with a towel around my waist, carrying two bags of rubbish, and a driver had shouted "tuk tuk" at me from across the street. I couldn't even laugh about it. The heat, the horror, the delusional characters on the Hill were destroying me.

I had to get out. I had less than $3,000 left. It was barely enough to buy a tiny bar on Karaoke Street, and that wouldn't turn a profit. I had to go back to the UK, and earn some money. The thought of going back terrified me.

I wandered along the broken road and met Josh at his restaurant. He was drinking tea from the $2,000 silver teapot he'd found in a Japanese recycling shop in Phnom Penh. It was the only antique he had left in the country. He was clutching a broken rib, and looked in a very sorry state. He hadn't had a drink for two days.

A week before, he'd finally broken up with Loung. He'd gone home sober, put a suit on the next day, and headed down to the police station to tell the chief he was leaving Loung. The next day, she went round to the station and told him Josh had kidnapped her and made her sign away the deeds to the restaurant.

The police interrogated her, realised she was lying, and told her to go back to her province and never come back again. She was back a week later, living in a mud-floored shack 100 yards from Josh's house. Whenever he walked past, she put her wrists together and made a handcuffs gesture. Every day, she lay outside the shack on a wooden bench. She couldn't walk more than a few yards. The bar girls said she was dying from AIDS.

211

A Scottish expat with a huge forehead and dreadlocks that made him look like the Predator was sitting on one of the bar stools. He'd been in a few days before when Josh and a few of his regulars had come back from a night fishing trip. The table was covered with cheese and bread they hadn't eaten on the boat, and soon the Predator was tucking in.

"Oh, that's a lovely piece of cheese," he kept saying, forever reaching over to cut more slices. He'd soon eaten the lot. His bar tab had come to $1, and he asked if he could pay the next day. He must have eaten $15 of cheese.

"Is the soup done?" he said.

Josh had made tomato and vegetable soup - a great cauldron of the stuff - for $1.50 a bowl and a baguette. It was my recipe. I thought back to the times I'd worked in that stuffy kitchen day after day banging out soup for those skinflints.

An incredibly tall man with a beard and hangdog expression walked in. He said he was the executive chef of a group of luxury hotels, and was soon telling everyone how difficult it was drumming the basics of hygiene into his Cambodian cooks.

We got chatting, and I told him about my dismal failure retraining as a chef and the book I'd written about my experiences. I told him how it all started when Rick Stein let me do a week in his Seafood Restaurant.

"He's one of my best friends!" the executive chef beamed. "He even sent me a long email when Chalky died. He loved that dog. He was devastated..."

He told me they'd done their chef training together in France, and hinted at the drunken nights they'd had. I listened on, but was thinking of something else. I'd been wanting to send the celebrity chef an email thanking him again for the opportunity he gave me, and how if he hadn't, my book would probably never have been written.

But I'd lost Stein's email address long ago and knew if I sent a message through his PR people, it would probably never get to him.

I'd have more chance of sending him a message in a bottle from one of Cambodia's Robinson Crusoe islands. So when the executive chef eventually paused to take a swig of beer, I asked if he'd mind passing my thank you letter on to Stein. He handed me a business card with his email on it.

"Not a problem," he said, "Oh, we had some times together!"

Then he stopped suddenly and looked angry and bitter.

"Do you know the difference between him and me? Do you know how he got to where he is and I didn't?" He didn't wait for an answer: "Luck!"

I WROTE a thank you letter to Stein and emailed it to the executive chef. I didn't hear anything back. Not even anything to say he'd received it. My suspicions were finally confirmed when I was in the Irish bar talking to Aidan.

He told me the executive chef had been in a few days before and tried some of his Irish stew - a dish described in his bar adverts as "probably the best Irish stew in Cambodia".

We'd been chatting about the best way to cook it because the price of lamb made it impossible to make. At least at a price the cheapskates were prepared to shell out for. Goat would have been the next best option, but we couldn't get hold of that, and when I jokingly suggested dog meat Aidan looked appalled.

"My dog would smell it! He'd never come near me again!" he whimpered.

So I told him to use beef instead, but to throw in a few anchovies to give it a richer flavour. He made the stew with the usual chunks of carrots, potatoes, and onions, and then showed me his secret of mashing up a few spuds and putting them in the bottom of each bowl, and pouring the stew on top. It was a clever touch and kept the broth high in the bowl while allowing people to thicken the liquor to their liking, without having to do the mashing themselves.

Aidan told me the executive chef had raved about it. He began laughing, his prawn-like eyebrows wiggling away.

"'Oh,' he said, 'that's a lovely bit of lamb! That's neck fillet isn't it?' Fucking lamb! And he's an executive chef! People were listening, so I just played on. What the fuck could I do? 'I love lamb!' he says. 'It's my favourite fucking meat.' What the fuck! You couldn't make that up now, could you!"

No wonder the bloke hadn't replied to my email. It wasn't even his business card. The real executive chef was probably thinking: "Who the hell is this idiot banging on about Rick Stein?"

DIRTY DEREK had arrived back in town after a month prowling the bars in Pattaya. During the day he lounged on the beach, soaking up his golden tan, and in the evenings he visited the beach bars, haggling over prices.

He went into Rodney's bar some nights, and would sit there nursing a single beer. Rodney used to joke that he was so mean he wouldn't give a fly to a blind spider. I'd once heard him on the beach getting irritated with a boy selling sunglasses.

"Look, if I buy a pair for $2, how much will you make?" Dirty Derek had said.

"2,000 riel," the boy replied.

"Well, here's 2,000 riel, now fuck off."

"Cheap Charlie!" the boy said as he walked off.

We were sitting there one night when we saw Dirty Derek walking towards us with a Vietnamese woman. He walked in, put his bottle of wine on the table, asked for two glasses, and started boasting about his usual tricks for saving money. This time, he told us he was cutting down on restaurant bills by cooking in his hotel room using a kettle.

"I must be saving about four bucks a day," he said. "You can tell I was born a pom - I've got short arms and long pockets."

214

He said he boiled an egg for breakfast, which he ate with a baguette, and then cooked some spuds, and ate them with a few slices of corned beef, tomato, and cucumber, for lunch. He even cooked soup in there when the mood took him. He put a centimetre of water in the bottom, and then added a tin of soup, flicked the switch, and stirred away continuously with a wooden spoon for five minutes.

"I've made some lovely soups in there. The best one was a tin of Heinz chicken and mushroom. I buy a baguette from the market, put some butter on it...chicken and mushroom soup mate - it doesn't get much better than that!"

"Yeah, but how do you wash the kettle afterwards?" I asked.

"In the bloody en-suite! I top it up with water so the remains of the soup doesn't stick inside, then I boil it up again, and that gets all the shit off the sides. Then I turn it off, and swill it out, and just rub the inside with a paper towel, and it's clean again. The next day I'm boiling it up to make my tea and coffee..."

His latest experiment was a foray into the grandeur of Italian cuisine. He boiled spaghetti in the kettle, drained it, then added a tub of pasta sauce to the kettle, heated it up, and mixed it with the pasta.

I decided I'd give it a go. The next morning, I got a moto down to the market, or at least a few yards up the road, and sat on the back as the driver chatted to a policeman friend who was investigating a domestic disturbance at one of the bars.

When I say investigate, I mean turn up and ask for $50. Even reporting a crime costs money in Cambodia. During the Khmer New Year, they all hit the streets, turning up at every bar looking for cases of beer and cash to see them through the festivities. It was always a dubious time of year to be in Cambodia. I heard one story about a drunken police chief who'd staggered around the bars on the Hill, threatening people with an AK 47, until his officers arrived to collect him.

Eventually we got to the market, and I headed into the sweaty labyrinth, looking for a kettle. No-one knew what I was talking about. But eventually I spotted one at a stall, run by an old woman. The kettle was perfect. There was no element inside to worry about when stirring - it was safely tucked away in the plastic base. And the top was wide, meaning you could get at your spuds quite easily. The only trouble was there wasn't a lead.

The woman went off for five minutes and then came back with a bag full of black cables. She tried a few but none of them worked. Eventually after a few wiggles, the red light came on, and as I found to my cost, the metal bottom was soon red hot. I was worried about the lead though - it fell out of the socket so easily I could tell it wasn't the one the manufacturer had in mind, but at $4 I couldn't really go wrong, or so I thought.

I then headed off in search of food to boil. There was a bubbling bowl of live crabs, and I could have probably got one in the kettle. But I'd promised myself to start with something simple. I'd give them a go when I'd got myself a bit more kettling experience. You can't rush these things.

Instead, I'd try one of Dirty Derek's tried and tested recipes. It was either boiled eggs, or boiled potatoes with corned beef. I looked around, but couldn't find any spuds. Then I spotted a mother and daughter selling crockery. I bought a plastic soup bowl, a small plate, a fork, and a large Thai-made knife that said "Kiwi Brand" on the label, but had "Kiwi Brandy" engraved on the blade.

What the hell, it wobbled a bit, was blunt as hell, and the join between the blade and the wooden handle had split, but it was only $1. Then I saw her mother had two huge bags of duck eggs she was taking home. I couldn't be bothered to search for potatoes, and asked if I could buy a couple.

Then I wondered whether they were the fertilised types that had 20-day-old duck foetuses inside - a popular street food snack in SE Asia. The brown liquor is drunk, the whole bird is spooned out and then dunked in tuk meric.

"They have small baby?" I kept saying.

Eventually the daughter seemed to understand and said they were just normal duck eggs. We rode back up to the Hill and I stopped off at a ramshackle shop and bought two potatoes, a green tomato, some chillies, a handful of snake beans, an onion, and a tin of corned beef.

I got back to my hotel and tried switching on the kettle. Nothing. After about two minutes of wiggling the lead, and expecting to be thrown across the room, the red light came on for a second. Considering the shoddy electrics in the place, which meant there were sparks every time I plugged my laptop adapter into the two-hole plug socket, I was taking no chances. I kept drying my sweaty hands on a towel before giving the lead another wiggle.

Eventually the red light stayed on, and there was a disconcerting roar from the electrics. I wondered whether that was how I'd be discovered - cooking in a kettle in a cheap hotel room, slumped over two black eggs, the water long dry in the kettle.

I remembered what Dirty Derek had said about making perfect soft-boiled eggs: "You wait until the water's too hot to put your finger in, you then put your egg in and leave it there for three minutes, and you've got yourself the perfect egg mate!" But I'd forgotten to buy a spoon, let alone an egg cup. They would have to be hard-boiled and eaten whole.

The red light had gone out again. I rubbed my hands on the towel, and started wiggling. The kettle fired up, and after a few minutes the water was bubbling away ferociously, which was when I discovered there wasn't a cut-out switch either.

The angled red light I'd taken for a switch was just a light. The only way you could turn it off was either to remove the lead from the socket - which meant losing the right wiggle connection - or pulling the plug out of the wall, with the accompanying flash and fizz of electrics. Using my Kiwi Brandy blade, I carefully lowered the eggs into the water along with a burnt match to stop them breaking.

I boiled them for three minutes or so, and left them in the water. They would be far harder boiled than I'd have liked, but as I still wasn't sure whether they contained duck foetuses or not, I wanted as much cooking as possible.

I rolled the eggs up the side of the kettle and lay them in my new bowl. It was the moment of truth. Did they contain baby ducks? I tapped away at the shell. They were as tough as dinosaur eggs. I chipped away with a fork, and a chunk came free. I peeled more away, and was relieved to see white albumen rather than brown jelly.

Not that I'd looked that much the last time I tried them. I'd just shut my eyes, whacked the thing in my mouth, and swallowed as quickly as I could, trying to banish the thought of dark feathers tickling my tonsils, and beak crunching between my teeth. Then I downed a tequila.

I teased the top open with my fork. I didn't want to bite into it, just in case. I remembered a friend who went to an expensive boarding school. He told me a tale about a pupil who'd dug into a soft-boiled egg, found a chicken foetus inside, and died on the spot from a heart attack.

A little bit more, and I could see the orangey yolk, with no hint of alien life form. Then I realised there was no salt and pepper, so I nipped across the road to a cafe, bought a bottle of water, and poured some salt and pepper into a napkin when they weren't looking. Then I set about my delicious duck eggs.

THE NEXT night, I drank into the early hours in Rodney's bar. The 30-seater restaurant next door was for sale. It had a bedroom and broom cupboard kitchen at the back, and no customers. But Rodney was convinced I could "clean up". The only problem was customers had to walk through the kitchen to get to the toilet. But Rodney said if I took it on, they could use his.

He said the owner had run out of money and was desperate to sell. He reckoned he might even take $2,000 for it. There were two-and-a-half years left on the lease, and the rent was $350 (or 450 beers) a month. Rodney spent the rest of the night convincing me to buy it.

"You've got to do it - enough of your talk! See your money - put it where your fucking mouth is! I tell you what - you'll fucking clean up. Take the gamble! Don't talk about it - fucking do it!"

I looked at the hole-in-the-wall bistro, with its chained-up chairs and tables outside. It was called The Coconut Tree - it didn't even have a frigging coconut tree. The nerves and indecision were already setting in.

"You can lose a lot of money doing that, following your heart..."

"Yeah, if you've fucking lost, you've lost, you go back home. But at least you've fucking tried, and that's the fucking difference. If you don't try, don't take the gamble, you're sitting there all your life. Ber ber ber ber ber! Who gives a fuck? Take the gamble!

"If it works, lovely jubbly! If it don't work - tough luck! But it will work. This is a prime spot, they know where I am, word of mouth, they're all coming round here. It's famous this bar - I've done it. I don't even have to look back. Take the bloody gamble! It's up to you, you're the chef, go and do some grub..."

Rodney was right - it was time to finally nail my colours to the mast. The bistro was far from perfect, but at least I'd be near Serendipity Beach, and wouldn't have to deal with the misers on the Hill.

I got back at 4am, absolutely famished. None of the restaurants were open. So I cooked myself something in the kettle. I'd been planning on boiling some diced potatoes and sliced snake beans, and then serving them with a few slices of corned beef and tomato for my next experiment - a tweak on the recipe Dirty Derek had recommended.

"I have a couple of slices with my potatoes, which I cook in my hotel room with my little electric kettle, with some slices of cucumber and tomato, and I always bring a genuine pot of English mustard when I fly in from Australia - I'm in heaven!" he'd said.

He used to bring Colman's Mustard wrapped in cling film, smuggled in with his hand luggage, along with a stash of Oxo cubes he'd sometimes hand to restaurants to make gravy for his pies. But when I picked up the tin of corned beef, I saw the key had fallen off. I wasn't going to search for a tin opener on an unlit street during robbery season, and the handle of my Kiwi Brandy blade was far too flimsy to stab into the tin.

219

So I decided to go for soup. I had two potatoes, a tomato, four red chillies, a handful of snake beans, an onion, and the napkin of salt and pepper. It didn't look too promising, but I was too hungry to care. Then I remembered the head of garlic I'd been using in the ridiculous belief it would ward off snakes.

Someone had found a small one in one of the rooms. It must have wriggled under the door, and I was on the bottom floor and was taking no chances. When I heard that a backpacker had been sunbathing on the balcony when a large serpent had crawled over the back of her legs, I'd have taken any advice on the matter.

So I found myself listening when a Khmer friend told me that snakes don't like garlic. They don't go near the stuff, apparently. I don't know if it's the sight or smell. I didn't ask. It was hard enough getting that much. But she said many people in her village left garlic around in their houses, especially during the rainy season, when rising waters bring pythons to the area.

Perhaps the snake had come up through the toilet? And how big did they mean by small? A small one wouldn't have been able to get up there, would it? I checked, and the toilet lid was still down. Then I put a couple of books on top just to make sure.

I staggered around the badly-lit room looking in the corners, trying to hide the thought of snakes from the rest of my mind. Rodney was right - it was time to act. I'd go round to speak to the owner the next day and offer him $2,000. I'd finally have my own place. I'd finally conquer my habitual indecision - my eternal, volitional deliberation. There would no longer be retching and no vomit.

Then I remembered what I was doing, and poured 250ml of water into the kettle. Not that I had a measuring jug or anything. I know because I used pretty much all of a 330ml bottle, and when I downed the rest there was little more than a double in there. You wouldn't complain about the measure, put it that way.

But the problems started again when I tried to switch on the kettle. I kept wiggling the lead in the socket, but the red light wouldn't go on. For minutes I tried, changing plug sockets, with the accompanying sparks, and pushing the lead into all sorts of contortions, until I found that the light went on briefly if I jammed the socket upwards and twisted slightly. The dodgy electrics roared up, the light went on, then off, then stayed on again for a minute.

But every time I let go, the lead fell out. I jammed a pen under the socket but it was too wide. Eventually I found the perfect device - one of those tiny toothpaste tubes they give you in hotels. The light stayed on. And then the water started to bubble.

I used a ledge by the sink to deal with the vegetables, listening out for the faint, pleasing roar. In my drunken haze, with my stomach gurgling, and the fan making its wheezing, scraping sound, it was difficult to hear the kettle from the bathroom.

I darted out a few times, delighted each time I saw the red light. I examined the veg. I'd left them tied up in a plastic bag on the bed, because I didn't want ants running up and down the walls. They'd eat anything those bastards - even toothpaste.

The snake beans were a putrid, sludgy grey and looked more like a bag of mouldy prahok. And one of the potatoes was rotten. I sliced the peel off the good potato, cutting on a split, plastic bag on the sink. I thinly sliced it and carefully added the pieces to the kettle, terrified any ripple would knock out the lead.

I roughly chopped the onion and added it gingerly. I cut off the few remaining green bits from the snake beans. There was hardly anything there. But I sliced them anyway, thinking it would be good for the colour. Then I did the same with the tomato. I chopped up two of the four chillies and added the lot to the kettle. It was bubbling away nicely and the potatoes were softening.

Then I sliced the garlic and started hearing cracking noises. The bedside cupboard the kettle was perched on had a glass top, but I couldn't see any cracks. I looked at the sign on the bathroom door. It said "no weapons, explosives, gambling and prostitutes". But I couldn't see anything about cooking in the room. No, I was wrong: "Don't cock or using iron pot electronic in bedroom."

I stood there swaying, now more hungry than drunk. The smell was incredible. It's amazing what hunger does to your taste buds. There's nothing like building up an appetite on a Sunday morning walk and then finishing it off with a decent roast in a proper pub. The anticipation is everything.

I wondered if they were thinking the same down the corridor. I lifted the lid carefully. The potatoes had broken up nicely, thickening the soup, which had now taken on a brown colour I hadn't notice at first with the poor lighting. There was another crack. Or was it a pop?

I looked at the glass top again. Surely the surface was designed for a kettle? I gave it another careful stir. I pulled the socket out and gave the kettle a few shakes, then stabbed the potatoes and tomato to break them up. I added some salt and pepper and waited for the soup to cool.

It was hard judging the seasoning. I didn't know what ratio of salt to pepper was in the mix. And when I dabbed one side of the napkin it was mainly pepper, but then I'd try another side and it smacked of salt. But there was definitely far more pepper. I'd done the cafe manoeuvre so quickly, it was impossible to know, and with the white napkin you had no hope of spotting the salt-rich areas in that light. It would have to have a very peppery kick to get the salt right.

I gave the broth a good stir and added more seasoning, and tried it again. It could take more salt. I chopped up the other two chillies and threw them in, and added more of what I now knew was basically pepper. I stirred again, and tried another mouthful. I was trying to eat soup with a fork. It had come to this. I had one of those moments when you look at yourself and wonder what happened. Then I thought about the bistro again.

I let the kettle sit there for another few minutes, cooling and thickening. I would have done anything for some bread - a couple of thickly-buttered hunks of granary crust, seasoned with celery salt and a dusting of cayenne pepper. Not that it needed extra spice. The soup was explosive enough already, but it definitely needed more salt. I tossed in the last of the pepper mix. The chilli and pepper came at you like wild dogs, one distracting as the other took hold, and soon the sweat was running down my face. It was absolutely delicious.

I was so hungry, I wolfed it down, trying to lap up as much of the broth as I could with the prongs of the fork. As I got further down, I began swigging from the kettle, swilling it round like a fisherman's mug. Then as I got lower, I noticed black marks at the bottom where the veg had caught. It was a salutary lesson in the overlooked art of hotel room cocking.

But if anything, it had given the broth the sort of juice-scraping succulence that stock-cube peddler Marco Pierre White would be proud of, the sort of notes you get from frying a white mirepoix of onions, celery, garlic, and leek whites for 30 minutes. Not to that colour admittedly. I'd be sacked for doing that.

But I wasn't in a professional kitchen, stainless steel gleaming under the eternal lights. I was cooking in a mouldy hotel room using a kettle with a dodgy socket. I told myself that the autumnal colour was not just down to burning, but the generous handfuls of pepper.

I finished the soup with sweat running down my chest and back, and I'd begun hiccupping. Even sitting directly in front of the second fan I'd bribed the one-armed security guard into giving me made no difference. I had one can of beer left, but it was far too warm to drink.

I took off my scallop shell, had a shower, tipped the last bits of soup I couldn't fork down the sink, and washed the kettle out with the tap trickling away like an incontinent mouse. I thought about the restaurant again. The Coconut Tree! The name would have to change for a start. The Scallop Shell? The Seafood Shack? What's Khmer for scallop?

I filled the kettle with water, remembering the way Dirty Derek had told me to clean it, and tried to connect the lead again. I wiggled away, and a massive numbing pain shot up my arm to my chest. I flew back and slipped on the wet floor. I couldn't open my eyes. The electricity was in my head - it felt like it was crushing my brain - and I plunged into an inky, black void of forgetfulness.

About the Author

Alex Watts is a travelling journalist and sometime cook. He has written for TV, radio, and national newspapers in the UK, America, and Australia. He also writes the blog Chef Sandwich - a journal of his food/travel writing.

Twitter: http://twitter.com/alexwatts

Blog: http://chefsandwich.blogspot.com

226

8652845R00138

Printed in Great Britain
by Amazon.co.uk, Ltd.,
Marston Gate.